CRIME AND CONFLICT
IN THE COUNTRYSIDE

ENVIRONMENT AND COUNTRYSIDE LAW

The Environment and Countryside Law Series provides a forum for the publication of studies and research relating to distinctly 'rural' issues. The Series has a strong focus on environmental law and nature conservation, and on related issues of rural land use. However, other well-established areas of legal study, such as criminal law and property law, also raise distinct problems when studied in a rural context, and the scope of the Series also includes subjects such as rural crime, rural housing and access to justice in rural areas. The Series therefore seeks to promote and publish research into all aspects of the law as it applies in the countryside.

CRIME AND CONFLICT
IN THE COUNTRYSIDE

edited by

GAVIN DINGWALL

and

SUSAN R. MOODY

UNIVERSITY OF WALES PRESS
CARDIFF
1999

© The Contributors, 1999

British Library Cataloguing-in-Publication Data.
A catalogue record for this book is available from the British Library.

ISBN 0–7083–1510–0

Typeset at University of Wales Press
Printed in Great Britain by Bookcraft, Midsomer Norton, Avon

Preface

In the past criminology scholars have focused heavily on 'urban' crime, its causes and origins. 'Rural' crime has received relatively little attention as a distinct subject. Scant attention has been paid to the distinct problems and methodologies of research into rural criminology, and the very concept of 'rural' crime as a distinct area of criminological study has been left undefined, except insofar as it is viewed as a mirror image of 'urban' crime.

In this, the fourth collection of essays in the Environment and Countryside Law Series, Gavin Dingwall and Susan Moody have brought together a wide range of specialist contributors in order to address both the theoretical basis and definition of 'rural' criminology as a discipline, and a number of practical issues and problems specific to crime and disorder in rural areas. The Environment and Countryside Law Series is devoted to promoting the study of the distinct legal problems of rural areas in their widest sense, be they issues of environmental law, countryside management, access to justice or crime and disorder in rural areas. This collection is a welcome addition to the series, not only for its own merits (which are considerable), but because the contributions emphasize the breadth of subject matter which must be addressed if we are to arrive at a true understanding of the distinctive problems facing the law in rural areas.

Christopher Rodgers,
Centre for Law in Rural Areas,
University of Wales, Aberystwyth.

Contents

Foreword

PAUL WILES

Criminology developed as a subject in response to the problems of social order which attended industrialization and the growth of crime in industrial cities. The result is that criminology has always essentially been the study of urban crime and its social control. As some of the essays in this volume record, there have been spasmodic attempts to study rural crime but these have been largely parasitic and often applied the methods and theories of urban criminology to rural situations. None of this has amounted to a rural criminology.

It could be argued that this does not matter, on the grounds that place may not be a critical explanatory variable for criminality or crime. For a significant part of criminology's history that would have been a common position because the dominant theories concentrated on social space to the exclusion of the geographical. After the pioneering work of the Chicago school criminology largely lost interest in the spatial patterning of crime. However, a new interest in spatial patterning (in part because of new digital means for analysing spatial phenomena) means that this would now be a difficult position to sustain. We know how important variations in place are to the amount and patterns of crime and criminality in urban areas. All the evidence suggests that there is a difference between urban and rural crime, even though police-recorded crime may somewhat distort the picture. Furthermore, as a number of the essays in this volume point out, there are variations in crime and place *between* rural areas. This does not mean that we ought to develop geographical theories of crime *per se* – or at least we must be careful to avoid a geographical determinism. However, it does mean that criminological theories need to take account of and be capable of explaining spatial patterns. Criminology, therefore, needs to study crime in the countryside as well as urban crime in order to develop adequate general theories.

Ironically, whilst we do not have a developed rural criminology, nevertheless rural crime has played an important role in urban criminology. That role has essentially been that of antithesis. Urban crime is defined as high *relative* to rural crime; urban informal social control is judged to be weak *compared* with rural informal social control. Such a role would be unproblematic were it based on sound evidence, but the lack of a rural criminology means that it is not. As the rest of this book demonstrates, a simple urban/rural antithesis as a model for understanding crime just will not do.

Because rural crime has been seen as the antithesis of urban crime, it has also been held out as the model of where the solutions to urban crime problems are to be found. For example, it is often stated that cities, relative to villages, lack a sense of 'community' and have high crime – therefore reducing urban crime depends on strengthening or rebuilding communities in cities. This one example of urban/rural antithesis has generated endless crime reduction programmes aimed at 'strengthening', 'rebuilding' or 'empowering' communities in high-crime urban areas. The centrality of the urban/rural antithesis has been so important that even the very poor success rate of such programmes has not led to a re-examination of the underlying assumption. Criminology has had at its heart an urban/rural distinction in crime which, because it has not been properly examined, has distorted the conceptualization of crime and social control. Rural crime has been largely an ideal type – but a mythological ideal type.

Even more alarming is that the mythical role which rural crime has played in criminology has actually distorted even the study of urban crime. Cities relative to rural areas do have higher crime rates, but it does not follow that all places in cities have higher crime rates than all rural areas. This simple fact has often been ignored, so that criminology largely has been not just the study of urban crime but of high-crime places within urban areas. Models of low-crime areas do not have to be a mythical rural idyll but can, in fact, be found in both urban and rural areas. However, the mythical ideal type of rural crime has been so powerful in thinking about crime that it has not only impeded the development of a rural criminology but also the study of low- crime areas in cities – a suburban criminology. Indeed, there are probably fewer studies of suburban low-crime areas than there are of rural crime. This lack of attention to rural and suburban crime has meant that criminology has made little use of the comparative method in spite of its obvious epistemic utility.

Unfounded beliefs about the rural are not unique to criminology. Indeed, the reason why the mythical nature of the beliefs has gone unchallenged is because they are so widely shared. The essays in this volume attest to the importance of the myths even to the social fabric of life in the countryside itself. Whilst careful scholarship might puncture the myths about rural crime, mere knowledge will not remove the social significance of the myths. We have a powerful myth that 'village = low crime' so that urban areas with low crime frequently refer to themselves as village-like. In a similar way, in the USA, myths about black crime have meant that for many (white) Americans 'black = crime' and no amount of careful analysis of the relationship between race, place and social structure has destroyed that simple equation. This is unfortunate since it has diverted attention away from the important question of why there are (relatively) high- and low- crime areas in urban, suburban and rural places. In order to answer that question we will have to deconstruct categories such as 'inner city', 'urban', 'suburban' and 'rural' so that underneath the myths we can see the complexity of the social structures and relations which explain crime and criminality in different places.

Each of the essays in this book is important because they get behind the myth to reveal differing aspects of rural crime and its control. That in itself is a significant achievement, and together the essays make an important contribution to criminological knowledge. However, the collection has another and wider importance. The present volume is a start at carrying out the much larger task of deconstructing one of the central categories of much existing criminological thinking, so that a more accurate and general set of theories about crime and criminality can be developed.

The Contributors

Simon Anderson is Associate Director of System Three, Edinburgh.

Pam Davies is currently working on a Home Office-funded research project into child abuse.

Gavin Dingwall is a Lecturer in Law at the University of Wales, Aberystwyth.

Daniel Gilling is a Senior Lecturer in Social Policy at the University of Plymouth.

Richard Hester is the County Community Safety Officer for Warwickshire County Council.

Laurence Koffman is a Reader in Law at the University of Sussex.

Ciaran McCullagh is a Lecturer in Sociology at University College, Cork.

Susan R. Moody is a Senior Lecturer in Law at the University of Dundee.

Jill Peay is a Senior Lecturer in Law at the London School of Economics and Political Science.

Harriet Pierpoint is a Research Assistant at the University of Plymouth.

Kevin Stenson is a Professor of Social Policy and Criminology and Director of the Social Policy Research Group at Buckinghamshire Chilterns University College, High Wycombe.

Paul Watt is a Senior Lecturer in Social Policy Research at the University of East London.

Paul Wiles is Professor of Criminology at the University of Sheffield.

Brian Williams is a Senior Research Fellow at De Montfort University, Leicester.

Introduction
'Mean Streets' Myopia: Challenging Criminology's Boundaries

GAVIN DINGWALL and SUSAN R. MOODY

This book aims to stimulate debate about a major gap in contemporary criminological research. Although the impact of environmental factors on criminality has long been acknowledged, criminology has largely failed to examine crime and criminal justice in a rural setting, and has concentrated almost exclusively on the more visible problem of urban criminality. Indeed, the sites for criminological research have, as Paul Wiles points out in his Foreword to this collection, not only been almost exclusively metropolitan-based but have also narrowed their focus to encompass certain types of urban environment only. Even the more theoretical literature tends merely to compare the rural with the urban and fails to engage in a more analytical discussion of rurality and its significance for the discipline. This failure to consider the concept of rurality diminishes the importance of complex sociological, geographical and demographic phenomena, and helps perpetuate a simplistic distinction between the crime-ridden urban and the crime-free rural.

The reasons for this 'mean streets' myopia merit brief exploration. One easy exit route from criminological studies of the rural is to claim that there are no differences between the experience of crime in the city and crime in the countryside. Globalization, it is claimed, has led to homogeneity – we all inhabit the same spaces now (Giddens, 1991). However, as the contributions to this book make clear, there are differences, both quantitatively and qualitatively. Studies of urban criminality alone cannot do justice to the diversity and complexity of crime, its effects and its control.

Other, more pragmatic influences have adversely affected the development of rural criminology. The social problems approach to criminality has, not surprisingly, concentrated on those areas where the problem seems most acute, namely those inner cities and peripheral estates where recorded crime is high. Increasingly, political concern about crime has sought solutions to the difficulties presented by these 'black spots', which have come to represent disorder and decay. It is clear that urban residents regard crime as more serious than their rural counterparts and have become increasingly vociferous in their demands for 'something to be done about crime'. At a time when citizens are in fact faced with much more ubiquitous fears than the threat of criminal victimization in a world increasingly pervaded by global dangers (Beck, 1992), politicians and policy-makers must seek to show that at least the 'crime problem' is under their control. Media coverage of crime has encouraged this urban focus. The generation of news about crime is both easier and more immediate in a tightly constructed urban area, where crime itself (or certain types of crime) and the impact of such crimes are more visible, than in the countryside where spatial dimensions and cultural features may serve to hide criminal activity.

Practical difficulties have also discouraged empirical research in this field. It is more difficult to obtain funding for studies of rural crime, mainly because policy-makers want to target resources where the need is seen to be greatest and where the pay-off is likely to be most advantageous. It has therefore been much easier to obtain funding for urban crime studies. In addition, empirical work is likely to be more expensive, time-consuming and complex where the population is more dispersed, the crime rate more diffuse and people less attuned to the demands of social science research.

Perhaps the most important reason for the lack of rural crime studies, however, rests with criminologists themselves. They have not regarded crime in the countryside as sufficiently interesting or challenging to be an attractive site for study. With most academics being based in metropolitan areas or large towns, the countryside has been kept at a distance, useful for leisure pursuits but not a focus for work. The study of crime in an urban setting may have elements perceived as exciting and dangerous, which criminologists can enjoy vicariously and in safety. The countryside, on the other hand, offers few such incentives!

This neglect contrasts markedly with other disciplines, particularly geography, where there is now a keen critical interest in the rural, arising out of the changing nature of the countryside and encompassing such emerging trends as counter-urbanization, immigration and commodification. As a concept, rurality is inherently diverse, complex and evolutionary in character. Quite simply, criminology has a great deal to learn from the methodological and theoretical sensitivity of other disciplines.

The project started when the editors, both of whom had independently been researching aspects of crime and criminal justice in the countryside, made contact after an article on research activity in the Law Department at Aberystwyth featured in the Society of Public Teachers of Law Newsletter. We wanted to stimulate interest in the rural dimensions of crime and crime control, and to this end we contacted the British Society of Criminology whose members encouraged us to convene a section on Crime and Rurality at their conference at Queen's University, Belfast in July 1997. We are grateful to the conference organizers for their encouragement and assistance. The session generated considerable interest, and it was clear that a number of participants shared our belief that rurality deserved further criminological exploration. Several of the chapters in this collection have their genesis in papers presented at the conference. The enthusiasm of the contributors, the originality of their work, and the contribution that we felt could be made to an understanding of crime and conflict in the countryside led to our decision to edit a collection. The University of Wales Press, which has a distinguished tradition of publishing work on the operation of law in rural areas, shared our belief that this was a timely venture, and we thank them for their commitment to the project, and time, assistance and skill in producing the final collection. We also gratefully acknowledge the help that we received from the Centre for Law in Rural Areas at the University of Wales, Aberystwyth, and from our respective departments which provided the necessary financial backing to allow us to edit a collection with editors based over 400 miles apart, in mid-Wales and Tayside. Towards the end of the project Kevin Bates, a research assistant at Dundee University, prepared the final manuscript with great competence and good humour. The value of this book, however, derives from the work of our contributors, and the editors would like publicly to acknowledge their commitment, enthusiasm and assistance in the genesis, evolution and completion of *Crime and Conflict in the Countryside*.

It is difficult to convey the breadth of the collection in a short introduction, but a number of central themes emerge. The first is that the popular perception that there is no 'crime problem' in rural areas is as misleading as it is enduring. Contrary to the belief of many, there is objective evidence that the prevalence of crime is a significant problem in the countryside, even if the risk of actual victimization is lower than in urban areas (Anderson, chapter 3; Koffman, chapter 4). From a more subjective standpoint, such views are changing, with rural residents becoming increasingly concerned about crime (Anderson, chapter 3; Stenson and Watt, chapter 5). Anderson attributes a heightened fear of crime amongst rural residents to a process of globalization, caused largely by the immediacy of contemporary media imagery (see Ericson, 1995), despite anecdotal evidence from police officers that the situation has not deteriorated markedly. Yet the mythical rural idyll has an enduring appeal in the popular consciousness: myths about the countryside should not blind us to its symbolic importance which is reflected in the construction of criminality in rural areas (Moody, chapter 1; McCullagh, chapter 2; Anderson, chapter 3; Stenson and Watt, chapter 5). In both the United Kingdom (Peay; chapter 11) and the Republic of Ireland (McCullagh, chapter 2) the imagery associated with rural tranquillity has been invoked to powerful political effect. And when a serious offence occurs in the countryside it creates disproportionate concern because it shatters this potent imagery. Perceptions of rurality do not just affect rural residents. McCullagh argues that the rural plays an important part in the national psyche (at least in the Republic of Ireland) and that, as a consequence, rural crime is of great symbolic importance: highly publicized incidents of violent crime in rural Ireland were taken as a sign that crime was indeed a serious national issue and this led to fundamental changes in the criminal justice system.

A second perception, namely that rural communities enjoy a high degree of stability and consensus, is also both enduring and misleading. The rural is all too often described as an undifferentiated 'other' (Moody, chapter 1; Stenson and Watt, chapter 5; Hester, chapter 8; Peay, chapter 11). In fact, within the countryside one finds different groups with very different experiences of crime and the criminal justice system: the Aberystwyth crime survey (Koffman, chapter 4) demonstrates clearly that different groups of rural residents experience different rates of victimization; Stenson and Watt (chapter 5) show how two areas within the same Buckingham-shire village are conceptualized differentially both by residents and by criminal justice personnel; Hester (chapter 8) documents the conflicting values of New Age Travellers and other countryside residents, whilst Peay (chapter 11) explores the resolution of a community conflict in a southern English village generated by a clash of personalities, class and interests. This perception of community equilibrium masks a vivid reality of marginalization and conflict (Stenson and Watt, chapter 5; Hester, chapter 8; Peay, chapter 11). As Moody comments (chapter 1), the rural environment provides criminologists with a clear focus to study conflict and dispute resolution in contemporary society.

This perception of stability and consensus leads to a view that rural communities make great use of informal methods of social control. There is clearly some basis for this in reality: Anderson (chapter 3) notes the use of informal cautioning by police officers in rural Scotland; Stenson and Watt (chapter 5) recognize the variety of informal modes of governance operating in 'Outville' and the implications that this has for official criminal justice agencies; Gilling and Pierpoint, in their analysis of crime prevention in rural areas (chapter 7), suggest that attempts to formalize self-reliance are very much in line with the approach traditionally taken by rural communities to social organization, whilst Peay (chapter 11) notes how the community she studied made frantic efforts to avoid police intervention. Yet it would be a mistake to assume that rural communities avoid conflict through a desire to conform to an informal set of shared values. In truth, tight social control mechanisms operate (Stenson and Watt, chapter 5), and the fear of being shamed (Davies, chapter 9; Peay, chapter 11) or ostracized remains strong.

These theoretical issues also give rise to a number of practical questions regarding the provision of criminal justice services in rural areas. If one accepts that there is something distinct about such regions, to what extent does current practice accommodate this diversity? It would appear that, despite an increasing trend towards centralization and managerialism in recent policy initiatives (Dingwall, chapter 6; Gilling and Pierpoint, chapter 7; Williams, chapter 10), there are qualitative differences in the way that criminal justice personnel operate in the rural environment. This distinction may be resource-driven, in that services may have to be rationalized to take account of demographic factors, but there is evidence to suggest that cultural factors may also be of direct relevance (Davies, chapter 9; Williams, chapter 10). And these cultural differences may in turn be affected by aspects of geography in that firstly, services are often dependent upon fewer personnel in rural areas which may lead to a strengthening of collegiate solidarity, and secondly, the geography means that staff often operate with less visible supervision than their urban colleagues, again allowing variations in practice to develop. These cultural factors are also important at the sentencing stage. Owing primarily to a more restricted occupational base in country areas, the lay magistracy, who sentence the majority of rural offenders in England and Wales, often represent a narrow range of occupations which share a traditionally conservative role in the rural community: their perceptions of the concerns of the local community may well differ from those of other rural interest groups with possible consequences for sentencing practice (Dingwall, chapter 6).

If rural communities do have particular crime concerns to what extent are they being addressed both at a national level, in terms of governmental action, and at a local level, in terms of the priorities of local criminal justice agencies? The two major British empirical studies (Anderson, chapter 3; Koffman, chapter 4) into crime in rural areas both demonstrate that country residents are generally satisfied with policing arrangements, although levels of popular dissatisfaction clearly exist. Minority groups such as New Age Travellers, however, may well have justifiable grievances regarding the discriminatory manner in which they are dealt with by rural forces (Hester, chapter 8). Once again, the practical operation of the criminal justice system can be seen to affect different groups in different ways, demonstrating the variety of conflicting values to which the police have to respond. Another source of concern is the apparently widespread perception amongst criminal justice personnel that the move towards centralization is primarily a political response to urban disorder, and that the measures contained in recent criminal justice legislation are ill suited to the rural terrain (Dingwall, chapter 6; Davies, chapter 9). The result is an assumption that rural residents do not receive criminal justice services that are as satisfactory or as appropriate to their needs as those living in the city (Stenson and Watt, chapter 5; Williams, chapter 10).

These practical concerns provide a useful focus for a far larger debate about the provision of criminal justice in contemporary society, a debate characterized by delimiting the respective roles of the state, the community and the individual in controlling delinquent behaviour. This collection makes a number of observations which are of considerable relevance to this more general debate. Firstly, there is a clear sense that increased state involvement in criminal justice implementation via a process of centralization has not always resulted in uniformity of action but rather has exposed the difficulties of finding all-embracing solutions to complex, and inherently diverse, social phenomena (Dingwall, chapter 6; Gilling and Pierpoint, chapter 7; Davies, chapter 9; Williams, chapter 10). Secondly, several contributions have highlighted both the practical extent of informal social control in rural communities (Anderson, chapter 3; Stenson and Watt, chapter 5) and the potential for community involvement in dispute resolution (Peay, chapter 11). Thirdly, the collection challenges the notion that the countryside is the stereotypical cosy community where common values are shared and conflict is rare (Moody, chapter 1; McCullagh, chapter 2; Anderson, chapter 3; Stenson and Watt, chapter 5; Hester, chapter 8; Peay, chapter 11). Rather there is a recognition that the countryside contains those with diverse and competing interests which the criminal law, and the local population, have to police. The contributions seek to puncture the myth of an undifferentiated countryside, which is 'other' to the city. In fact, rural spaces contain as much variety in 'others' as urban areas.

Finally, and perhaps most importantly, despite the claim that postmodern society is becoming increasingly globalized, this collection demonstrates that there is something distinctive about crime and criminal justice in the countryside: criminal justice policy-makers as well as criminologists need to recognize and respond to the key issue of locality. When one recognizes the futility of searching for all-embracing solutions, one is forced to reassess the roles of the state, the community and the individual in responding to the social problems associated with late modernity. Rural communities provide criminologists with the opportunity to test notions of community and to assess the variety of social control mechanisms in operation in contemporary society. It is an opportunity that should not be wasted.

It is our hope that this collection advances theoretical discussion about crime and conflict in the countryside and encourages other researchers to give rurality the importance it deserves in criminological analysis.

References

BECK, U. (1992) *Risk Society: Towards a New Modernity*, London: Sage
ERICSON, R. (ed.) (1995) *Crime and the Media*, Aldershot: Dartmouth
GIDDENS, A. (1991) *Modernity and Self-Identity: Self and Society in the Late Modern Age*, Cambridge: Polity Press

1

Rural Neglect:
The Case Against Criminology

SUSAN R. MOODY

Anybody can be good in the country. There are no temptations there.[1]

Introduction[2]

The countryside is significant in contemporary criminology mainly because of its absence. Look for indigenous studies of crime in rural areas, rural crime, rural criminal justice in the twentieth century, and you come across a very limited number, most of which are only marginally concerned with the notion of rurality (for example, Shapland and Vagg, 1988; Tuck, 1989; ACRE, 1995; Husain, 1995; Loader, 1996). Research projects on public perceptions of crime and fear of crime sometimes include reference to differences between the rural and the urban (Skogan, 1986; Crawford et al., 1990; Mirrlees-Black et al., 1996), but the significance of location is never fully developed and serves merely as a backdrop to consideration of other, more global issues. The Aberystwyth Crime Survey was the first to focus specifically on victimization in rural areas (Koffman, 1996 and chapter 4). The most recent empirical work on crime in the countryside looked at rural Scotland (Anderson, 1997 and chapter 3). For the most part, however, criminologists in the United Kingdom have ignored the rural dimension to crime, seeing inner cities or peripheral housing estates as the key areas for analysis.

In spite of this neglect (and perhaps partly because of it) there are sound justifications for work on rurality and its significance for criminology. First, precisely because it is so undeveloped it may offer fertile ground for testing out new hypotheses about crime or for

---

[1] Oscar Wilde, *The Picture of Dorian Gray* (1891), ch. 19.
[2] My thanks to Stephen Feltham, research assistant at the University of Dundee, Summer 1997, for his help in the literature search for this chapter.

refuting or confirming existing ones. Rural area studies in the United States have been used to test out general theoretical approaches to crime, such as Shaw and McKay's social disorganization theory (Petee and Kowalski, 1993), Sutherland's differential association theory (Clinard, 1960), Cloward and Ohlin's strain theory (Laub, 1983), Hirschi's control theory (Natalino, 1982) and Felson's routine activity hypothesis (Carter et al., 1982). One of the most interesting studies of rural crime to come out of the United States applies ideas about the impact of technology on the production and distribution of illegal drugs in rural Kentucky (Weisheit, 1993). In their investigation of crime in rural Australia, O'Connor and Gray (1989) use their data on the fear of crime to highlight certain conceptual difficulties in the literature on fear of crime.

The differences which exist between the experience of crime in the countryside and in the city are still highly significant (although the gap appears to be narrowing). For instance, Anderson's analysis of the Scottish official crime figures from 1980 to 1995 shows that the ratio of rural to urban offending is 1:3 for recorded criminal incidents, but that the steady decrease in offending during the 1990s has been particularly significant in city areas. This, he suggests, largely accounts for the apparent increase in recorded crime in rural areas (Anderson, 1997). The same trends are evident in Scottish Crime Survey data although the differences are less pronounced (MVA, 1997). In England and Wales official statistics and crime-survey data also reveal major differences between levels of recorded and of unreported crime in rural and urban areas. For example, the incidence of burglary in agricultural areas was 20 per cent of the national average (Mayhew et al., 1993). There are parallels with the gender differences which have become such a key aspect of criminological work over the last twenty years (Smart, 1977, 1995; Heidensohn, 1996; Naffine, 1995). The distinctions between rural and urban crime rates could shed light on the effectiveness of informal and formal social control mechanisms, in the same way as studies of female criminality may aid our understanding of what encourages certain groups in society to conform (Carlen, 1983; Gelsthorpe, 1989; Worrall, 1990). Location plays as important a part in the construction of crime as gender, race or class, and yet the locations chosen for criminological research are almost always urban-centred. Might not a focus on the rural encourage a more imaginative look at crime and explanations for crime?

Crime in the countryside is also important for practical reasons. Crime rates in rural areas have risen, fear of crime has increased and rural communities are looking for assistance with their 'crime problem' (Koffman, 1996; Anderson, 1997). Certain types of rural crime, such as the theft of farm machinery and agricultural subsidy fraud, have an adverse effect not only on the rural economy but on the nation as a whole (National Farmers' Union, 1995). The reputation of a rural area as one with high crime rates may put off tourists and new residents (Krannich et al., 1989).

At a more abstract level, perceived problems in the countryside may serve to undermine confidence in the stability and safety of society generally, particularly at a time when insecurity and uncertainty appear to pervade the national psyche (Beck, 1992 and see also McCullagh, chapter 2). If crime is becoming commonplace even in 'England's green and pleasant land' what hope is there for 'the dark Satanic mills'? And what if 'the countryside strikes back' against its urban masters to protect itself from urban dilution, as apparently happened with the Countryside March in the spring of 1998?

In spite of these theoretical and practical justifications for undertaking research on crime in rural areas, the landscape of rural crime studies is, for the most part, flat and colourless. The next part of this chapter is an analysis of some of those studies, locating them in a myopic empirical tradition (rurality as matter) which I believe has undermined the possibilities for a more imaginative look at crime and the rural from within criminology itself. I then go on to dissect rurality as myth, and to question the assumptions which are made about crime and the countryside. From there I move away from criminology and look elsewhere for inspiration, to geography, and in particular rural geography, focusing on the meaning of rurality. Here the rural becomes a perplexing, sometimes breathtaking but always engaging space. I conclude by revisiting crime and the rural, and suggesting ways in which the significance of rurality for criminology may best be understood and further explored.

Rurality as Matter

While in the United Kingdom there has been very little written about twentieth-century crime in rural areas (historical studies deserve separate consideration and will be dealt with in the next section), the United States has seen a profusion, if not a wealth, of research. These studies can be most usefully considered as three waves, the first in the late 1920s, the second in the late 1970s/early 1980s, and some rekindling of interest in the 1990s. A literature search suggests that there are well over 300 pieces of research which have resulted in publications. I use the term 'matter' to describe this literature since the vast majority of studies are empirical in the positivistic tradition, and are in response to perceived concern, particularly on the part of government and law-enforcement agencies, about the 'problem' of crime in rural areas. In asking what is the matter with the country-side today they inevitably find that crime is embedded in the answer.

I do not propose to spend much time on these studies, worthy as they may be. For the most part, they are pedestrian, conservative and well-meaning, rather like the stereotype of an American Midwest farming family (the Waltons perhaps?), all pot-luck suppers and children who are naughty but never nasty. However, I think it is useful to illustrate what little progress has been made in this area over the last seventy years by comparing a number of studies from each of the three time periods.

First wave of crime studies in rural America: 1920s–1930s

The first wave of studies in the 1920s and 1930s is set in the context of the development of urban sociology, particularly with the emergence of the Chicago School from 1915 onwards. The ideas of Park and Burgess had much to offer the aspiring criminologist, and attempts were also made to incorporate mainstream sociological ideas, from Durkheim, Simmel and Tönnies, in studies of crime in rural areas.

These influences are clearly discernible in a major meta-analysis by Sorokin, Zimmerman and Galpin, which surveyed the literature on crime in the rural areas of fifteen countries (the United Kingdom, the United States, Australia, British India and eleven other European states) between 1857 and 1920 (Sorokin et al., 1930). Their findings are prefaced by references to changes in the nature of social control, particularly the reduction in the influence of the family and other informal neighbourhood groups, and the 'greater psycho-social heterogeneity of the city population', which have occurred as a 'result of the complication and urbanisation of society' (p. 264). These factors have affected rural as well as urban areas, they claim, but the system of rural social control continues to be more efficient and therefore the crime rate is lower in the countryside. Sorokin et al. established nine propositions, which can be summarized by stating that there is less crime in the countryside, fewer criminals are born or live there, their crimes are less sophisticated and recidivistic, but there are distinctions between different types of crime. Thus crimes of violence are proportionately more likely to occur in rural areas than crimes against property, and certain crimes, namely arson and cattle stealing, are predominantly rural crimes. The class differential is reflected in the fact that the agricultural class, although the most law-abiding of the 'occupational' classes, is nevertheless more criminal than the professional and official classes.

This early study sought to define the factors that distinguish the rural from the urban, citing occupational and environmental differences, population density, migration patterns and the size of communities, differentiation in socio-psychological characteristics, social stratification, social mobility and the system of social interaction as between the city and the countryside. It is interesting to note that the authors drew attention to the changing face of country life and considered that urban and rural communities were becoming increasingly convergent, particularly in western Europe. The authors also highlighted problems in defining what is rural, problems which have continued to be key issues for the more discerning studies of crime in rural areas.

A contemporaneous study by Smith (1933), claimed to be the first study of crime in rural areas ever published in the United States, provides some interesting material. Smith's approach offers a subtlety which is sadly lacking in some of the more recent research about crime in rural areas. Firstly, he has a developed sense of history, not a feature of many criminologists in the subsequent 'Walton' tradition. He draws on Victorian studies of crime in England, the Webbs' analysis of local government, and work by Lombroso and Aschaffenburg to underline both the urban/rural divide and also the considerable variations over time in the crime rates of rural areas. In his consideration of crime in the rural United States he applies the ideas of the Chicago school to the cattle ranges of the Northwest and the mining country of Montana in the 1860s, which were affected by 'the great waves of migration which rolled from east to west across the continent' and resulted in 'a species of rural crime which originated in the shifting about of large numbers of people' (Smith, p. 14). Secondly, he is aware of the difficulties in mapping crime patterns at a time when few rural areas in the United States were covered by the US Department of Justice's Uniform Crime Reports, and when the definition of 'rural' was unclear. He also notes the danger of assuming a simplistic relationship between crime rates and population density:

> The policies and official activity of the police in making arrests, of prosecutors in bringing defendants to trial, of juries in finding verdicts, and of judges and others . . . all exercise an influence . . . as the collection of criminal statistics becomes more and more remote, in a procedural sense, from the commission of the criminal act itself, the less value does it have as an index of the actual volume and incidence of crime. (Smith, pp. 25–6)

He points up a significant feature of rural life, namely that the figures for homicide in some rural areas, particularly in the Deep South, are proportionately greater than in city areas. Most importantly for the purposes of this chapter his ideas on the impact of social change on crime in the countryside are in line with much current thinking (O'Connor and Gray, 1989; Anderson, 1997), for instance:

> As a direct consequence of such developments [an intricate network of highways, the use of the motorcar, the employment of mechanical devices at home and on the farm] the rural dweller has been brought into intimate contact with both favourable and unfavourable urban influences. He has forsaken the cross-roads for the market town [read shopping centre]; widened the circle of his acquaintance, experienced the city dweller's frequent urge to rapid accumulation of wealth [and] suffered a distinct loss in his sense of economic security . . . these changed patterns have also involved a certain amount of dislocation which in turn has created new problems. There has also been a profound change in the social concept of crime, which has extended its scope to include various forms of irregular conduct not heretofore classed as criminal . . . effort is made to enforce additional regulations of human behaviour in city and country alike. (Smith, pp. 3–5)

Second wave of crime studies in rural America: the 1980s

Nearly fifty years later these same themes are reworked in a study (Cronk et al., 1982) funded by the US Department of Justice. In a review of research from 1933 to 1978 Warner notes that many of the problems associated with work on crime in rural areas, which were identified by Smith, have not been resolved. For instance, the definition of rural has been derived mainly from what the United States Census Bureau omits from its definition of 'metropolitan areas', that is, all communities with a population of under 9,999 or, according to the FBI, 'that portion of a county outside the Standard Metropolitan Statistical Area'. However, communities between 2,500 and 9,999 are classed as small towns. This applies both to the Uniform Crime Reports classification and the categories used in the National Crime Surveys.

Warner is also aware of the problems encountered in using official statistics as an accurate guide to crime patterns, just as Smith was fifty years before. Nevertheless, Warner's summary of work on crime in rural areas draws on Quinney's attempt (1966) to explain crime rates, a study which is based on official statistics. The explanation for the differences are derived, Quinney claims, either from structural issues, such as population density, or cultural factors, including a greater propensity to violence. While he does acknowledge the significant impact of criminal justice policies and practices on official crime rates he fails to explore this fully, and the areas selected for analysis are much too large to offer real insight into rural/urban differences. In addition, this work remains firmly located in the positivistic tradition of criminological research and offers no ethnographic or appreciative understanding of rural or indeed urban life. In passing it is interesting that another of the *enfants terribles* of criminology, Marshall Clinard, also carried out work on the rural/urban divide in crime (Clinard, 1960). Sadly, little of note appears in his research in this area. Nevertheless, it is clear from the volume of work around this time that crime in rural areas was increasingly regarded by American criminologists as a fruitful area, both in terms of research funding and virgin territory, particularly for those based in the Midwest.

Third wave of crime studies in rural America: the 1990s

To conclude this summary of criminological literature on crime in rural areas brief consideration will be given to the most recent wave of crime studies from the rural United States, which includes the work of Bachman on crime rates (1992), Weisheit et al. on rural crime and rural policing (1994) and Thompson on the nature of crime in rural areas (1996). In particular, the work of the doyen of rural crime studies in America, Joseph F. Donnermeyer, provides a useful example of current research concerns and will therefore be examined in more detail here (Donnermeyer et al., 1995). Accepting that definitional problems have not been resolved and that 'rural areas are incredibly diverse' (p. 2), he begins his analysis by noting that global factors – population mobility, urbanization, interdependence – shape crime trends in rural areas just as they do in urban areas. However, he soon leaves such abstractions behind, preferring to concentrate on a very broad statistical mapping exercise which fails to deal with the definitional issues and does not acknowledge complexity and diversity. By focusing on a comparison between the rural and urban areas of states he falls into the very traps that he himself has identified. His main findings are that there are still major differences between levels of crime in rural and urban areas, that violent crime is on the increase right across America, and that rural areas are now experiencing the levels of crime which were found in urban areas in the early 1960s.

Donnermeyer pinpoints substance abuse, gangs and political terrorism as matters of growing concern in rural areas. His explanation for this increase revolves around six factors (none of which are developed or substantiated): culture, poverty, urbanization, rapid change, organized crime, and urban export. Underpinning these factors is an understanding of crime causation in which the breakdown of traditional sources of authority, the family, the school and religion, is reinforced by encouragement to engage in deviant behaviour.

This brief review of the criminological literature is unlikely to encourage anyone to linger long – dinner with the Waltons may be filling and wholesome but *haute cuisine* it is not. Instead this body of research appears to be politically naïve, methodologically simplistic and philosophically unengaged. Nevertheless it is worth exploring the significance of rurality for crime further, particularly if one leaves criminology behind.

Rurality as Myth

The American studies of crime in rural areas considered in the last section tend to be ahistorical, fail to tackle key definitional issues, draw a crude divide between rural and urban, and are insensitive to residents' own perceptions of crime and the importance of geographical location. They feed off myths about rurality, based on a rural idyll of bygone days, the homogeneous, undifferentiated countryside, egalitarian rural communities and shared under-standings of country and city life.

Some of these myths surrounding rurality and crime are revealed through historical work. In the wonderfully titled *The Unquiet Countryside* Mingay (1989) brings together a formidable array of debunkers, involving studies of property crime, poaching and agrarian unrest, which demonstrate that crime in rural areas of the British Isles was a major problem before 1850. The image of a peaceful rural society is punctured by contemporaneous accounts painting a fearful picture of 'the tyranny of the countryside' where violence and malicious damage were sometimes more common in villages than in large neighbouring towns. Agrarian unrest was widespread, with 'Captain Swing' wreaking havoc to hay ricks and travellers in England, and 'Rebecca' following suit on the Welsh borders (Jones, 1989). Emsley (1987) describes villages which were said to be unsafe after dark and where gangs of young men roamed. An observer of the time, John Glyde, came to the shocking conclusion that '[t]he simplicity and innocence of peasant life exists only in imagination' (1856, pp. 146–7). And the further back we go the worse it gets. 'In the seventeenth century men killed, tortured and executed each other for political beliefs; they sacked towns and brutalised the countryside' (Sharpe, 1984, p. 185). Davey uncovers descriptions of village youths in late eighteenth-century Lincolnshire 'assembled in a riotous and unlawful manner to pull up gates and fences, throw stones at windows and harass people they did not like' (1994, p. 133). Of course these histories may themselves contain myths, often ignoring, for instance, the role of women in agrarian unrest and the ways in which perceptions of crime in rural areas were shaped by contemporary political and religious rhetoric. Nevertheless, they offer a valuable antidote to the pre-twentieth-century rural idyll.

Contemporary rural geographers have demonstrated very clearly that there are current as well as historical myths about rurality. Howard Newby's outstanding study of social change in rural England (1979) looks beyond the façade to the function and sees a rural landscape very different from that portrayed in *Country Life* or retirement-home literature. The village no longer has the function it once had as an occupational centre for farming arts and crafts. Instead, what is left of farming has become agribusiness, and that represents a diminishing share of the employment cake in rural areas. The unique, timeless, close-knit nature of rural communities is disappearing and Newby notes the 'gradual absorption of rural life into the mainstream of English society' (p. 273), something which urban dwellers and incomers observe with 'rural retrospective regret' (p. 155). His analysis also cuts across the traditional view of rural life epitomized by writers like Frankenberg, a way of life characterized by role diversity, breadth of role definition, small social networks, simple economy, little division of labour, and social integration which minimized conflict (1966). Instead Newby's rural settlements are not organized around a disembodied spirit of community; as he asserts, localities which are visually pleasing are not necessarily normatively so. He is critical of the notion of 'community' in any case, citing a study by Hillery (1955) which provides ninety-four different definitions of community with only one thing in common: they all involve people!

The uncritical coupling of the two social constructs, 'the rural' and 'crime', to create 'the rural community' lends itself to the creation of a conjoint myth. A more sophisticated analysis breaks down rural communities into various 'fractions' characterized by, for instance, occupation, age, household composition and length of residence (Cloke and Thrift, 1990). This analytical approach demonstrates clearly that conflict is often a key feature of rural life, and that it is not confined to the traditional landed/landless division or the more recent local/incomer distinction. Class, ethnic and gender divisions play an increasingly important role in defining groups in rural society.

In addition, recent Scottish and English studies of poverty and disadvantage in rural areas have punctured the myth of a comfortable country life. Schucksmith, for instance, in his observations on Scottish rural areas sees clear signs of severe disadvantage, which in many ways is more intractable and damaging than deprivation in urban areas (Shucksmith et al., 1994). Poverty in rural areas is nothing new, but Shucksmith notes the end of 'the mutuality of the [rural] oppressed' (Williams, 1973) with social isolation, the absence of service provision, and social divisions between incomers and locals causing deeper divisions between the haves and the have-nots. The notion that poverty is more bearable in the country, the myth of 'psychic income' where material disadvantage is compensated for by the uplifting nature of rural living, has encouraged greater acceptance of low incomes and increased the invisibility of the rural poor (Cloke et al., 1997).

The very notion of a distinct rural space is itself under challenge in the wake of immigration to the countryside and globalization. Indeed many would now claim with some authority that 'differences between rural and urban society may remain, but they are relatively unimportant' (Barrett, 1994, p. 24). The rural–urban continuum described by Wirth (1938) has been severely criticized, not least by its own adherents, such as Pahl (1965 and 1968) and Cloke (1977, 1990). 'The terms "rural" and "urban" are used habitually, yet the criteria employed in their definition have often been of a vague and intuitive nature' (Cloke, 1977, p. 31). A recent book on legal provision in the rural environment of Wales (Harding and Williams, 1994) notes that the definitions will depend on the nature of the enquiry and that there will therefore be 'shifting senses of rural, depending on the kind of questions asked' (p. 39). (For this point see also Anderson, chapter 3.)

Hoggart (1990) goes so far as to say that the broad category 'rural' is detrimental to the advancement of social theory. According to this critic, focusing on such a geographically based sub-field detracts from our understanding of the 'general rules of the game' (p. 246). Attempts to group together very different areas under the banner of a common rurality are doomed at best to failure and at worst to producing misleading results. Instead studies should focus on actual shared characteristics, such as socio-economic structures, since causal forces are not distinctive in rural areas and such a false distinction 'smoothes over the complexity of extra-local interchanges with an aura of intra-rural similarity' (p. 249). There is real danger of reification here, that 'locality becomes abstracted from the more substantive concerns of recounting the structuration of people's lives in it . . . Place . . . in this manner takes priority over people' (p. 253).

Most research studies of crime in rural areas, therefore, have neglected to explore the key issue of whether it is still possible to distinguish between urban and rural and, if it is, to break down what lies behind an undifferentiated notion of rurality. They have also failed to take account of general crime trends on the one hand and of rural residents' own perceptions and experiences on the other. O'Connor and Gray (1989) provide a notable exception in one of the most interesting studies which has been conducted of crime in rural areas. In a balanced, somewhat tongue-in-cheek description of a small town and its hinterland in New South Wales the writers suggest that

> we cannot spin a story about the horrors of the crime problem from the official evidence. Neither can we contrast the idyllic rural environment with the nasty urban milieu of violence on the streets . . . the safety of rural communities and the dangers of urban life have both been exaggerated. The possibility of criminal victimisation is a fact of life, but the likelihood of serious victimisation is small. The good news is that this is true whether you live in a city, in a small town or on an isolated rural property. (p. 18)

They make some interesting observations on the causal and mediating effects of locality on attitudes to crime, drawing on Max-field's work (1984). They also consider the role of locale in providing a support network, that elusive notion of 'community'. They make the crucial distinction between 'fear of victimization' and 'concern about crime' and argue strongly for a focus on 'central constructs of rural sociology, such as community and locality' (p. 170). They conclude that the images of the peaceful countryside and the dangerous city are largely myths. 'The difference in crime rates between urban and rural areas isn't that great' (p. 78). Shapland and Vagg's study of informal and formal policing in rural and urban areas in the early 1980s also suggests that, on the one hand, urban and rural respondents shared similar problems in their day-to-day life, and on the other, experience of crime and disorder was very diverse and very location-specific (1988, pp. 64–5).

Finally, geographers have dispelled the myth of rural isolation by reminding us that the countryside is as much affected by the national and international economy as the city. While rural areas are still experiencing depopulation, they are also undergoing population growth and repopulation (Rogers, 1993). Champion's work on immigration and counter-urbanization demonstrates that these are complex processes, which on the one hand reflect wider social trends and on the other are highly place-specific (Champion, 1989). These phenomena are global, as is much of the pain which accompanies such upheavals. In a study of social change in an Ontario small town, which is given the pseudonym of 'Paradise', Barrett demonstrates the impact of immigration on perceptions:

> For the past two decades there has been a steady influx of incomers . . .
> According to the locals, these newcomers . . . have ruined the community.

Crime has escalated, community spirit has disappeared, and with it everything that was pleasing and charming about rural life. In short, from the perspective of the people who were born and raised in the town, Paradise has been lost. (1994, p. 1)

Rurality as Meaning

Rural human geography has suffered, as has the study of crime in rural areas, from a lack of interest on the part of scholars, who have preferred to concentrate on urban issues and locate the countryside on the margins of their work. This urban ethnocentrism means that discussion about key developments is still relatively new but there has been a significant growth in academic interest within the last ten years. In addition, a public debate has begun to emerge about the 'real' nature of the countryside, prompted by a combination of very diverse issues of concern, such as proposals to outlaw field sports, factory farming, the spread of disease through the food chain, the destruction of natural habitat, inadequate public transport, the closure of village schools and the availability of rural housing. This in turn has led to resurgence in the notion of a distinct rural culture, both as a social phenomenon worthy of study and as a cause worth fighting for. The cause is not the province of one particular group or political persuasion, and so-called defenders of the countryside include farmers, the remnants of the landed aristocracy, New Age Travellers, field-sports enthusiasts, environmentalists, incomers and many city-dwellers also.

The question remains, however, whether rurality or ruralities exist at all. Is there any link between a distinctive rural 'way of life' and the undoubted difference in crime rates in the city compared with the countryside? Are the actions and perceptions of rural residents affected by where they live? Are ruralities experienced as different from urban environments by outsiders? Urban sociologists from Wirth to the present day have tried to convince us that the answer to all of these questions is yes. Even those who are critical of the urban/rural divide (such as Hoggart) nevertheless still seem to accept that some distinction is warranted.

One useful way into this issue is the public/private distinction. Lofland pioneered this approach in the early 1970s and it has been further developed by Fischer (1981), Freudenberg (1986) and Tittle (1989). A key issue for contemporary society is the protection of citizens, who appear to be particularly vulnerable to crime in public places, and the use made of public space by individuals or groups regarded as deviant. Young people causing annoyance on the streets, homeless men drinking and congregating in parks, New Age

Travellers seeking access to public sites (see Hester, chapter 8) have all become a focus for concern. They represent, using Wilson and Kelling's approach, signs of social disorder, and modern policing methods increasingly see them as a key target (Wilson and Kelling, 1982). Urbanism, it is claimed, leads to increased contact with 'unfamiliar, annoying and threatening people' in public space and this fosters estrangement and conflict between different groups within the city (Fischer, 1981). It is not, then, the breakdown of intimate relations that leads to social instability and crime but the difficulties in sustaining positive interaction with strangers. As Freudenberg shows, it becomes more difficult to control deviance when there is a decline in the density of acquaintanceship, that is where the proportion of people known to each other decreases (Freudenberg, 1986).

Critical rural studies, while rejecting the parochialism of traditional rural geography and adopting a 'political economic' approach, also recognize the importance of the physical and the metaphorical spaces within which 'the "communicative" aspects of social life' take place (Phillips, 1994, p. 91). In this framework the notion of the 'public sphere', 'a sphere of private people coming together as a public' (Habermas, 1989, p. 27) can usefully be applied to illuminate social interaction in rural spaces. This idea is both an old one, owing much to Adam Ferguson's notion of 'civil society' (1767), and has received new impetus from Habermas in his *Structural Transformation of the Public Sphere* (1989).

For the purposes of this chapter it is particularly important that the public sphere can be interpreted as having a spatial dimension since there appears to be a significant variation between the delineation of public and private in rural as contrasted with urban areas. The public spaces within the countryside – the village green, the village fair, the parish hall, the country pub, the meeting in the fields – may have no equivalents in urban life, either materially or metaphorically. They appear to occupy a position midway between the purely private and the entirely public, as an 'intermediate public sphere',which may give them particular significance in rural communities. It has been suggested that because there may be 'fewer unremittingly "public" public spheres in rural communities . . . it may be much harder to become an anonymous subject: a person with no private history' (Phillips, 1994, p. 103). In addition, it may also be much more difficult for country people to 'retreat into a completely private sphere in that the village publics regularly call on people to become active in a community' (ibid.). The role of women in rural communities, who may be more firmly located in the private sphere than they are in cities, may both encourage their conformity and provide them with greater opportunities to act as the moral guardians of 'village life' (Little,

1997). Thus communicative interaction in physical and symbolic rural space may, if Phillips is correct, both insulate people from strangers and lead to greater scrutiny by others whose approval is important, providing social control mechanisms which are not so readily accessible to city-dwellers. The implications for criminology of this perspective on rural spaces deserves further scrutiny.

In addition to their focus on delineating distinctions between the spatial dimensions of rural and urban spaces, critical rural geographers have done some useful and relevant work on the cultural dimension to rural problems, what might be termed metaphorical rural spaces. While crime is not included specifically in this analysis a focus on 'cultures of rurality' does offer a way into consideration of crime and deviancy in the countryside (Cloke and Milbourne, 1992). This approach argues that the rural idyll is a powerful one, but that in spite of its mythological qualities it is possible to discern 'a number of different cultural influences which interconnect in the changing lifestyles of people in rural areas' (p. 359). It accepts that the notion of a rural 'space' with distinctive rural functions is no longer tenable on a simplistic level. Local communities have ceased to be autonomous (because of mobility), the local economy has been superseded by national and global imperatives, rural areas increasingly are used in ways which draw in people from outside those areas, counter-urbanization has led to much more diversity in rural populations, and the insular nature of the countryside has gone for ever. However, the idea of rural cultures is resurrected in the form of social constructs which have a powerful influence on the way people think, decide and act, and on a cultural domain which impacts upon the processes of constructing those meanings. 'Rural becomes a world of social, moral and cultural values in which rural dwellers participate' (p. 350).

This approach does not lead us back to the undifferentiated rural idyll, however. These constructs of the rural are many and varied and, as we shall see shortly, they conflict and compete with each other for dominance. In fact such 'intra-rural' conflicts inevitably express themselves in part in the form of crime and disorder. The policing of New Age Travellers, the militancy displayed by both sides in the conflict over field sports, disputes over rural housing, and environmental protests can all be understood as expressions of different ruralities. Using this strategy, the myth of rurality is not discarded, it is deconstructed, and in the process its significance for criminology is manifested. It is difficult to do justice to the breadth and complexity of the critical geographers' work on rurality and the cultural dimension, and even more problematic to apply their arguments to crime. However, the following are some preliminary thoughts arising from their analysis.

Notions of stability, timelessness and security are embedded in the dominant notion of the rural at a national level (see, for instance, chapter 2 for a detailed analysis of the role of rurality in constructing a national identity for the Irish Republic). This myth offers 'a key to a door behind which lies a secret land; it will let you in but it is not the land itself . . . once beyond the door, only you can find it' (Fowles, quoted in Cloke and Milbourne, 1992, p. 351). This is a landscape dominated by patriotism, conservatism, patriarchy, ethnic preferences and class relations in which youth, alternative lifestyles and the shock of the new are particularly threatening. Whereas the urban myth prioritizes youth, dynamism and diversity, this rural myth has a fundamental mistrust of youth culture (reflected in concerns about raves and cannabis cultivation) and of alternative cultures (expressed in the strong measures used against New Age Travellers; see Hester, chapter 8). Some of these concerns were explicitly addressed in the provisions of the Criminal Justice and Public Order Act 1994. The idea of preserving the traditional notion of the rural from pernicious 'new' influences is also illustrated by the responses to the more diffuse threats to the countryside perceived, for example, in the abolition of hunting.

Rurality offers identity, seeking a clear delineation between the bucolic, law-abiding us and the lawless urban-import other. Studies of rural residents' perceptions about crime suggest that they are unwilling to accept the statistical evidence that most crime in rural areas is committed by rural dwellers (Anderson, 1997). Even though there is now greater room for doubt and increasing dissatisfaction among rural residents about crime in their area, a sense of a fundamental distinction, a rural/urban divide, still persists. Even the under-reporting and underestimates of crime in rural areas may be constructed as an oppositional to perceptions of urban crime. Paradoxically, it also appears to be possible to have *rus in urbe*, an urban area which residents regard as 'honorary countryside', a part of the landscape of Middle England, indelibly associated with low crime rates, a sense of security and the 'construction of benign-ness'. Even where the remnants only of a traditional English village exist, incomers particularly will cling fiercely to the idyll of a 'pastoral enclave'. An example is the village of Prestbury, very much exurbia as a village suburb of Macclesfield, where 'established, affluent residents are immensely proud of their village' and its reputation for a certain kind of pastoral 'Englishness' (Loader et al., 1998, p. 393). Here 'causing disorder' is especially troubling because it threatens this escape from the outside world of crime and incivilities.

The importance of 'otherness' in critical rural studies also has something of value to offer criminology. The 'Mr Average' of the countryside is 'white and probably English, straight and somehow without sexuality, able in body and sound in mind, and devoid of any other quirks of (say) religious or political affiliation' (Philo, 1992, p. 200). While the rural is seen as the converse of the urban, in fact we see ourselves reflected in the country-dweller, and Mr Average has been described as a mirror image of the academics who study him (ibid.). Therefore, to go beyond the rural, which is itself the 'other', and encompass otherness within the countryside is a very difficult task. As with traditional depictions of criminals and deviants, the 'other' in rural studies has generally been the undifferentiated other and there has been a failure to acknowledge the diversity of others who inhabit rural spaces. Studies of rurality, including studies of crime, should be open to describing and giving expression to the variety of others who live in the countryside, many of whom are excluded and marginalized from the official public sphere.

Finally, constructs of the rural provide a means of understanding and unpacking ideological conflicts which derive from contested and competing meanings attributed to the countryside (see Stenson and Watt, chapter 5). The landed gentry and landless farmworkers, whose conflicts over the true meaning of rurality have been a part of the landscape for centuries, are now joined, and in some cases superseded, by other groups, from commuters, agribusiness industrialists and back-to-the-landers to urban rejects and surplus elderly. Conflicts between these groups manifest themselves nationally over environmental issues and animal rights, regionally through White Settler campaigns and locally in disputes over housing and local amenities. Struggles over the control of rural spaces offer a valuable means by which criminologists can study issues about the differential distribution of power and control within societies, and this is well illustrated in Peay's chapter on the village pond dispute (chapter 11).

Conclusion

The criminological tradition has offered little of theoretical significance in its analysis of crime in rural areas. Attempts to explain the distinctions in crime rates and also in rural residents' perceptions of crime have fallen back on global explanations and have failed to present a more incisive view which is attuned to rural/urban differences. While problems persist in defining the rural and in describing the variety of rural domains, much more could be done by criminologists to illuminate this forgotten terrain.

The differential uses of material and metaphorical space in rural and in urban areas can provide a useful analytical tool for understanding crime in the countryside. The variety of meanings which attach to the rural, which are of course heavily dependent on class, race, gender, age and income, as well as specific locality, inevitably impact on the perceptions and actions of rural residents. Conflicts between different rural 'fractions' should be a developing field for criminology.

Criminology could contribute to our understanding of social relations in rural areas in a variety of ways. For instance, the rich tradition of ethnography in criminological research including such classics as *Luke Street* (Gill, 1977), *Wine Alley* (Damer, 1974) and more recently an English *Middletown* (Loader, Girling and Sparks, 1998) could be used as a resource for similar studies in rural areas. (See also chapter 11 of this book.) The development within criminology and socio-legal studies, firstly of feminist perspectives and then of theoretical approaches informed by debates about gender, could also be further extended to encompass crime and conflict outside the city. And the influence of postmodernism on criminological thought, which can be seen in the work of criminologists like Alison Young (1996), could fruitfully be applied to the criminal and deviant 'others' of the countryside.

Yet the field of rural criminology remains largely unexplored, at least in any analytical or critical sense. The reasons for this are diverse, including the absence of funding for rural studies, a desire on the part of the policy-makers to concentrate on urban areas, logistical difficulties in doing fieldwork with geographically dispersed populations, and a social problems approach to criminology which is constrained by its own parameters to focus on 'the mean streets' rather than 'the green fields'. Nevertheless, a few studies (most notably Anderson, 1997 and chapter 3; O'Connor and Gray, 1989; Shapland and Vagg, 1988) have shown that these difficulties can be overcome. The main problem continues to be the lack of engagement on the part of criminologists themselves with the rural. While critical rural geographers ten years ago could castigate their colleagues for ignoring rural studies and needing an 'urban fix' to excite their interest, that is no longer the case, with some of the best and most innovative work in geography being undertaken in this area. However, criminologists do not appear to have moved in the same direction. Although the uncritical, myth-laden approach of much American rural criminology is to be deplored, this chapter has tried to show that other more imaginative perspectives on the rural could be applied to research on crime and conflict in the countryside.

So rurality has something of significance to offer criminology. Sadly, however, criminology has offered little in return.

References

ACRE (Action with Communities in Rural England) (1995) *Rural Crime*, Cirencester: ACRE

ANDERSON, S. (1997) *A Study of Crime in Rural Scotland*, Edinburgh: Scottish Office Central Research Unit

BACHMAN, R. (1992) 'Crime in non-metropolitan America: a national accounting of trends, incidence rates, and idiosyncratic vulnerabilities', 57 (4) *Rural Sociology*, 546

BARRETT, S. R. (1994) *Paradise: Class, Commuters and Ethnicity in Rural Ontario*, Toronto: University of Toronto Press

BECK, U. (1992) *Risk Society: Towards a New Modernity*, London: Sage

CARLEN, P. (1983) *Women's Imprisonment*, London: Routledge and Kegan Paul

CARTER et al. (1982) *Rural Crime: Integrating Research and Prevention*, Montclair, NJ: Allanheld, Osmun

CHAMPION, A. G. (1989) *Counterurbanisation: The Changing Pace and Nature of Population Deconcentration*, London: Arnold

CLINARD, M. (1960) 'A cross-cultural replication of the relation of urbanism to criminal behaviour', 25 *American Sociological Review*, 253

CLOKE, P. (1977) 'An index of rurality for England and Wales', 11 *Regional Studies*, 313

CLOKE, P. (1990) 'Political economy approaches and a changing rural geography', 1 *Rural History*, 123

CLOKE, P., GOODWIN, M. and MILBOURNE, P. (1997) *Rural Wales: Community and Marginalization*, Cardiff: University of Wales Press

CLOKE, P. and MILBOURNE, P. (1992) 'Deprivation and lifestyles in rural Wales, II: rurality and the cultural dimension', 8 (4) *Journal of Rural Studies*, 359

CLOKE, P. and THRIFT, N. (1990) 'Class and change in rural Britain', in Marsden, T. et al. (eds.), *Rural Restructuring*, London: David Fulton

CRAWFORD, A. et al. (1990) *Second Islington Crime Survey*, London: Middlesex Polytechnic

CRONK, S. D., JANKOVIC, J. and GREEN, R. K. (1982) *Criminal Justice in Rural America*, Washington DC: US Department of Justice

DAMER, S. (1974) 'Wine Alley: the sociology of a dreadful enclosure', 22 *Sociological Review*, 221

DAVEY, B. J. (1994) *Rural Crime in Early Modern England 1550–1750*, Hull: University of Hull Press

DONNERMEYER, J. (1995) *Crime and Violence in Rural Communities*, Internet: http://www.ncrel.org/sdrs/areas/issues/envrnmnt/drugfree/v1donner.htm

EMSLEY, C. (1987) *Crime and Society in England, 1750–1900*, London and New York: Longman

FERGUSON, A. (1767) *An Essay on the History of Civil Society*, Edinburgh

FISCHER, C. S. (1981) 'The public and private worlds of city life', 46 *American Sociological Review*, 306

FRANKENBERG, R. (1966) *Communities in Britain*, Harmondsworth: Penguin Books

FREUDENBERG, W. R. (1986) 'The density of acquaintanceship: an overlooked variable in community research', 92 (1) *American Journal of Sociology*, 27

GELSTHORPE, L. (1989) *Sexism and the Female Offender*, Aldershot: Gower

GILL, O. (1977) *Luke Street, Housing Policy, Conflict and the Creation of a Delinquent Area*, London: Macmillan

GLYDE, J. (1856) *Suffolk in the Nineteenth Century: Physical, Social, Moral, Religious and Industrial*, London

HABERMAS, J. (1989) *The Structural Transformation of the Public Sphere: An Inquiry into a Category of Bourgeois Society*, Cambridge: Polity Press

HARDING, C. and WILLIAMS, J. (eds) (1994) *Legal Provision in the Rural Environment*, Cardiff: University of Wales Press

HEIDENSOHN, F. (1996) *Women and Crime*, 2nd edn, Basingstoke: Macmillan

HILLERY, G. (1955) 'Definitions of community: areas of agreement', 20 *Rural Sociology*, 111

HOGGART, K. (1990) 'Let's do away with rural', 6 (3) *Journal of Rural Studies*, 245

HUSAIN, S. (1995) *Cutting Crime in Rural Areas: A Practical Guide for Parish Councils*, Swindon: Crime Concern

JONES, D. (1989) *Rebecca's Children: A Study of Rural Society, Crime and Protest*, Oxford: Clarendon Press

KOFFMAN, L. (1996) *Crime Surveys and Victims of Crime*, Cardiff: University of Wales Press

KRANNICH, R., BERRY, E. and GREIDER, T. (1989) 'Fear of crime in rapidly changing rural communities: a longitudinal study', 54 (2) *Rural Sociology*, 195

LAUB, J. H. (1983) 'Patterns of offending in urban and rural areas', *Journal of Criminal Justice*, 129

LITTLE, J. (1997) 'Employment marginality and women's self-identity', in Cloke, P. and Little J. (eds), *Contested Countryside Cultures: Otherness, Marginality and Rurality*, London: Routledge

LOADER, I. (1996) *Youth, Policing and Democracy*, London: Macmillan

LOADER, I., GIRLING, E. and SPARKS, R. (1998) 'Narratives of decline: youth, disorder and community in an English "Middletown"', 38 (3) *British Journal of Criminology*, 388

MVA Consultancy (1997) *The 1996 Scottish Crime Survey*, Edinburgh: Scottish Office Central Research Unit

MAXFIELD, M. (1984) *Fear of Crime in England and Wales*, Home Office Research Studies No. 78, London: HMSO

MAYHEW, P., AYE MAUNG, N., MIRRLEES-BLACK, C. (1993) *The 1992 British Crime Survey*, Home Office Research Study No. 132, London: HMSO

MINGAY, G. E. (1989) *The Unquiet Countryside*, London: Routledge

MIRRLEES-BLACK, C., MAYHEW, P. and PERCY, P. (1996) *The 1996*

British Crime Survey, Home Office Statistical Bulletin No. 19/96, London: HMSO

NAFFINE, N. (ed.) (1995) *Gender, Crime and Feminism*, Aldershot: Dartmouth

NATALINO, K. W. (1982) 'Family, peers and delinquency: a rural replication of urban findings', in Carter et al. (eds), *Rural Crime: Integrating Research and Prevention*, Montclair, NJ: Allanheld, Osmun.

NATIONAL FARMERS' UNION (1995) 'Rural crime: the true picture', *British Farmer* (October)

NEWBY, H. (1979) *Green and Pleasant Land? Social Change in Rural England*, London: Wildwood House

O'CONNOR, M. E. and GRAY, D. E. (1989) *Crime in a Rural Community*, Sydney: Federation Press

PAHL, R. E. (1965) *Urbs in Rure*, London: Weidenfeld and Nicolson

PAHL, R. E. (1968) 'The rural/urban continuum', in Pahl, R. E. (ed.), *Readings in Urban Geography*, Oxford: Pergamon Press

PETEE, T. and KOWALSKI, G. (1993) 'Modelling rural violent crime rates: a test of social disorganisation theory', 26 (1) *Sociological Focus*, 87

PHILLIPS, M. (1994) 'Habermas, rural studies and critical social theory', in Cloke, P., et al. (eds.), *Writing the Rural: Five Cultural Geographies*, London: Paul Chapman

PHILO, C. (1992) 'Neglected rural geographies: a review', 9 *Journal of Rural Studies*, 193

QUINNEY, R. (1966) 'Structural characteristics, population areas, and crime rates in the United States', 57 *Journal of Criminal Law, Criminology and Police Science*, 45

ROGERS, A. (1993) *English Rural Communities: An Assessment and Prospect for the 1990s*, London: Rural Development Commission

SHAPLAND, J. and VAGG, J. (1988) *Policing by the Public*, London: Routledge

SHARPE, J. A. (1984) *Crime in Early Modern England 1550–1750*, London and New York: Longman

SHOEMAKER, R. B. (1991) *Prosecution and Punishment: Petty Crime and the Law in London and Rural Middlesex, c. 1660–1725*, Cambridge: Cambridge University Press

SHUCKSMITH, M. (1990) *The Definition of Rural Areas and Rural Deprivation*, Research Report No. 2, Edinburgh: Scottish Homes

SHUCKSMITH, M. et al. (1994) *Disadvantage in Rural Scotland: How is it Experienced and How should it be Tackled?*, York: Joseph Rowntree Foundation/Rural Forum

SKOGAN, W. G. (1986) 'Fear of crime and neighbourhood change', in Reiss, A. J. and Tonry, M. (eds), *Communities and Crime*, Chicago: University of Chicago Press

SMART, C. (1977) *Women, Crime and Criminology*, London: Routledge and Kegan Paul

SMART, C. (1995) *Law, Crime and Sexuality: Essays on Feminism*, London: Sage

SMITH, B. (1933) *Rural Crime Control*, New York: Columbia University Press

SOROKIN, P., ZIMMERMAN, C. and GALPIN, C. (1930) *A Systematic Sourcebook in Rural Sociology*, vols. 1–3, Minneapolis: University of Minnesota Press

THOMPSON, K. M. (1996) 'The nature and scope of rural crime', in McDonald, T. D. et al. (eds), *Rural Criminal Justice: Conditions, Constraints and Challenges*, Sheffield: Sheffield Publishing Company

TITTLE, C. R. (1989) 'Influences on urbanism: a test of prediction on three perspectives', 36 *Social Problems*, 270

TUCK, M. (1989) *Drinking and Disorder: A Study of Non-metropolitan Violence*, Home Office Research Study No.108, London: HMSO

WEISHEIT, R. A. (1993) 'Studying drugs in rural areas: notes from the field', 30 (2) *Journal of Research in Crime and Delinquency*, 213

WEISHEIT, R. A. (1994) *Rural Crime and Rural Policing*, Internet: http//www.ncjrs.arg: 71/0/4/1 pubs/wr/crim.asc

WILLIAMS, R. (1973) *The Country and the City*, London: Chatto and Windus

WILSON, J. Q. and KELLING, G. (1982) 'Broken windows', *Atlantic Monthly*, 29

WIRTH, L. (1938) 'Urbanism as a way of life', 44 *American Journal of Sociology*, 1

WORRALL, A. (1990) *Offending Women*, London: Routledge

YOUNG, G. A. (1996) *Imagining Crime: Textual Outlaws and Criminal Conversations*, London: Sage

2

Rural Crime in the Republic of Ireland

CIARAN McCULLAGH

Introduction

The prospects for a significant chapter on rural crime, or on crime in rural areas, in Ireland are initially at least unpromising. As we shall see below, the predominant feature of crime in the Republic of Ireland has been the degree to which it has been and continues to be concentrated in urban areas and particularly in Dublin, the capital city. This was true in the late nineteenth century and continues to be true today. Crime in rural areas, which between 1922 and the late 1960s was negligible, continues in the more recent period to be low.[1]

Thus rural crime appears to be an unpromising site for criminological or sociological investigation. However, such pessimism confuses quantity of crime with symbolic and political importance. The lack of significant crime in rural areas conceals the role which rural crime has played in the construction of crime as a problem and as a public and policy issue in the Republic of Ireland. The argument in this chapter is that rural crime or a number of highly publicized rural crimes have been of greater significance in creating a sense that there is a crime problem in Ireland than the quantitatively greater issue of urban crime.

This chapter is divided into two parts. In the first the limited amount of material on crime in Ireland is analysed to establish the patterns of rural and urban crime. This section is based on a small number of historical studies, some analyses of police statistics on

[1] The term 'rural' is used in this chapter to refer to those parts of the Republic of Ireland which are outside the major cities of Dublin, Cork, Waterford, Galway, Limerick and Sligo. The size of these cities reflects very much the pattern of urban primacy found in less developed countries, with the major city, Dublin, being almost eight times larger in population terms than the next largest city, Cork (see McKeown, 1986). While some of the smaller cities have acquired media reputations for certain kinds of crime (the association of Limerick, for example, with violent assault), these images are not well supported by official statistics.

crime, the results of the only victim survey done in Ireland that was national in scope, and the results of a more limited victim survey that looked at the incidence of domestic violence. The dearth of material is a reflection of a number of aspects of Irish political and academic life, most notably what was until recently a low level of concern with crime and a low level of funding of academic research generally. The second section explores the issue of rural crime through an analysis of the role that a particular version of rurality has played in the construction of national identity in Ireland. It examines the way in which a number of violent rural crimes undermined this image and the way in which they created a sense that crime is indeed a problem that requires a serious policy response.

Analysing Rural Crime

Let us begin, however, with a look at the overall pattern of crime in Ireland and with the place of rural crime in it. (For a useful historical review of crime in Ireland see Brewer, Lockhart and Rodgers, 1997). The major source for such an analysis is the statistics of the Gardai[2] which in their present form go back to 1947, but which exist in an utilizable form back to the 1920s. Most analyses of crime, though, such as those by Rottman (1980) and by Lockhart and his colleagues (1995), go back to the late 1940s and early 1950s, while the analysis by Paul O'Mahony (1993) goes back to 1973. When we supplement this with some historical material we can show how certain features of crime have remained constant. For the purposes of this chapter the key one has been the degree to which crime has remained primarily an urban phenomenon, and within this primarily a problem in Dublin.

In the nineteenth century and more specifically between 1870 and 1895 Dublin was the location of over half the indictable crime in the country.[3] The period is significant, as it was a time of major disorder in rural Ireland associated with the widespread and often violent agitation by tenant farmers over ownership rights (for a sociological account see Clark, 1975). But nevertheless even then crime was an urban phenomenon. In 1910 figures suggest that only one major city in what was then the British Isles had a crime level that exceeded

---

[2] The Irish police are known officially by their name in the Irish language, the Garda Siochana, which translates into English as 'guardians of the peace'. They are also known by a series of colloquial names that they share with police forces on a worldwide basis.

[3] Crime figures for the years up to 1921 refer to the island of Ireland. Figures from 1921 onwards refer to the Republic of Ireland.

Dublin's, and that was Liverpool. Dublin, for example, had 852 indictable offences per 100,000 of the population, compared with 253 in London (O'Brien, 1982).

An analysis of Irish crime statistics from 1860 to 1914 by Finnane (1995) does not directly focus on the rural and urban aspects of crime in which we are interested here. But overall the data tend to confirm the centrality of Dublin in crime statistics. They also imply that the relationship between location and crimes of violence may be more complex than some arguments suggest. Thus Rottman (1980) argues that crimes against the person are more common in rural areas, but the historical data suggest that for one kind of violent crime at least Dublin was important. Assaults on the police in the early 1860s were five times the rate of the closest county or urban area. This gap has narrowed and there is some evidence that this offence is now more pronounced in rural areas.

Where homicide is concerned, there is some evidence that in the early part of the twentieth century it was predominantly a small-town or rural offence. Rottman (1980) found that this was still the case in the 1950s, but by the 1970s, the period when his analysis of homicide statistics ends, urban centres accounted for almost half the homicides in the country. While there have been no more recent attempts to analyse murder statistics in these terms, most observers would argue that murder has become increasingly an urban crime. However, even this needs to be put into context. Though Dublin may now be a significant location for homicides in Ireland, the homicide rate is still by international standards very low. A 1985 comparison showed that the rate of murder in Dublin was 8 per million while those of Amsterdam, Paris, Hamburg and London were 290, 100, 50 and 20 per million respectively (see O'Mahony, 1993).

Traditionally the low levels of crime outside the urban centres were explained by the safety valve of emigration. Those most likely to be from what criminologists would term the crime-prone age groups simply left the country in search of economic and social opportunities. Indeed some historians have linked variations in the level of disorder in rural areas to the degree of ease with which landless males from rural areas could emigrate to the United States in particular. They argue that restrictions on emigrants to the US coincided with, if not produced, rural disorder (see Finnane, 1995).

The period from the 1920s to the 1950s was characterized by a steep decline in crime everywhere in Ireland, and one observer concluded that crime rates outside Dublin were so low as to be negligible (Rottman, 1988). Crime began to rise with the increase in economic prosperity produced by industrialization in the late 1960s. We can see this in a cursory look at crime statistics (for more detail see Rottman,

1980; O'Mahony, 1993; and McCullagh, 1996). In the 1950s and 1960s there were on average 15,000 indictable offences per year recorded by the Gardai. This rose to the 95,000 or 100,000 offences that annually characterize the current period. This change has been described as a structural transformation rather than simply a numerical increase, making the possibility of a return to previous low levels unlikely. However, this has not diminished the capacity of people who believe in the need for moral rearmament to delude themselves into setting it as a policy aim.

What is interesting, for present purposes, about the trends after 1964 is that they have been experienced fairly evenly across all parts of the country. According to Rottman (1984, p. 91), crime rose in Dublin and in other urban centres, but it also increased in rural areas. 'Such unevenness', he argues, 'is unusual as most post-industrialisation rises in crime began in the major urban areas and only after a substantial interval filtered down to small cities, towns and villages.' This means that rural crime rates did increase, but the effect was to raise the rates from negligible to low. The crime rate in Mayo, a typical rural area, is a fairly good example. In 1995 it stood at 7.95 per 1,000 of population compared with the rate in Dublin North Central of 222 per 1,000.

This is confirmed in the only national victim survey done in Ireland over a period in 1982/3 (Breen and Rottman, 1985). The authors concluded that 'rural rates of victimisation are extremely low except in areas in close proximity to Dublin and to certain other major urban centres'. Indeed parts of rural Ireland, such as the West, are 'virtually free of crime' (p. 53). Referring to the 57 per cent of the population who reside in places designated as rural areas (that is, with less than 10,000 population), Rottman (1988, p. 98) argues that 'they are exposed to a negligible risk of becoming crime victims'.

The other effect of the evenness of the increases has been to retain the dominance of Dublin as the location for crime in Ireland. Typically over the past twenty to thirty years 50–60 per cent of indictable crime occurs in Dublin, a city that in 1991 contained only around 30 per cent of the population. The results of the 1982/3 victim survey confirm this. Rottman (1988, p. 98) illustrates the extent of urban concentration through a comparison between London and Dublin. 'A family living in Dublin's inner city', he says, 'has 12 times the risk of becoming a burglary victim than someone living in rural Ireland; the typical family in inner city London has a 5-fold greater risk than their rural counterpart.'

These points are based on aggregate interpretations of crime figures and on the results of only one victim survey. More sophisticated analyses, yet to be done, would involve a more detailed examination of the trajectory of specific offences, in particular the distribution of crimes of violence. It has been suggested, for example, that there is one offence for which rural rates have remained consistently higher, and that is assaults on Gardai.

Such analyses would also allow us to put the crime pattern in rural areas in some sort of comparative perspective. At the national level, analyses based on police statistics show that Ireland continues to have one of the lowest crime rates of countries in the European Union and one of the highest detection rates. The results of the victim survey disputed some aspects of this, but as the survey has not been repeated its findings lack the comfort of replication. However, rural crime rates have never been placed in a comparative perspective and hence have not opened speculation as to whether they may be lower than those of other countries and, if so, why.

One kind of crime that was not considered in the national victim survey was that of violence against women, or more specifically violence against women in intimate relationships. An attempt to rectify this was made in a national survey in 1995 (Kelleher and O'Connor, 1995). Working with a definition of violence that embraced mental, physical and sexual violence, it surveyed a sample of 1,483 women over the age of eighteen and it had a 46 per cent response rate. On this basis it concluded that 18 per cent of the women in intimate relationships had been victims of some form of domestic violence by either a current or a former partner. When classified in terms of rural or urban location, the figure for women in rural areas was 17 per cent and 18 per cent for women in urban areas. Unfortunately for our purposes, this is the only point in the research at which location was used in the data analysis, and indeed it is unclear from the published report how the rural/urban distinction was constructed. The figures are also difficult to interpret, as the report gives no indication of the numbers of rural and urban women in the sample.

The report includes an analysis of incidents of domestic violence reported to the Gardai for an eight-month period in 1994. The figures cover the full range of Gardai divisions in the country. They show the urban dominance in such reports. Almost 75 per cent of incidents reported were in the Dublin metropolitan area. Moreover if the statistics allowed for a more sophisticated breakdown by rural and urban location they would show a much higher incidence of violence against women in urban areas.

These data tend to suggest significant differences in the way in which domestic violence is dealt with in the different locations, both in terms of comparisons between Dublin and rural locations and, probably more significantly, between rural locations themselves. Thus overall there was a higher percentage of arrests, charges and convictions in incidents of domestic assault outside Dublin. But a rural area like Sligo/Leitrim had two convictions out of 55 incidents, while a somewhat similar rural area like Clare had 29 incidents and also two convictions. These figures suggest that among other things police practices in responding to domestic violence may vary significantly from one rural area to another.

International and cross-cultural comparisons are difficult in this area as they raise complex issues of methodology, particularly in relation to definitions of domestic violence. However, fairly basic comparisons would suggest that at an aggregate level domestic violence may be somewhat lower here than in other countries. Of the 18 per cent of women who experienced domestic violence in this study 58 per cent experienced actual physical violence (i.e. 11 per cent of the total). This compares with figures of 25 per cent in Canada and 25–30 per cent in the United States (see Kelleher and O'Connor, 1995, pp. 139–40).

Overall, then, what all of these sources confirm is that the level of crime in rural Ireland is low. Despite this, however, the social and sociological significance of rural crime is not fully circumscribed by its numerical qualities. To understand this we need to move our discussion from the numerical to the cognitive arena in society. We need to place crime in the context of issue awareness and the creation of social problems. The increase in crime in Ireland was predominantly an increase in urban areas, but such numerical changes were not sufficient in themselves to produce awareness that crime had become a problem. There was a gap between the existence of crime and the awareness of crime as a social and political issue. Urban crime has not been sufficient in Ireland to unite the two, but rural crime was. This is what we turn to in the next section.

Rural Crime as a Cultural Problem

Consider this. There were three unrelated murders in January 1996 in three separate rural areas. The first was of a farmer, Patrick Daly, who was murdered on 18 January. He had been missing for some days and the Gardai had been looking for him. His body was found at the bottom of a well. It had been hidden there and covered with black plastic sheeting. Five days later the body of Tommy Casey, a farmer who lived in a rural area of County Galway, was found at his home. He had died as a result of injuries sustained in an assault by intruders. The same day, Joyce Quinn, a shop-owner in a small village in County Kildare and a mother of three, was murdered. She had been reported as missing and her body was found two days after she had been killed. Like all murders, these were brutal crimes, but beyond this they had little in common other than their temporal coincidence and the fact that they occurred in rural areas.

Yet these provoked a level of public response that was unusual in its intensity, and a level of Gardai response that was exceptional. An opinion poll conducted at the end of January 1996 by the national evening newspaper found that 97 per cent of respondents 'did not feel safe on their own and felt that crime was out of control'. The Gardai called in helicopter support to cover the countryside in the search for the alleged murderers, they set up checkpoints on an extensive scale nationally and in an act that had few precedents in peacetime Ireland they set up road blocks on major bridges across the River Shannon. These were staffed by armed officers and effectively controlled traffic flows into and out of the west of Ireland.[4]

There is no doubt that the three murders were serious, but equivalent offences in urban areas did not provoke the same level of response. Similarly the responses were disproportionate, in that normal police work identified the offenders in all three cases (and did so within just over a week in two of the cases and three weeks in the other). In two of the cases the alleged offenders were local to the areas in which the crimes were committed. One of them was the 71-year-old brother of one of the victims. So why this level of response? To answer this we need to understand the image of the rural in the Irish consciousness, and the cultural and ideological significance of the particular version of rurality that dominates in Irish society. As will be seen below, the rural is the repository of the sense of true Irishness, and this is one of innocence, beauty and tranquillity. If violent crime could come to such areas, then crime really was a serious problem in Irish society and one that needed an urgent response.

Thus, while crime had been rising in Ireland since the middle of the 1960s and had become particularly pronounced in a number of areas of Dublin, where it was accompanied by and had a somewhat symbiotic relationship with a rising level of heroin use, this did not create a sustained sense that crime was something that needed an intensive national response. There was also a certain sense in which crime was what you would expect in Dublin, and so was somewhat less urgent in nature.

This was particularly so in relation to drugs. Heroin use and abuse had taken hold in a limited number of seriously deprived areas in Dublin. But, despite the efforts of community activists and a small number of politicians, it never succeeded in provoking the kind of policy response that might have nipped the problem in the bud and

---

[4] The information on the crimes in this section is taken from the relevant issues of *Irish Times* newspapers for the period. These can be consulted on the Web page of the newspaper.

prevented the rise of a number of drug gangs who amassed large sums from the drugs trade. Rural crime simply had a kind of cultural resonance and induced a kind of culture shock that urban crime did not seem able to produce. To understand why this may be the case requires us to look at Irish identity and the place of the rural in it. For that we need to begin with the formation of the new Irish State in the 1920s.

One of the initial and decisive crises that a new nation faces is the attempt to create a sense of identity, an ideology of nationhood, or, more pertinently, a new way of imagining itself that can command the loyalty of its subjects. The nationalism of the new Irish State was not untypical of many forms of nationalism in post-colonial societies in that the identity that was constructed was reactionary: it was everything that the colonial power was not. The key defining elements of the colonizer were used as the focus point from which an alternative sense of identity could be created. This meant that the sense of what a new Irish nation would be was everything the British Empire, the colonizing power, was not. Thus Britain was perceived to be secular or Protestant (in the eyes of many Irish people at the time, a distinction that makes no difference); therefore Ireland would be Catholic. Britain was English-speaking; therefore Ireland would be Gaelic-speaking. Britain was urban and industrialized; therefore Ireland should be rural and agricultural.

These qualities did not spring into being with political independence in 1921 but had been present in embryonic form in nineteenth-century Ireland, particularly through the writings and teaching of major figures in the nationalist tradition. Thus the importance of the Gaelic language to the nature of Irishness was an idea that had been adopted from nineteenth-century European romanticism, particularly that of the German kind, and was a major influence on the formation of the Gaelic League in 1893. Their objective was to save the Gaelic language, which by then was spoken only along the west coast of Ireland. For them, as Daniel J. O'Neill (1987) put it, 'language was not simply a tool of communication: it was a unique product of a people's history and experience and a link with their forebears.' Language in their view, he continued, 'provided a chain of being. To abjure one's traditional language and assimilate to that of another people was to compromise one's nationality.' A minister in the first government said, 'there was no doubt that a country without a language was not a country at all. At best it was a province' (quoted in Brown, 1981). In this way, as O'Neill and others argue, Ireland had a sense of nationhood before it acquired statehood. Indeed it was a sense of nationhood which even then ignored the section of the population in the north-east of the country who did not and are still reluctant to subscribe to it, namely the Unionists in Northern Ireland.

These markers of identity and nationhood informed many of the policies of the new state and many of the ways in which the new state chose to present itself. Thus the close identity of Irish and Catholic was written into the constitution of 1937. In Article 42 it explicitly recognized the special position of the Catholic Church in the Irish State, a position that many believed was also reflected in the close level of consultation between Church and State on matters of social policy, particularly in the areas of health and education. The most striking example of this closeness was the capacity of the Catholic Church to prevent the State introducing what the Catholic bishops perceived to be socialized medicine, a controversy known in Ireland as the 'Mother and Child' scheme (see Keogh, 1994, pp. 208–13).

The central role of the Irish language was also recognized in Article 8 of the Irish constitution, which declared that it was the 'first official language' of the State. Irish had been taught in the schooling system prior to independence. But in 1924 this was taken a significant step further when the learning of the language was made a compulsory school subject, and a capacity to speak and work in it was made a requirement for employment in the civil service and many other State positions. This situation continues to exist and continues to be a point of some contention in Irish cultural and educational politics. State policy did little to halt the decline of the language, but this decline did little to affect the position that the language occupied in the pantheon of Irish identity. In these matters the relationship between symbols and empirical reality is often a matter of little consequence.

The situation in relation to the rural dimension of Irish identity is similar. 'The equation of rural life with all that was truly Irish' (the phrase is from Gibbons, 1984), which became a defining feature of the new sense of Irishness, had its roots in the cultural nationalism of the nineteenth century. A vision of what has been described as 'rustic dignity and rural virtue' (Brown, 1981) was made popular through the writings of luminaries such as the poet W. B. Yeats. But it was more widely diffused through the work of lesser-known and less talented writers such as the novelists Canon Sheehan and Charles Kickham. They wrote of farmers and peasants in rural Ireland as simple, though not in a pejorative sense, and as unspoiled and virtuous.

They wrote about rural Ireland as exemplifying the essential virtues and essence of the truly Irish. In particular they singled out the west of Ireland as the enclave of traditional values, and the desire of native government to halt the economic decline of the west was as much a cultural as an economic project. In this way, they reinforced Irish society 'in the belief that rural life constituted an essential element of an unchanging Irish identity' (Brown, 1981, p. 84).

This idealization of rural life, or as it is often called 'rural fundamentalism' (see Commins, 1986), saw the family farm and rural life as the source of political stability. The ideal of the family farm and the ideal of having as many as possible working on the land are enshrined in Article 45 of the constitution. This was linked to and supported by Catholic social thought of the time, which believed in the intrinsically moral nature of agricultural work. These views were echoed in the thought of Eamon De Valera and 'his evocation of a frugal pastoral utopia' (Murphy, 1983). They were given significant academic support by the work of Arensberg and Kimball (1968). The picture these anthropologists presented of an integrated set of relationships within families, and between families, kin groups and neighbours in rural Ireland was more a product of their theoretical interests in functionalism than of their somewhat more recalcitrant empirical material (see Bell, 1983). But the acceptance and popularity of their ideas was not a purely academic issue. Their work, as Bell (1983, p. 22) argues, provided a theoretical discourse 'to complement the ideological self-understanding of the new nation (or at least its nationalistically inspired intellectual elite)'.

Sport was also an important instrument through which Irish identity was promoted, and the radio was the key medium for the dissemination of images of sport and the cultural assumptions that sport embodied. It became a means through which Irishness could be asserted and, according to Boyle (1992, p. 634), 'media sport was an uncritical projection of what Irish culture supposedly was and was not'. Central to that was the pride of place given to the broadcast of Gaelic games in the radio sports schedules, and the relevant sporting body, the Gaelic Athletic Association (GAA), expected the media to devote large amounts of time to the live broadcast of matches. This was an expectation with which broadcasters were happy to comply. Their games were projected on radio as the opposite to the urban sports of industrial Britain, mainly soccer. That is, they were 'Irish, rural and celebrated the moral worth of the peasant' (Boyle, 1992, p. 626). Such was the strength of this antipathy to soccer that the refusal of the GAA to allow the Irish soccer team to play in Croke Park, the headquarters of the organization and the largest stadium in Ireland, continues to this day.

This discourse of rurality continues to be influential in Irish society. Writing in the 1950s in the report of a government commission to see what could be done to halt the haemorrhage of people from rural Ireland a Catholic bishop said that the rural 'has always been and is still, the best place to rear a family' (quoted in

Commins, 1986, p. 53). The centrality of the family farm also figures in the pronouncements of farm leaders in the current concerns about the future reform of the agricultural policy of the European Union. It is through its effects on family farms that the policy is being opposed. Like other aspects of national identity and ideology it too has remained relatively impervious to the empirical reality of rural decline, especially among those most idealized in the rhetoric, the small farmers of the west of Ireland. It has also remained impervious to the fact that the majority of the population now live in urban centres like Dublin and Cork.

The contemporary manifestations of this discourse can be seen in the means through which the Irish Tourist Board tries to market Ireland as a tourist destination. As O'Connor has pointed out, rurality is used as a selling point and is indeed one of the dominant motifs in tourist literature on Ireland. This literature has 'been instrumental in constructing Ireland and the Irish people as "other" to the modern industrial metropolitan centres of Europe and the US . . . a land of natural beauty and tranquillity and as a premodern society' (O'Connor, 1993, pp. 76, 82). It is also an image of Ireland that is particularly resilient to changes in tourist markets from being predominantly aimed at Americans to more European-orientated marketing strategy. Desmond Bell (1995) has analysed a specific incidence of this – the literature aimed at German tourists – though there is little reason to believe that his example is in any way untypical of how Ireland presents itself as a tourist destination generally. Here, he argues, the promotional literature emphasizes the backwardness of the countryside and its essentially undeveloped, unspoiled and unpolluted nature. Thus it offers panoramic views of the boglands of Connemara, the Blue Stack Mountains of remote Donegal and images of Glendalough in County Wicklow. The latter is a monastic site within easy driving distance from the capital city and is one of the most visited tourist sites in the country. Yet it is presented in the tourist literature as 'a mist-shrouded ancient ruin devoid of humanity but infused with a spirit of the past' (Bell, 1995, p. 50).

O'Connor (1993, p. 69) accepts that tourist imagery may be more or less effective in shaping identities, but argues that in the case of Ireland it plays 'a significant role in providing a native self-image'. She offers three reasons why this should be so. These are the length of time Irish people have been exposed to touristic representations of themselves, the pervasiveness of such representations in the culture and the high level of interaction between tourists and Irish people which makes them aware of how they are perceived by outsiders. For example, John Hinde, a photographer whose picture postcards of the

Irish landscape are an exemplar of the mythical features of the Irish landscape, is probably the best known of what might be termed visual artists in the country.

The contemporary relevance of such a construction of an image of Irishness can and is being contested primarily under the influence of economic and social changes, conventionally summarized by the term 'Celtic Tiger', used to depict the current growth of the Irish economy. The growing importance of foreign multinationals and the rise in the electronics industry have displaced the role of agriculture as the mainstay of the material and indeed the cultural economy. This can be seen in the attempts to depict Dublin as a major European capital city and to develop certain areas of the city such as Temple Bar as particularly worthy of visitors' attention because of their cultural significance (Corcoran, 1998).

However, the extent and significance of this contest can be questioned. It is very much in the nature of identity that 'disparate and contradictory images coexist without inconvenience' (Peillon, 1984, p. 167). The ability to present Ireland as a modern country does not necessarily require it to abandon its self-presentation as rural idyll. The images that it presents to attract foreign investment do not simultaneously require the abandonment of other aspects of its self-image. Thus, while the former may require an emphasis on the nature of the environment that it offers for business, such as a modern, youthful, educated labour force and a developed physical and technological infrastructure, this can and does sit alongside the image of the rural idyll without the latter being overwhelmed, undermined or indeed significantly contradicted.

Similarly Catherine Nash (1993) has written about the degree to which the cultural centrality of the rural and the image of the west as representative of true Irishness have been contested in recent years. There are two related grounds for such attacks. One is from those who argue that the symbol is in itself a distortion of the nature of rural life, and the other is that its centrality effectively hides or obscures other more appropriate or more contemporarily relevant ways of constructing Irishness. The music of the rock group, the Pogues, has, for example, been analysed in these terms. It has been presented as a critique and deconstruction of the myth of 'green innocent romantic Ireland' (see Keohane, 1990). Attacking symbols because of their inadequate relationship with empirical reality is in a sense a redundant exercise because national symbols at this level always involve silencing the more troubling aspects of the world they are intended to reflect. What is of more substantial significance is the timing and the extent of the circulation that these attacks achieve. Yet Nash (1993, pp. 108–9) suggests that 'the amount of time spent in contesting its ascendancy in contemporary Irish culture suggests the strength and resilience of its symbolic power as embodying the nation'. Thus, while the Pogues critique the myth, the degree to which they have escaped its hold can be questioned. Their reconstruction of more positive features of Irish community tends still to be rural rather than urban in nature.

Conclusion

What you had in Ireland, then, was a culture which, while identities were being reconstituted in many ways, still clung to a vision of rural Ireland as the real and essential Ireland. What the kinds of crimes mentioned at the beginning of the last section did was to pierce this image. When the media carried striking images of rural crime, such as bodies being carried from rural dwellings for forensic examination, they critically undermined the image of rurality that was at the heart of Irish identity. The tranquil rurality that was believed to be ever present suddenly became something that needed to be reconstructed and reclaimed. A coherent state response to crime was presented as a key element in this reconstitution.

A useful way of conceptualizing the impact of these crimes is by analogy with the role that Thomas Kuhn (1964) argues anomalies play in the rejection of established scientific theory and established ways of looking at the world. The 'unexpected discovery', Kuhn says (1964, p. 7), 'is not simply factual in its impact'. It is something that violates 'the expectations implicit' in established procedures and ways of looking at the world. What these crimes did was to violate the implicit understanding of the Irish people that the rural was tranquil and peaceful, and to reconstitute it as a place that was dangerous and where socially valued sections of Irish society, such as the elderly, were at risk of violent crime.

This led to a quickening of the policy process and gave an urgency to the development of a package of major initiatives to respond to the crime problem. These included policies aimed directly at drugs, such as the establishment of the Criminal Assets Bureau which has the radical power to confiscate assets it believes to have been acquired by criminal means, and a range of proposals aimed at introducing mandatory ten-year sentences for drugs-related offences. The policies also included measures intended to deal with more conventional crime, such as limiting access to bail, a measure that required constitutional amendment, and a major policy of building more prison places, a policy that may result in the virtual doubling of the capacity of the prison system.[5] Finally, and specifically relating to rural crime, it led to the introduction of a range of financial incentives to encourage the elderly to bank their savings and to install alarms in their homes.

Many of these represent fundamental changes in the policy armoury available to the state in Ireland. The pressure to make them came from the social-psychological impact of a number of rural crimes. The shooting of a Garda and a journalist in the summer of 1996[6] kept up this pressure, and by the end of that year all of these policies were significantly advanced, in that they were the stated and accepted policies of all of the major political parties in the state.

In this chapter we have outlined the situation in relation to crime in rural Ireland. The analysis has been limited by the dearth of research and by the rudimentary nature of official crime statistics. The conclusion such an analysis leads to is that crime in rural Ireland is low in very many areas and negligible in others. To a degree that is unusual by international standards crime is concentrated in the capital city, Dublin. However, a number of highly publicized rural crimes have been significant in preparing the public space within which major changes in crime policy could be introduced. These crimes were shocking both in themselves and also because they happened in rural Ireland, a place where, according to official mythology, such incidents should be unthinkable. The fact that they happened there was taken as a sign that crime had become a serious issue, and that the time was right for fundamental changes in the state's response to crime. In this way rural crime was one of the major engines that drove crime from a background issue into the foreground of Irish political life.

[5] There is no one source which deals with all of these changes in a systematic way. However some of these are dealt with in editorials in the *Irish Law Times*, particularly vol. 14, Nos. 6, 7 and 11.

[6] The Garda was Jerry McCabe who was murdered by a paramilitary group in an attempted robbery of a security van. The journalist was Veronica Guerin, an investigative journalist with a national newspaper, the *Sunday Independent*. She had a reputation for revealing the identities of drug dealers in Dublin and appears to have been shot by some of them to prevent further revelations. A series of cases related to her murder are still proceeding through the courts.

References

ARENSBERG, C. A., and KIMBALL, S. T. (1968) *Family and Community in Ireland*, Cambridge, Mass.: Harvard University Press

BELL, D. (1983) 'Community studies: the social anthropological heritage and its popularity in Ireland', 1 (1) *International Journal of Sociology and Social Policy*, 22

BELL, D. (1995) 'Picturing the landscape: Die grüne Insel', 10 (1) *European Journal of Communication*, 41

BOYLE, R. (1992) 'From our Gaelic fields: radio, sport and nation in post-partition Ireland', 14 *Media, Culture and Society*, 623

BREEN, R. and ROTTMAN, D. (1985) *Crime Victimisation in the Republic of Ireland*, Dublin: Economic and Social Research Institute

BREWER, J., LOCKHART, B. and RODGERS, P. (1997) *Crime in Ireland: Here Be Dragons*, Oxford: Clarendon Press

BROWN, T. (1981) *Ireland: A Social and Cultural History 1922–1979*, London: Fontana

CLARK, S. (1975) 'The political mobilisation of Irish farmers', 4 (2) *Canadian Review of Sociology and Anthropology*, 483

COMMINS, P. (1986) 'Rural social change', in Clancy P. et al. (eds), *Ireland: A Sociological Profile*, Dublin: Institute of Public Administration

CORCORAN, M. (1998) 'The re-enchantment of Temple Bar', in Peillon, M. (ed.), *Encounters with Modern Ireland: A Sociological Chronicle, 1995–1996*, Dublin: Institute of Public Administration

FINNANE, M. (1995) 'A decline in violence in Ireland? Crime, policing and social relations, 1860–1914', paper read to American Criminology Conference

GIBBONS, L. (1984) 'Synge, Country and Western: the myth of the West in Irish and American culture', in Curtin, C. et al. (eds), *Culture and Ideology in Ireland*, Galway: Galway University Press

KELLEHER, P. and O'CONNOR, M. (1995) *Making the Links*, Dublin: Women's Aid

KEOGH, D. (1994) *Twentieth-Century Ireland: Nation and State*, Dublin: Gill and Macmillan

KEOHANE, K. (1990) 'Unifying the fragmented imaginary of the young immigrant: making a home in the post-modern with the Pogues', 9 *Irish Review*, 71

KUHN, T. (1964) *The Structure of Scientific Revolutions*, Chicago: University of Chicago Press

LOCKHART, B. with BREWER, J., RODGERS, P. and FOWLER, D. (1995) 'Crime in Ireland since World War II: a preliminary report', paper read to British Criminology Conference

McCULLAGH, C. (1996) *Crime in Ireland: A Sociological Introduction*, Cork: Cork University Press

McKEOWN, K. (1986) 'Urbanisation in the Republic of Ireland: a conflict approach', in Clancy, P., et al. (eds), *Ireland: A Sociological Profile*, Dublin: Institute of Public Administration

MURPHY, J. A. (1983) 'The achievement of Eamon DeValera', in O'Carroll, J. P. and Murphy, J. A. (eds), *DeValera and his Times*, Cork: Cork University Press

NASH, C. (1993) 'Embodying the nation: the West of Ireland landscape and Irish identity', in O'Connor, B. and Cronin, M. (eds), *Tourism in Ireland: A Critical Analysis*, Cork: Cork University Press

O'BRIEN, J. (1982) *'Dear Dirty Dublin': A City in Distress, 1899–1916*, Berkeley: University of California Press

O'CONNOR, B. (1993) 'Myths and mirrors: tourist images and national identity', in O'Connor, B. and Cronin, M. (eds), *Tourism in Ireland: A Critical Analysis*, Cork: Cork University Press

O'MAHONY, P. (1993) *Crime and Punishment in Ireland*, Dublin: Round Hall Press

O'NEILL, D. (1987) 'Enclave nation-building: the Irish experience', 15 (3) *Journal of Ethnic Studies*, 1

PEILLON, M. (1984) 'Tourism: a quest for otherness', 8 (2) *Crane Bag*, 165

ROTTMAN, D. (1980) *Crime in the Republic of Ireland: Statistical Trends and Their Interpretation*, Dublin: Economic and Social Research Institute

ROTTMAN, D. (1984) *The Criminal Justice System: Policy and Performance*, Dublin: National Economic and Social Council

ROTTMAN, D. (1988) 'Crime in geographical perspective', in Carter, R. W. G. and Parker, A. J. (eds), *Ireland: A Contemporary Geographic Perspective*, London: Croom Helm

3

Crime and Social Change in Rural Scotland

SIMON ANDERSON

Introduction

Like many other social problems crime has tended to be seen as primarily an urban concern. This was not always the case. Indeed, until the last few hundred years violence and unrest were often associated with rural areas, which were home to marauding gangs (the Border Reivers, for example) against whom towns and cities felt it necessary to construct defensive walls. From the time of the Industrial Revolution onwards, however, there has been an increasing tendency to mythologize the 'dangerousness' of the big cities and idealize life in our rural communities.[1]

As with most stereotypes, these images undoubtedly have their roots in reality. There is little question that the highest concentration of crime in Scotland is to be found in urban areas, or that, for the most part, rural communities are relatively safe places to live. There are a number of reasons, however, for resisting the conclusion that crime is a problem *only* for urban areas. These include the fact that crime may be rising in rural areas, may be *perceived* to be rising, or may take forms which are specifically rural (e.g. poaching, farm crime or crimes against wildlife). There is also a theoretical case to be made for studying areas where problems are notable by their relative absence, since this may tell us something about the essential character of such problems and how they might be addressed elsewhere.

The material in this chapter draws on the results of a research study, commissioned jointly by the Environment and Home

---

[1] This forms part of a long tradition of 'anti-urbanism' in British cultural life, identified by Glass (1989) and Williams (1973), among others. Examples of this tendency are, arguably, to be found in literature, from Dickens's *Hard Times* onwards, and in recent political and media debate on the inner cities and the alleged growth of an urban 'underclass'.

Departments of the Scottish Office, and intended to provide an overview of crime in rural Scotland. The research drew on a variety of sources of information, including existing literature; police-recorded crime statistics and crime survey data; and a series of qualitative interviews with residents of four study areas (Wester Ross, Harris, North/East Ayrshire and Angus), local police officers and representatives of agencies with an interest in rural affairs.

The published report on the study (Anderson, 1997) covers a very wide range of issues. In this chapter, I want to focus on just four main sets of issues. First, is there actually a problem of crime in Scotland's rural areas, or can criminology's virtual blindness to the issue be justified? Secondly, if there is a problem, is it getting worse – either in absolute terms or relative to the experience of more urban areas? Thirdly, what, if anything, is distinctive about policing in rural areas? Finally, how can the issue of crime be located in the context of broader debates about social change from rural sociology and beyond?

A Note on the Definition of Rurality

'The rural' is a concept which, as one commentator has noted, is 'invisible only to the clever' (Halfacree, in Shucksmith et al., 1996). In other words, the term is employed easily at a common-sense level but, on closer inspection, proves very difficult – even impossible – to define.

Conventionally the urban and the rural have been seen as straight-forward empirical and mutually exclusive categories. Such an approach lends itself neatly to administrative purposes, where a simple urban–rural classification may be useful in terms of data analysis or resource allocation. The key issue here is how and where the boundary should be drawn. Areas can be defined as rural in a number of ways – for example, on the basis of settlements below a certain size, population density or employment in 'rural' activities such as agriculture. Although there is no 'correct' definition, for statistical purposes one in particular has been widely used in Scotland in recent years. This is known (after its originator) as the Randall definition and is based on population density at the level of local authority areas or districts. It defines as rural those local authority areas with an average population density of less than one person per hectare. This schema has two principal advantages: first, it is simple to apply; and, secondly, its use of local authority boundaries maximizes the range of social and economic data which can be considered.

A case in point are the statistics of crimes recorded by the police, compiled by the Scottish Office, which can be disaggregated to local authority level but not beyond. Consequently, the analysis of crime statistics contained in this chapter takes the Randall definition as its starting-point.

But, while a rigid definition of rurality is necessary for any form of statistical analysis, it is important not to reify 'rural Scotland' as a wholly distinct and homogeneous entity. Hoggart (1990) and other commentators in rural geography and sociology have warned of the dangers of empirical analysis which treats rural areas as if they possess a unitary character, preferring instead a second and slightly different way of conceptualizing the relationship between urban and rural – that is, as poles at opposite ends of a continuum running from 'most urban' to 'most rural'. Others, however, have pointed out that 'ways of life do not coincide with settlement patterns' (Newby, 1980). While it may be possible to locate communities at a particular point on the continuum in terms of population density, employment profile or environmental characteristics, this does not mean that social structures and behaviours will conform to neat urban/rural stereotypes. It may be more useful, then, to see communities as tending more towards the urban or rural pole in relation to specific characteristics, but not as having a fixed position on a continuum.

While the nature of the available statistics made it difficult to reflect the diversity of rural experience in Scotland in the quantitative element of the project, the subsequent studies of different areas using qualitative techniques were able to do so more effectively – through a focus on life in the 'urban fringe' and small towns within easy reach of the larger cities as well as remote Highland and Island communities characterized by their geographic and economic isolation.

Ultimately, it is necessary to have a flexible understanding of the rural, since simple conceptions of urban and rural may obscure more than they reveal in relation to crime.

Is there a Problem of Rural Crime?

Are rural areas the essentially crime-free idylls of popular imagination? If not, what kinds of problems do they experience and how do such problems compare in type and volume with urban areas? There is little doubt that absolute risks of *crime* in rural Districts are significantly lower than in most urban areas. In terms of numbers of incidents recorded by the police, the character of Scotland's crime problem is overwhelmingly urban – for every crime recorded in a rural area there are four in an urban locality. It is worth noting, however, that the ratio of rural to urban offending is markedly lower (at 1:2.3) for *offences*. This is largely accounted for by the distribution of motor-vehicle offences which, not surprisingly, often take place on roads passing through rural areas, though they do not necessarily involve local residents.

Table 3.1   Proportion of police-recorded crimes by area type, 1995

Crime category	City	Other urban	Rural	All Scotland	Ratio rural:urban
	%	%	%	%	No. of crimes	
Total crimes	**44.9**	**36.1**	**19.0**	**100.0**	**527064**	**1:4.3**
Non-sexual crimes of violence	48.4	37.4	14.3	100.0	19774	1:6.0
Crimes of indecency	53.7	28.2	18.1	100.0	5998	1:4.5
Crimes of dishonesty	45.9	36.1	18.0	100.0	350346	1:4.6
Fire-raising, vandalism etc.	37.6	39.4	23.0	100.0	88543	1:3.3
Other crimes	47.7	32.1	20.2	100.0	62403	1:4.0

Note: Area types have been defined on the basis of the Randall definition. The 'rural' category includes those local authority areas with a population density of less than one person per hectare.

Table 3.1 gives a sense of the absolute scale of the crime problem in Scotland's rural areas in terms of numbers of incidents. To what extent, however, does this apparent urban bias simply reflect the fact that greater numbers of people live in such areas? For many purposes a more useful indicator than absolute numbers of incidents is the rate of victimization, expressed as the number of incidents per 10,000 head of population. This is calculated simply by dividing the crime rate for an area by its mid-year population estimate and multiplying the rate by 10,000. If one looks at rates of crime per 10,000 population, police-recorded crime risks are much greater in Scotland's four City authorities and slightly greater in 'other urban' areas than in rural Districts, as Figure 3.1 shows. In 1995, for example, the top eight Districts in crime terms were all urban and the bottom 17 all rural.[2]

But while rural residents are generally less likely to become victims than people living in urban areas, it is worth noting that the actual profile of crime types (whether based on police or crime survey figures) is very similar. In other words, people living in rural areas do fall victim to car crime, housebreaking, domestic violence and so on. These are by no means exclusively urban phenomena. However, the

---

[2] Since these figures date from 1995 they are based on Scotland's local authority boundaries prior to reorganization.

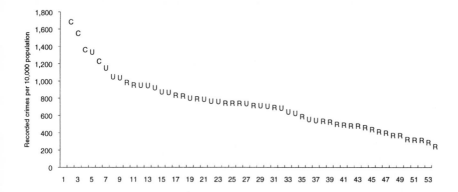

Figure 3.1   Recorded crimes per 10,000 population by District, 1995
Source: Scottish Office Criminal Justice Statistics Unit, GRO mid-year population
estimates
Key: C=City authority U=other urban authority R=rural authority (defined on the
basis of the Randall definition)

experience of such incidents may be very different in a rural context,
since the impact of crime may be exacerbated by physical or social
isolation, a lack of services for victims, poor transport or simply the
assumption that 'close-knit' communities will look after their own.
There are parallels here with the provision of services to minority
ethnic communities.

It also has to be remembered that there are two aspects to the
construction of the 'problem of crime': what actually happens and
what people think and feel about crime. And, although there is little
evidence that rural residents are in the grip of a panic about crime –
indeed, in the qualitative phase of the project the issue was rarely
mentioned spontaneously in connection with the problems of rural
living – there is an underlying and widespread belief that crime is
rising in rural communities, and a sense of heightened vulnerability,
especially to property crime committed by people from outwith the
immediate area. These 'away-day' criminals are generally seen as the
source of most serious crime problems in rural areas, though resident
'incomers' were also associated with 'trouble' by many longer-
established residents. This often coincided with a widespread and
sustained concern about problems involving young people. A group
of older women in Ayrshire, for example, linked the emergence of
certain problems – vandalism, drug misuse, under-age drinking and
'people hanging around' – explicitly to 'people who have come into
the village':

It's all scraped and vandalised. Now we would never have touched that – with a knife, a pencil or anything. We were brought up to be proud of the village, but the weans [children] now – they're not proud of the village, because there's that many of them been brought into the village. It's just somewhere for them to stay. (Females, 50 plus, Ayrshire)

We return to the issue of the impact of social change on the construction of the crime problem in rural areas below.

Is the Problem of Rural Crime Getting Worse?

The evidence from the research suggests, then, that there is (and there probably always has been) a problem of crime in Scotland's rural areas, albeit one which, in absolute terms, is significantly lower than in most urban areas.

The next question, then, is whether the problem of crime in rural areas is getting worse. There has, over the years, been sporadic concern about the spread of 'urban problems' into the countryside. This has a long history. In England and Wales, for example, the report of the Royal Commission on the County Constabulary in 1841 reported concern that serious crime in country areas was increasingly the work of 'strangers from the great towns' who were using the newly opened rail and canal networks to target rural communities. In recent years, there have been occasional media scares about 'shattered idylls' or villages under threat.[3]

Overall, the evidence is equivocal. Many of the problems which are now being 'discovered' in rural areas have probably always been there, albeit at a lower level than in the cities. As recorded crime rates have risen across the country as a whole, so too have they risen in rural locations. Moreover, there is some evidence that between 1980 and 1995 rates of recorded crime rose slightly faster in rural areas than elsewhere, with the result that there was a slight narrowing of the gap in absolute terms. Those trends are displayed in Figure 3.2.

But there are a number of caveats worth noting here. First, this is a very recent and possibly temporary phenomenon. As anyone who has used them will know, police-recorded crime statistics are full of unexplained blips and booms, and it would require a longer time-frame to be convinced that we are looking at a real change. Secondly, this slight convergence of rural and urban experience actually coincides with a period of static or falling crime rates across the

---

[3] See, for example, 'Farming communities buckling under blight of rural crime', *The Scotsman*, 5 February 1996; 'Dealers move into rural areas to sell off city drug glut', *Scotland on Sunday*, 17 December 1995.

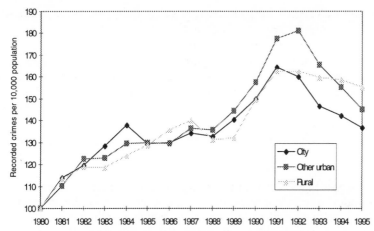

Figure 3.2   Trends in police-recorded crimes per 10,000 population, urban and rural Scotland 1980–1995 (1980=100)

Source: Scottish Office Criminal Justice Statistics Unit, GRO mid-year population estimates.

country as a whole. What we are seeing are sharper *falls* in urban crime, rather than particularly steep increases in rural areas.

Finally, it needs to be remembered that police-recorded crime statistics are just that – a measure of incidents recorded by the police – and not a straightforward reflection of crime reality. This raises the possibility that what we are actually witnessing are changes in the relative propensity of members of the public to report incidents or of the police to record them across urban and rural areas. This brings us on to the fourth area I want to look at – policing in the rural environment.

Policing in Rural Areas

Since rural crime in general has suffered from a lack of attention, in both academic and policy circles, it is not surprising that our images of rural policing are also conditioned more by fictional representations (*Hamish Macbeth* or *Heartbeat*, for example) than by any serious study (but see Cain, 1973; Shapland and Vagg, 1988; Young, 1993). Is there any truth in such images? It has been fashionable in recent years to dismiss ideas of 'golden age' policing. However, many of the core elements of such images are still present, albeit to varying degrees, in many rural communities. As part of the research, interviews were carried out with police officers in each of the four study areas, from which it was possible to build up a picture of the main characteristics and challenges of policing in rural areas, and also of the ways in which it is changing.

In all four areas the police claimed a significantly closer relationship with the local community than would be found in urban areas. This was particularly so among officers working in village stations, but even in the small lowland towns there was a belief that the police benefited from a high level of respect and co-operation from the public. One officer, who had previously worked in London, contrasted the experience of being an officer there and in his present posting:

> The biggest thing is that in these areas you're living in a community, and in London you were anonymous . . . You went in, you did your eight-hour shift or whatever, and 99 per cent of the people you dealt with you'd never come across before. And that was it, you forgot about them, and you'd probably never see them again in your life. Here, it's completely different. You're plonked in this community, and you're doing the same sort of job, but you're living with them. Your family are identified by you . . . they're 'the policeman's children' or 'the policeman's wife'. . . You have to be very aware of how you behave, how you act and how people are seeing you. (Police officer, Wester Ross)

Great emphasis was placed on the importance of personal contact with the local community. Officers stressed the value of at least being able to speak to most potential troublemakers or criminals on first-name terms, even in those communities where it was no longer possible to know 'everyone'.

In the smaller communities, whether in highland or lowland areas, there was a widespread feeling that the police operated as a broadly based community service, rather than in a simple law-enforcement role. This was felt to have significant advantages in strengthening police-community relations and making it easier to tackle crime problems when they did emerge.

All of the officers interviewed were conscious of the fact that police resources were stretched in rural areas. An important implication of this was felt to be that policing had to be pragmatic in approach, since, in the absence of immediate back-up, officers could not afford to let situations escalate. Far from being a frustration or disadvantage, however, rural officers tended to see this as one of the key features of the job, since it encouraged them to develop an ability to defuse situations and to find consensual solutions.

This touches on a further important characteristic of policing in many rural areas, namely its informal character. Although the use of discretion plays a part in policing in any community it is particularly important in a rural context. Rather than acting as strict law-enforcers, rural officers often find themselves in a mediating role – for example, agreeing not to report a vandal to the procurator fiscal on condition that he or she apologizes to the victim and pays for the damage caused. Particularly in the more remote areas, there is almost an expectation that petty offenders will not end up in court, at least not on the first occasion. As one member of the public in Wester Ross put it, 'When I came out here, there was a code in the West – you didn't get done unless it was something dire.' Another officer commented:

> Most folk around here like to take a warning and they quite accept the fact that if they haven't abided by the warning that you've given them and you catch them the next time, they're quite happy for you to take out your notebook and put them in front of the courts and all the rest of it. (Police officer, Angus)

This type of solution is often felt by officers to have advantages for all concerned, though the limitations of such an approach (in terms of more serious crime, or the need for all parties to be open to it) are also widely recognized. Particularly in the smaller communities, there was an evident desire to prevent young people from gaining 'a reputation' which might reinforce the original problem and, more generally, to defuse tension between local people, tension which otherwise might lead to a series of ongoing problems. If this can be accomplished through the use of informal channels then rural officers are likely to use them:

> I can count on one hand the number of times I've been to court in the last ten years, simply because if you do it with these guys – it's quite a string of things you've got here, but we could forget about that, we'll sort this out if you pay him back or give him back that and sort it out. He'll [the victim] be quite happy to get his things back. So it's maybe just two charges at the end of the day. The boy holds up his hands, guilty, that's fine. I don't have to sit and write statements, I don't have to go to court. Witnesses don't have to go to court. And the guy's got his stuff back. (Police officer, Angus)

The often informal character of policing in rural areas also appears to be reflected in the way that local people convey information to the police. Most of the officers interviewed felt that rural residents were often reluctant to report incidents (particularly petty incidents) formally. The reasons given for this varied, though they seemed to be informed more by a general reluctance to be seen to be 'playing a part in someone else's downfall' than by a fear of reprisals from the

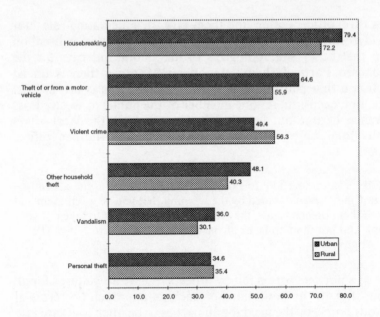

Figure 3.3   Rates of reporting to the police, urban and rural Scotland, 1992
Source: 1993 Scottish Crime Survey.

offender. The qualitative evidence on this point appears to find support in the results of the 1993 Scottish Crime Survey, illustrated at Figure 3.3 above, which indicates that people in rural areas are generally less likely to report incidents of victimization to the police.

There is evidence that local residents tend to have a less rosy picture of police–public relations than do the police themselves. Many claimed to have had little or no contact with local officers, and there was widespread cynicism, particularly in the lowland areas, about the 'local' character of policing. Among the most common complaints were that it is often difficult to contact the local officers because they are on duty elsewhere, and that when called the police take too long to respond.

How did the police themselves view the crime situation in the four areas, and how did their views compare with those of the public? In none of the study areas did the police feel that there was a very serious crime problem or that levels of crime were rising significantly. In the mainland areas, however, there was a widespread perception that problems associated with young people (including drug and alcohol misuse) had become more common, and that, as road networks had developed, the problem of travelling criminals had worsened.

In general, officers felt that public anxiety about crime was a greater problem than crime itself, and that there was a disproportionate fear of certain types of victimization (especially street crime). This situation was blamed on a number of factors, including the influence of national media, the arrival of city-dwellers with a 'siege mentality', and the fact that stories of those incidents which do happen are spread far and fast by local gossip:

> There's a lot of heads shaking, you know, 'it never used to be like this when I was a youngster', but I think people are very selective in their memories. We've got old incident books, and if you look through . . . quite a lot went on twenty or thirty years ago. I've got a book going back to 1871, and people were being locked up in 1871 for various thefts and dishonesty and frauds and assaults. It's hard to tell. I think people tend to look through rose-coloured glasses a bit at the past. Their perception is that it's getting worse, but I doubt it is. (Police officer, Wester Ross)

In most areas (though again with the exception of Harris), the nature of policing and the character of the relationship between the public and the police were felt to be changing rapidly. This was seen to be the result of changes in policing itself (notably, the fact that officers are now much less likely to live in the communities they police, or to stay in postings for more than a few years at a time) and changes in the character of rural communities (such as population growth, increasing turnover and the growing number of residents with an 'urban perspective'). As a consequence of these changes it has become more difficult to sustain community-oriented policing, and the possibilities for resolving issues informally have been reduced. This latter point may help to explain, at least in part, why there has been a slight narrowing of the gap between urban and rural areas in terms of police-recorded crime.

Crime and Social Change in Rural Scotland

In this final section I want to try to locate the issue of rural crime in the context of three sets of related debates about the character and direction of rural social change.

The first of these is specific to rural sociology and concerns the reversal of the traditional move away from the countryside towards the towns and cities. This process, which has been particularly evident in Scotland in recent decades, has come to be known as 'counterstream migration' (see Jedrej and Nuttall, 1996; Shucksmith et al., 1996). Former city-dwellers have taken themselves off to all corners of the Scottish countryside in search of the good life, or have simply relocated to rural areas within commuting distance of the large conurbations. In either case, they could be said to be living in what Pahl (1965) calls 'villages of the mind' in that they are pursuing an image of rurality which never existed, no longer exists, or which their very presence is helping to change. What possible consequences may this development have for the construction of the problem of crime in such areas?

There is a strong case to be made for 'urban baggage' – in other words, the possibility that people bring with them at least some of their urban fears and urban responses. For example, while women who had grown up in rural areas were generally content to walk around their community by themselves at night, others who had moved from the cities were much less willing to do so, some linking this explicitly to previous habits and ways of thinking:

> The attitudes that I brought with me from being in Aberdeen and Dumbarton . . . I prefer to walk my dog when I can see where I'm going. I like walking on my own, but once it starts getting winter and it's night, I think, well, I don't know who might have been in the hotel. So when I walk past there I'm a bit quicker and I've trained my dog in certain ways . . . And people laugh at you a bit, but it's just something you bring with you. (Mixed group, 25–44, Wester Ross)

If the way that people think and feel about crime in rural areas is increasingly coloured by an urban mindset, then their actual responses to incidents are also affected. Clearly, this has implications for the way in which the police deal with incidents. First of all, more incidents are likely to result in formal reports, with a correspondingly greater expectation of prosecution on the part of victims; and secondly, informal mediation is less likely to succeed because there is no relationship to build on in the first place. As one officer in a rural community in lowland Scotland commented:

> Still by far the greatest amount of policing we do is conflict resolution. But it sometimes doesn't work as effectively I would say now as it used to. Because, before, what you were getting was someone who was complaining about a neighbour who they had possibly grown up with all their days and, okay, they had fallen out with them, but maybe they had been friendly six months before; six months down the line they might be friendly with them again. Now what you're getting is strangers telling strangers. So people are quite happy to pick up the phone and complain about a neighbour. Whereas, before, they might have went and chapped the door and said, 'Look, your kid's causing me grief every night, what are you going to do about it?', now, they'll pick up the phone and report that to the police . . . There's nothing there to gel them together. (Police officer, Ayrshire)

The second broad theme of obvious relevance to discussion about rural crime is the debate around globalization and the increasingly interconnected character of geographically distant communities. Rural communities are not only physically much more accessible than ever before (through improvements in road and other transport networks); they are also increasingly exposed to global cultural and economic systems. This has led to a gradual flattening out of local cultures and to an increasing tendency for world-views to be shaped not solely by immediate experience and community but by events and cultures from far away. Clearly, this is hugely important in terms of the construction of public perceptions about crime. Quite simply, the idea that it *could* happen here has been implanted in the minds of people living even in some of our most remote areas, even if their immediate, day-to-day experience gives them little cause for alarm (or alarms!).

The debates about globalization are perhaps especially salient in relation to young people in rural areas. There is little doubt that this section of the population is, through the mass media, more attuned than any other to national and international cultures. At the same time, however, they are also – through their lack of access to money and transport – peculiarly fixed in one place. This central irony surely needs to inform the way that we understand the complaints of young people in rural communities about their lack of access to services and facilities and the way in which they actually behave.

The issue of the impact of global events on local consciousness links to the third theme that I want to address, namely the nature of risk and anxiety in late-modern society. As numerous commentators have noted, we live in an age of increasing uncertainty. We are bombarded with information but, at the same time, can actually be sure of less and less. As a society, we are increasingly preoccupied with risk and its regulation – with the 'colonisation of the future' (Giddens, 1991, p. 111) – yet increasingly confronted by social change and an apparent lack of control. In such a context, as Hollway and Jefferson (1997) have pointed out, 'law and order' discourses provide a particularly rich focus for our anxieties not just about crime but about the pace and direction of social change more generally. The emergence of a significant 'fear of crime' discourse in our rural communities may, therefore, be a reflection of broader anxieties about the changing character and composition of those communities, rather than a direct reflection of 'actual crime risks'.

Conclusions

There is, and has always been, crime in Scotland's rural areas. While absolute risks may be lower than in the cities, rural residents do fall victim to the same types of crime as people elsewhere and suffer the same types of problems. Moreover, those problems may be compounded by other aspects of rural life – for example, the lack of services, physical isolation or poverty.

Whether crime in the countryside in Scotland is getting appreciably worse in terms of actual prevalence is more difficult to say. Although there is some evidence from police statistics of a narrowing in the gap between urban and rural districts, this may prove to be a temporary phenomenon or may simply reflect a change in the relative willingness of rural residents to report incidents to the police. Moreover, it has occurred during a period in which crime rates have been falling across Scotland as a whole.

There is some evidence, however, that the 'problem of crime' – defined in terms of the conjunction between 'things that happen' and the way that, as individuals and communities, we react and respond to those things – may have intensified. While rural residents do not appear to be in the grip of a panic about crime, there is a widespread perception that crime rates are rising in rural areas and a perception of increasing vulnerability, especially to property crime committed by outsiders. While there is not widespread or sustained anxiety about 'serious' crime, there is a pervasive concern both for and about young people, revolving in particular around the issues of drug misuse, under-age drinking and the associated problems of vandalism and disorder.

To some extent, the apparent worsening of the crime problem in rural areas relative to other parts of the country may reflect greater potential for conflict and a reduced capacity for informal social control brought about by population growth and change in the countryside. Such factors, along with changes in the structure of policing itself, have also reduced the scope for traditional rural policing methods in all but the most remote communities.

The issue of crime needs, therefore, to be understood in the context of broader social change in Scotland's rural areas. For those looking to address it, the answers may lie as much in the reinforcement of rural communities' capacity to absorb or deal with their own problems as in the traditional crime prevention measures adopted elsewhere.

References

ANDERSON, S. (1997) *Crime in Rural Scotland*, Edinburgh: Scottish Office
CAIN, M. (1973) *Society and the Policeman's Role*, London: Routledge and Kegan Paul

GIDDENS, A. (1991) *Modernity and Self-Identity: Self and Society in the Late Modern Age*, Cambridge: Polity Press

GLASS, R. (1989) *Clichés of Urban Doom*, Oxford: Basil Blackwell

HOGGART, K. (1990) 'Let's do away with rural', 6 (3) *Journal of Rural Studies*, 245

HOLLWAY, W. and JEFFERSON, T. (1997) 'The risk society in an age of anxiety: situating fear of crime', 48 (2) *British Journal of Sociology*, 255

JEDREJ, C. and NUTTALL, M. (1996) *White Settlers: The Impact of Rural Repopulation in Scotland*, Luxembourg: Hardwood Academic Publishers

NEWBY, H. (1980) 'Trend report: rural sociology', 28 (1) *Current Sociology*, 1

PAHL, R. (1965) 'Class and community in English commuter villages', 6 *Sociological Review*, 5

SHUCKSMITH, M. et al. (1996) *Rural Scotland Today: The Best of Both Worlds?*, Aldershot: Avebury

SHAPLAND, J. and VAGG, J. (1988) *Policing by the Public*, London: Routledge

WILLIAMS, R. (1973) *The Country and the City*, London: Chatto and Windus

YOUNG, M. (1993) *In the Sticks: An Anthropologist in a Shire Force*, Oxford: Oxford University Press

4

Crime in Rural Wales

LAURENCE KOFFMAN

Introduction

It is often assumed that crime is a predominantly urban problem and that a relatively crime-free existence is one of the advantages of rural life. If this is so, it would seem that such low-crime areas are worth studying to see what lessons can be learnt from them by those areas with a more serious crime problem. For example, to what extent do some communities rely more heavily on informal methods of social control? However, the conventional view of a relatively crime-free rural life needs to be examined. There was some evidence in the early 1990s that the overall rise in crime, based on recorded police statistics, was greater away from the inner cities.[1] For example, while the crime rate was falling in London, Liverpool and Newcastle, certain rural areas, including Cheshire, Cambridgeshire and Devon and Cornwall, were experiencing significant increases in recorded offending.[2]

In the past, the vast majority of studies of both crime and victimization have concentrated on densely populated urban or inner-city areas. But today there is growing interest in investigating issues of crime, victimization and policing in rural areas, and there is more caution in accepting some of the traditionally held views about crime in rural areas. It is now accepted that recorded crime rates, on their own, provide a very incomplete picture of rural crime, as they tell us little about local communities' experience of crime, their levels of fear and their relationship with the police.

[1] Recorded crime patterns have changed over the last six years and, in particular, there has been a significant decrease in most areas of England and Wales. The most recent British Crime Survey also reveals a downward trend of 14 per cent between 1995 and 1997 (Mirrlees-Black, 1998). However, since this chapter focuses on a local crime survey which was conducted in 1993 it would be inappropriate to make comparisons with the most recent British Crime Survey, conducted four years after the Aberystwyth Crime Survey.

[2] See report in the *Guardian*, 4 November 1993, based on Home Office statistics.

One of the leading studies of crime and policing in rural communities, together with a comparison of crime in an urban area, was conducted by Joanna Shapland and Jon Vagg (1988). The researchers used observational methods and semi-structured interviews with residents of two groups of villages in the Midlands. The first of these ('Southton') was a large village of 2,000 residents, whilst the second ('Northam') was a group of villages with a slightly smaller population. In addition to these villages, Shapland and Vagg studied four small urban areas in a Midlands city. The researchers did not find the pronounced disparities in residents' perceptions of their respective areas that one might have expected. They found 'the difference between rural and urban areas to be matters of degree, rather than marks of a rural/urban divide' (ibid., p. 19).

In looking at the official crime figures for these areas the researchers found that the types of crimes committed in the villages were congruent with those in the urban areas, but that they occurred much less frequently. One interesting and surprising difference, however, was that in the rural areas property crimes were committed against private individuals in only around half of incidents, with the remainder being against shops, pubs, companies, the council and others. By contrast, the large majority of property offending in the urban areas was against private individuals. This is the reverse of what might have been expected and perhaps indicates the lower level of protection against theft, burglary and vandalism of commercial premises in rural areas.

Shapland and Vagg also studied the public's use of police services by looking at the messages received and recorded by the police in both urban and rural areas. In the rural areas calls from the public followed a roughly similar pattern in subject matter to those made in the urban areas but, in relation to the size of the population, the police received far more calls in the urban areas.[3] The researchers found that whilst reports of property offences were usually acted upon by the police, an official response was much less likely in relation to reports of disturbances. For example, in rural areas only about 9 per cent of such reported incidents were ultimately recorded by the police. In both urban and rural areas the police appeared to see their role in responding to reports of disturbances as one of defusing the situation and restoring the peace rather than one of strict law enforcement.

This research was of particular interest in addressing the traditional belief that rural crime follows a pattern which is qualitatively different from that of urban areas. Shapland and Vagg found no

---

[3] The police received over 9,000 calls per 100,000 population in the towns, compared to about 2,700 calls per 100,000 in the villages.

justification for this belief, stating that 'the types of problems and crimes affecting residents and business people seemed to be similar in towns and villages' (p. 43). Of course there were large quantitative differences between the urban and rural crime rates, but the types of crime committed followed broadly similar patterns.

It was found that fear of assault was not really a problem amongst village residents, but that urban dwellers thought that there was a greater possibility of being the victim of an assault. As well as asking respondents about their chances of being assaulted, the researchers also asked them how safe they felt going out alone after dark. In general, levels of fear were found to be higher amongst urban residents: almost one third of those in urban areas felt unsafe, in contrast to 13 per cent of village respondents. Generally, it was found that urban residents' views as to their likelihood of being assaulted were based not so much on local knowledge or direct experience as on second-hand information, such as media reports.

Shapland and Vagg found a generally high level of support for the police in all of their survey areas. This fairly high level of satisfaction with the police provides a significant contrast with other local survey findings, such as those in the Islington Crime Survey (Jones et al., 1986). More particularly, the findings from a number of local crime surveys have suggested that the public would like to see more foot-patrol police officers in their area. For example, Kinsey (1985) found that Merseyside officers shared the public's view on this matter in general terms, although the majority of officers did not want such a job for themselves! Shapland and Vagg also asked respondents for their views on the type of policing they wanted, and found that there was considerable demand for a local police officer who would be known to residents, especially in the urban areas. They found a greater level of satisfaction with policing arrangements in Southton, where two-thirds wished to see no change from the status quo. This can probably be explained by the fact that in Southton the local officer was a village resident and was known to the majority of respondents. This is an interesting finding, which suggests that residents want to see a strong local base to their policing, with identifiable officers who have some knowledge of local affairs. As with other local surveys, it was found that respondents preferred the idea of foot patrols.

In summary, Shapland and Vagg provided a detailed comparison of crime and policing in rural and urban communities. In doing so, they challenged some widely held beliefs about the differing nature of crime and related problems in rural and urban areas. Despite the fact that recorded crime rates were much lower in rural areas, offences were generally of a similar nature to those of the urban areas. They did not rely on recorded crime figures exclusively, but used observational and semi-structured interviews with residents. However, their study was not a crime survey in the sense that this term is applied either to the British Crime Survey programme (Mayhew and Hough, 1988) or to local victimization surveys such as Newham, Merseyside and Islington.[4]

Crime (or victimization) surveys, based on a sample of the population, either local or national, provide information about the number of crimes actually committed in a particular area within a specific period, as opposed to the number of crimes reported to and recorded by the police. Additionally, such surveys offer valuable information about the personal characteristics of victims. However, crime surveys have tended to concentrate on densely populated urban or inner-city areas, and local surveys have often focused on areas perceived as having a serious crime problem. There has been a paucity of victimization research in rural areas, employing methodology similar to the British Crime Survey (BCS). In an attempt to redress the balance, this writer decided to conduct a crime survey in the predominantly rural mid-Wales area. It is the findings and implications of this research which form the focus of attention for the remainder of this chapter.

The Aberystwyth Crime Survey (1993)

The author conducted a victim survey in Aberystwyth, a university town situated in the predominantly rural area of mid-Wales.[5] The town itself provides a clear contrast to the large urban areas studied by other researchers in the majority of crime surveys. Aberystwyth has a considerable rural hinterland, and the town and its surrounding area might be characterized as 'semi-rural'. The aim of this research was to contribute to our understanding of the nature and extent of crime in less densely populated communities, and to investigate fear of crime amongst the local population. Furthermore, it was hoped to provide a means of comparison with urban crime surveys and to provide practical information which would be of value to law enforcement, crime prevention and other social agencies. In pursuing these aims, it was intended to build up a more informed and accurate picture of local crime than the one presented by official crime figures based on reported offences.

The Aberystwyth Crime Survey (hereafter the ACS) was conducted

[4] Since the first British Crime Survey in 1982, there have been successive 'sweeps' of the survey in 1984, 1988, 1992, 1994, 1996 and 1998.

[5] Aberystwyth is a small holiday resort, with a population of around 12,000, excluding the student body.

in June 1993 using professional interviewers.[6] A total of 259 interviews were conducted, after contacting 340 addresses taken systematically and unclustered from the electoral register.[7] The sample was a
representative cross-section of the town's population, aged sixteen
and over, but it did not include institutional buildings, such as nurses'
or student halls of residence. The survey used a modified version of
the established BCS questionnaire, and where the screening
questionnaire revealed cases of victimization up to three victim forms
per respondent were completed. Briefly, the sample was made up of
the following: 108 males and 151 females; 87 in the 16–34 age group,
62 in the 35–54 group, and 107 aged 55 and over; 139 respondents
were in social categories ABC1 and 119 in C2DE; 103 respondents
lived in households of three or more persons, 89 in households of
two, with 67 living on their own; 102 respondents were in employment
and 38 of the sample were students; 155 either owned or were buying
their own house, 44 were council tenants and 47 rented
accommodation in the private sector. In all, the survey found that 76
respondents were victims of crimes covered by the survey during the
relevant fourteen-month period. A total of 116 victim forms were
completed for the survey and form the basis of its analysis of
victimization trends. A detailed summary and analysis of the main
findings of the ACS have been published in other works by the author
(Koffman, 1996 and 1997). This chapter aims to describe some of the
main findings of the survey and their significance for our understanding of crime and victimization in less densely populated and
semi-rural areas.

The population of Aberystwyth appears to be both stable and
reasonably content with where it lives. Although it should be
remembered that student halls of residence were not included in the
sample, it is striking that virtually two-thirds of respondents had lived
for ten years or more in the area (that is, within fifteen minutes' walk
of the town). A mere 7 per cent had lived in the area for less than one
year. It is not surprising, therefore, that 65 per cent of the sample
were satisfied with living in the area and 28 per cent were fairly
satisfied. Indeed, only 6 per cent felt fairly dissatisfied with living in
the area.

As fear of crime is regarded as a serious social problem in its own
right, crime surveys have attempted to investigate levels of fear
amongst respondents, and whether levels of fear are increasing: for

---

[6] Interviewing was carried out for the survey by NOP Social and Political, an
organization which had experience of work on some sweeps of the British Crime
Survey.

[7] The response rate of approximately 80 per cent is higher than that obtained by
the British Crime Survey.

example, see Maxfield (1984 and 1987) and Hough (1995). The notion of 'fear of crime' is employed to connote not simply the imminent apprehension of victimization but a more generic anxiety on the part of the respondent about crimes against the person and against property. Despite some misgivings about how accurately fear of crime can be measured by survey methodology the ACS included questions on this subject which were similar to those contained in the national survey.

Aberystwyth respondents were asked about their fear of crime in general, and in relation to certain specific offences. It is possible to compare the ACS findings with those of the BCS 1992 sweep in relation to the 290 Welsh respondents who formed part of the sample taken by the national survey in England and Wales.[8] Although there were no inner-city areas amongst the fourteen Welsh sample points used by the BCS, a number of urban areas, such as Swansea, Newport and Cardiff, were included, providing an interesting contrast to the ACS sample. It was found in the ACS that 39 per cent of respondents felt very safe walking alone in their area after dark, with 36 per cent fairly safe, 17 per cent a little bit unsafe, and 9 per cent very unsafe. In relation to the Welsh BCS respondents the corresponding findings were: 22 per cent very safe, 35 per cent fairly safe, 31 per cent a bit unsafe, and 11 per cent very unsafe. It seems that fear for personal safety on the streets in Aberystwyth is less prevalent than in more urban areas of Wales. It is tempting to conclude that, as three-quarters of all respondents felt safe on the streets at night, fear for personal safety is not a conspicuous problem in the town. Yet this should not be too readily assumed, especially in relation to certain sections of the local population. For example, a mere one in five of female respondents felt very safe and only one in three of all those in the 35–54 age group. The fact that 15 per cent of women and 16 per cent of all respondents aged over fifty-five felt very unsafe walking in their area after dark is a matter for concern. However, the proportion of Aberystwyth respondents feeling very or fairly unsafe out alone after dark (i.e. 26 per cent) was smaller than the corresponding proportion in repeated sweeps of the BCS, which rose from 34 per cent in 1982 to 36 per cent in 1994 (Hough, pp. 12–13).

As with the BCS, the ACS included questions about respondents' anxiety in relation to particular crimes. The results are summarized in Table 4.1.

---

[8] Further details of the methodology of this comparison and of the Welsh sample points used by the BCS can be found in Koffman (1996, p. 108).

Table 4.1 Worry about crime (percentages): 1993 Aberystwyth Crime Survey

	Burglary	Mugging	Rape	Car theft	Theft from cars
Very worried					
Men	15	8	N/A	12	9
Women	17	20	29	12	10
Total	16	15	-	12	10
Very and fairly worried					
Men	42	24	N/A	31	37
Women	53	46	52	28	24
Total	48	37	-	29	30

The results indicate that almost half of the respondents were worried about being burgled. The most worried group in relation to this crime – although not shown in Table 4.1 – were council tenants, amongst whom nearly two-thirds were either very or fairly worried. Respondents in social classes ABC1 were slightly less worried about burglary than people in social classes C2DE.[9] It seemed that there was little difference between male and female respondents in the numbers who were very worried about burglary, although a larger proportion of women were fairly worried about this offence. In conclusion, it appears that worry about burglary is less of a problem in Aberystwyth than in England and Wales as a whole: the 1996 sweep of the BCS suggests that 62 per cent of the total sample were either very or fairly worried, with 22 per cent very worried (Mirrlees-Black et al., 1996, p. 51). But in view of the infrequent occurrence of burglary according to ACS findings (see later), it is perhaps surprising that so many local residents were worried about this type of crime.

The ACS results were consistent with the BCS finding that more women than men worry about being mugged or robbed. Amongst Aberystwyth female respondents 20 per cent were very worried and 46 per cent were either very or fairly worried; whilst the BCS figures are 26 per cent very worried and 57 per cent very or fairly worried (Mirrlees-Black et al., 1996, p. 51). More than half of Aberystwyth female respondents were worried about being raped and 29 per cent were very worried. Women in the 16–34 age group were most worried about this crime, with two-thirds either very or fairly worried. More than half of the council tenants were very worried about rape, and it

[9] For details of corresponding BCS findings on fear of crime in relation to social class and housing area, see Hough, 1995, pp. 17–20.

is also significant that 90 per cent of students were either very or fairly worried. Findings such as these are important in lending support to those of local surveys, in urban areas, such as Islington (Jones et al., 1986), which have emphasized the need to focus on those groups which are especially vulnerable, as crime and fear of crime are not experienced equally throughout society. The ACS did not investigate female residents' experience of crime and harassment in the same depth as the Islington survey, but the extent of fear of serious sexual assault which it discovered is a matter for concern. These findings have important implications for crime prevention and security initiatives, particularly in relation to young women, council tenants and the student population. For example, they might lend support to those who favour the increased use of security measures in the town, such as the recently introduced closed-circuit television surveillance. On the other hand, it could be argued that such measures are themselves productive of increased levels of fear and are of questionable value in a town like Aberystwyth.

The ACS investigated another important issue, that of respondents' attitudes towards the police. As background to this discussion, it is worth noting that the BCS findings for the 1980s suggested a general decline in public confidence in the police during that decade (Skogan, 1994). In particular, the 1988 sweep of the survey reported a noticeable decline in confidence in the police in small towns and rural areas, and amongst women and the elderly (ibid., p. 5). This trend continued into the early 1990s, but appeared not to be worsening in the 1994 sweep. It might be expected in Aberystwyth, with its stable population and its relatively low level of recorded crime, that public confidence in the police would be high, but the results of the survey (see Table 4.2) do not bear out this supposition unequivocally.

Table 4.2   Do the local police do a good job (percentages)? 1993 ACS

	Male	Female	16–34	35–54	55+	All
Very good	18	15	13	13	21	16
Fairly good	49	47	56	58	35	48
Fairly poor	12	16	11	15	17	14
Very poor	7	5	7	3	7	6
Don't know	14	17	13	11	21	15
Very and fairly good	67	62	69	71	56	64
Very and fairly poor	19	21	18	18	24	20

As the police come to know about the vast majority of crimes through the public, and the willingness of victims to report incidents in particular, it is essential that the police maintain good relations with the local population. It could be argued that, with nearly two-thirds of ACS respondents thinking that the local police do either a very or a fairly good job, there is no cause for concern about police–public relations. But it is significant that a mere 16 per cent of all respondents thought that the police do a very good job. It might surprise many that the over-55 age group was less satisfied with police performance than the younger subgroups of respondents, but it should be remembered that this finding is consistent with BCS findings in the 1980s. Although not shown in Table 4.2, the ACS found also that council tenants were less satisfied with the work of the police than other groups, and that women were less satisfied than men with the police.[10] It is interesting that recent victims of crime were less impressed by the performance of the police than those who were not victims: a mere 9 per cent of victims were very satisfied with the work done by the police. This may suggest that the group which had the most direct contact with the police found them wanting in the performance of their main tasks. On the other hand, the police could be the focus for the dissatisfaction of victims and their grievances about other social agencies and the criminal justice system.

It is useful to compare the ACS findings on public attitudes to the police with those derived from a survey commissioned by the Dyfed Powys police, which was carried out in the same year as the ACS.[11] The Dyfed Powys Police Survey (DPPS) was not a crime survey like the ACS, but it asked respondents from eight different sample points within that police area – a total of around 1,000 respondents in all – a number of questions which can be compared to ACS findings (Koffman, 1996, pp. 110–13). Aberystwyth provided about one-tenth of the sample taken by the DPPS, and it is the results from this subgroup which are discussed here. Of these respondents 10 per cent thought that they were very well protected by the police, with half feeling quite well protected. The 25–36 age group felt less well protected than older age groups, and men felt less well protected than women. An interesting result was that Welsh speakers felt less well protected than non-Welsh speakers. In relation to the service provided by the police, the least satisfied respondents were those aged over fifty-five, a finding which is consistent with the ACS. However, the

[10] For further details of these results, see Koffman, 1996, Table 5.4, p. 132.

[11] The unpublished Dyfed-Powys survey was devised by the Police Quality Research Section and the Department of Social and Economic Studies at Swansea University.

DPPS found a slightly higher level of satisfaction with the work of the police than was revealed to the ACS.[12]

In keeping with BCS practice, the ACS asked its sample about their estimation of changes in the level of crime in their local area. Successive sweeps of the BCS have revealed that a majority feel that crime is on the increase in their area over the previous two years (Mirrlees-Black et al., 1996, p. 49). It is difficult to gauge how respondents form their opinions on this subject: that is whether their views are based on direct experience, opinions of others, or the preoccupation of the media (local and national) with crime stories. This uncertainty may call into question the usefulness of the responses to this particular question, but the findings are nevertheless interesting in view of the claims of the Dyfed-Powys police that the rate of recorded crime fell by 14 per cent in 1994 from the previous twelve months, and that this decrease included a 6 per cent reduction in the Aberystwyth division.[13] Slightly more than half of ACS respondents thought that crime had increased – either a lot or a little – over the last two years, and these results were almost identical to those obtained in the 1996 sweep of the BCS. In the ACS, 22 per cent thought there was now a lot more crime, 32 per cent a little more crime, and 35 per cent that the crime rate was about the same. It appears then that there is virtually no difference in perception about the growth of crime between a semi-rural area like Aberystwyth and the more urban and densely populated areas which comprise the bulk of the BCS sample. As respondents in both surveys were recipients of the same national media presentation of crime, both fictional and 'fact', these findings could lend support to the argument that popular perception of crime trends is not directly based on personal experience.

A major impetus for carrying out the Aberystwyth survey was to measure the extent of victimization in the area and to investigate the main correlates of victimization. The offences which respondents were asked about were broadly the same as for the BCS; these include 'personal' offences such as thefts from the person, robberies, assaults and sexual offences, and 'household' offences, such as burglary, vandalism and car-related crime. Respondents were asked about their own experience in relation to personal offences, and also asked more widely about events affecting any member of their household in relation to household offences. In phrasing questions about specific

[12] The ACS sample of 259 residents was considerably larger than the DPPS Aberystwyth subgroup of about 100.

[13] These figures are based on a report by the Dyfed-Powys Chief Constable delivered to a police authority meeting, as reported in the *Cambrian News*, 13 January 1995.

crimes interviewers explained the legal definition in non-technical terms so as to avoid any confusion for respondents.

During the survey period around 70 per cent of respondents were not victims of any offences included in the survey, and 30 per cent were victims (Koffman, 1996, Appendix). There was no significant difference between men and women in the rate of victimization, but there were fractionally fewer female victims than male. Age seems to be a more relevant factor, with the 16–34 age group the most frequently victimized (43 per cent were victims). In contrast, just 17 per cent of those aged fifty-five and over were victims. Interestingly in view of this group's fear of crime (discussed earlier) council tenants emerged as the least victimized group, with 86 per cent as non-victims. It must be admitted that these results are based on quite a small number of council tenants included in the sample, but tentatively it can be suggested that this subgroup's assessment of the likelihood of becoming a victim of crime, particularly burglary, is not borne out by these figures.

In a university town it is both conspicuous and worrying that students were the most victimized group in the sample; almost half were victims during the survey period. Students suffered the highest rate of victimization and multiple victimization, and this indicates the need for further investigation by the University authorities and the police. The University is a major employer in the area, and the competition amongst universities to attract students is becoming fiercer. One of the attractions of Aberystwyth for prospective students is the relatively safe environment in which to live, when compared to many urban and city institutions. If this is to be maintained, it may be necessary to provide further crime prevention assistance to students.

Further details of the number of incidents for each type of crime covered by the Aberystwyth survey can be found elsewhere (Koffman, 1996), but the proportion of ACS offences in different categories is set out in Figure 4.1. The large majority of ACS offences were against property, a finding which is consistent with successive sweeps of the BCS. It is in keeping with BCS results also that car-related crime was the commonest form of offending. For example, in the 1996 BCS, 32 per cent of all crimes involved either thefts of or from vehicles, or vehicle vandalism. In the ACS there was an even higher figure of 37 per cent of offences within this category. It seems that Aberystwyth suffers a higher than average rate of vehicle vandalism – excluding inner-city areas – and this offence was the most common one found by the survey. One in five Aberystwyth vehicle owners in the sample had their vehicle damaged or tampered with during the survey period. Taking the corresponding figures for the Welsh BCS respondents in

1993 only 15 per cent were victims of these offences. In contrast, the ACS revealed a lower rate of respondents having their vehicles stolen (1 per cent) than the 5 per cent of Welsh BCS respondents. There was a slightly lower rate of thefts from vehicles in the ACS than in the Welsh BCS sample.[14]

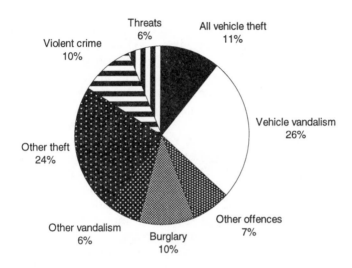

Figure 4.1 Proportion of ACS crimes in different categories

Figure 4.1 shows that 10 per cent of ACS incidents were violent, involving either a physical or a sexual attack on the respondent, and a further 6 per cent of the total consisted of threats of damage or violence. This is a slightly higher proportion of violent offences than the corresponding 1996 BCS figures (Mirrlees-Black et al., p. 13), and it represents quite a high rate of violent incidents. On the other hand, it is worth mentioning that one third of ACS victims of violence sustained no significant physical injury. Most victims were either slapped, punched or kicked, with only one case resulting in broken bones. But two-thirds of victims of violence suffered some form of bruising, and one in five suffered cuts. It is notable that there were no victims of violence in the over-55 age group, and that the 16–34 age group was by far the most at risk of violence. These findings are similar to those of the 1996 BCS in relation to the proportion of adult victims of contact crimes (Mirrlees Black et al., 1996, pp. 29–30).

[14] For a more detailed comparison, see Koffman, 1996, pp. 108–10.

Crime surveys have been less successful in measuring offences of violence than property crimes for a variety of methodological reasons. This is particularly so in relation to so called 'domestic' violence where an attack is carried out by one household member against another, such as an incident involving spouses, partners or relatives. BCS findings suggest that incidents of domestic and acquaintance violence represent the largest increase in contact crimes since the national survey began in 1981 (Mirrlees-Black et al., 1996, p. 28). The ACS asked respondents about domestic violence, and the results were interesting but inconclusive. Although 93 per cent replied that they had not suffered this type of incident it is possibly revealing that just 89 per cent of women, 87 per cent of students and 86 per cent of the 16–34 age group could say the same. Whilst no incidents of domestic violence were actually disclosed by respondents, the frequency of 'no-response' to this question was conspicuous. In the 16–34 age group, 14 per cent gave no response when asked whether a member of their own household had inflicted violence on them during the survey period. There was a similar no-response rate amongst students and council tenants. It may well be that younger respondents were inhibited from revealing incidents of their victim-ization owing to the fact that they were more likely to have other people present at home during the interview.

Through the use of detailed victim forms for each incident the ACS was able to build up a clearer picture of patterns of offending during the survey period. It was revealed that 90 per cent of all incidents took place in the Aberystwyth area, and about three-quarters of all offences occurred either during evening time or at night. It is notable that around one in four of all incidents took place either at or in the home of the victim. Victims were asked also for information regarding the offender or offenders, and more than a third had information to impart. From the replies of this subgroup, it appears that offenders were predominantly young and male. It was thought that 17 per cent were of school age, and that nearly two-thirds were in the 16–25 age group. The victim said that the offender was male in 83 per cent of cases, and in only 7 per cent of incidents was the offender thought to be female. It was thought that there were male and female offenders involved in a further 5 per cent of incidents. A single perpetrator was involved in around half of all cases where the victim could supply information, whereas 21 per cent thought that there were two offenders, and 21 per cent thought that at least three offenders were involved. Also, it seems that this subgroup of victims knew the offender (or offenders) prior to the incident in around half of all cases.

The ACS found that around four out of ten incidents disclosed to the survey involved something being stolen from the respondent or a member of the respondent's household. The items of property most vulnerable to theft appeared to be car parts, money, clothes, purses and credit cards. Although a quarter of incidents involved stolen items worth less than £10, it cannot be said that the majority of offences were trivial. Property worth between £11 and £50 was taken in 40 per cent of incidents and in 12 per cent of cases the property was valued at between £51 and £100. In around one in five cases of theft the stolen property was valued at more than £100. As with other local crime surveys, many ACS victims of acquisitive crimes were amongst the least well-off and the loss of what might appear to be a relatively small amount of money would have quite serious consequences for them. Moreover, 60 per cent of victims whose property was either stolen or damaged were not covered by insurance for the property in question.

A useful function of all victimization surveys has been to help reveal the 'dark figure' of unreported and unrecorded crime. The ACS found that the police were informed of ACS incidents in only 45 per cent of cases. This has clear implications for the recorded crime rate in Aberystwyth in that well over half of all offences disclosed to the survey were not reported to the police. Male victims were least likely to report incidents, with around a third notifying the police. Students and younger victims were also less likely to report offences, with just four out of ten incidents being brought to the attention of the police. A willingness to report offences appears to increase with the age of the victim, with over half of victims aged fifty-five or over reporting their incident. The most common reason given for non-reporting – in about 50 per cent of all cases – was that it was too trivial or not worth reporting. The reason given by 13 per cent was that the police could not have done anything about the crime. Men were more likely than women to want to deal with the incident themselves but, in all, only 6 per cent of respondents stated that this was their reason for not reporting the offence to the police. There is little evidence that fear or dislike of the police inhibited reporting in Aberystwyth, as a mere 5 per cent gave this as a reason, although 5 per cent also thought that the police would not have been interested in the incident. Where the police were informed two out of three victims were satisfied with their response. However, around a quarter thought that the police showed less interest than they ought to have done.

Conclusion

Most local crime surveys have studied crime as an urban, or even an inner-city phenomenon. The purpose of the Aberystwyth survey was to attempt to redress the balance by investigating crime, victimization and police–public relations in a less densely populated, semi-rural area. The sample taken by the ACS was admittedly of limited size, and this is particularly relevant when considering the findings in relation to certain subgroups within the sample. But in asking the same questions as the British Crime Survey it has allowed comparisons to be made between predominantly rural mid-Wales and more urban areas of England and Wales. The ACS provides an interesting insight into such matters as fear of crime, confidence in the police, rates of victimization and which groups are most at risk from offending. In turn, this information has implications for crime prevention initiatives, University authorities, the police, town planning and the security industry. A further value of such a study is that it may act as a corrective to public misconceptions about crime levels and risks of victimization, especially where these views are based on the media presentation of crime news. The ACS would be of even further value if repeated, enabling us to consider crime and victimization trends over a longer period.

The Aberystwyth findings suggest that a considerable number of offences go unreported, with over half of all incidents not brought to the attention of the police. This is important as the number of offences reported determines the workload of the police to a large extent and, in turn, the recorded crime figures for the area. The proportion of offences in different categories was broadly similar to the findings of the 1996 sweep of the BCS, but with a smaller proportion of vehicle thefts and a larger proportion of vehicle vandalism. Aberystwyth residents are less in fear for their personal safety on the streets than those who live in more urban areas of Wales, but fear amongst Aberystwyth women for their personal safety is quite high and a cause for concern. In relation to their fear of being raped, this is a serious problem in its own right, given the ACS findings, and more needs to be done in terms of crime prevention and security initiatives. This is a matter about which the police are aware and it will be interesting to see if any progress has been made in reducing the fear of women in Aberystwyth. The frequency with which students are victimized is another significant finding of the survey, and one which should be a source of concern to the University authorities.[15]

There is today a growing interest in rural life and the countryside, which has led to debates about the environment, transport, farming and even the entitlement to a certain way of life which might be

[15] The author is informed that there is now a resident police presence in the Students' Union in the form of a Student Liaison Officer.

culturally distinct from that of urban dwellers. It is possible that a burgeoning interest in rural crime, victimization and policing is part of this development. Although crime may be a more serious problem in large towns and cities in quantitative terms, there is much to be learnt from the study of crime in a predominantly rural environment.

References

HOUGH, M. (1995) *Anxiety about Crime: Findings from the 1994 British Crime Survey*, Home Office Research Study No. 147, London: Home Office

JONES, T. et al. (1986) *The Islington Crime Survey*, Aldershot: Gower

KINSEY, R. (1985) *Survey of Merseyside Police Officers: First Report*, Liverpool: Merseyside County Council

KOFFMAN, L. (1996) *Crime Surveys and Victims of Crime*, Cardiff: University of Wales Press

KOFFMAN, L. (1997) 'Key findings from the Aberystwyth Crime Survey', 28 *Cambrian Law Review*, 33–44

MAXFIELD, M. G. (1984) *Fear of Crime in England and Wales*, Home Office Research Study No. 78, London: Home Office

MAXFIELD, M. G. (1987) *Explaining Fear of Crime: Evidence from the 1984 British Crime Survey*, Research and Planning Unit Paper No. 43, London: Home Office

MAYHEW, P. and HOUGH, M. (1988) 'The British Crime Survey: origins and impact', in Maguire, M. et al. (eds), *Victims of Crime: A New Deal?*, Milton Keynes: Open University Press

MIRRLEES-BLACK, C. et al. (1996) *The British Crime Survey*, Home Office Statistical Bulletin Issue 19/96, London: Home Office

MIRRLEES-BLACK, C. et al. (1998) *The 1998 British Crime Survey*, Home Office Statistical Bulletin Issue 21/98, London: Home Office

SHAPLAND, J. and VAGG, J. (1988) *Policing by the Public*, London: Routledge

SKOGAN, W. (1994) *Contacts Between Police and Public: Findings from the 1992 British Crime Survey*, Home Office Research Study No. 134, London: Home Office

5

Crime, Risk and Governance in a Southern English Village

KEVIN STENSON and PAUL WATT

Introduction

The huge demonstration in London in March 1998 by representatives of diverse rural interests flagged up a range of issues. Among them were the neglect by politicians of the burgeoning problems of rural deprivation, the declining quality and scope of the social and economic infrastructure of the countryside, and the social problems to which these developments are said to give rise. This governmental neglect, if there is substance to the charge, is echoed by a paucity of recent interest by social scientists in issues of rural crime, disorder and crime control – seemingly trivial in comparison with the problems of the inner city and peripheral housing estates. Yet historians of eighteenth-century Britain have identified the crucial importance of issues of rural crime and justice in helping us to understand social change at that time, and this body of intellectual work is usually considered essential for the apprentice criminologist (Hay et al., 1975).

Then, the rise of agrarian capitalism and the enclosure of common land transformed class relations in the countryside, displacing much of the population into the cities and sharpening lines of acrimonious and sometimes violent social conflict between landowners and the new rural wage-earners. These changes were reflected in and re-inforced by the creation of new laws, attempting to prevent the combination of rural labourers in unions, and transforming property rights through the criminalization of poaching and access to the newly appropriated common land (ibid.).

The political economy of the British countryside has been transformed dramatically since then. In the information age the mechanisms for producing and allocating wealth, income and housing, and for determining the flow of populations are very different, not least because economic, political and cultural changes which impact on local environments are increasingly global in scope and intrude into even the sleepiest, leafy retreats (Marsden et al., 1990). Yet, at least two points of continuity can be discerned. Firstly, the period of great enclosure has left a legacy in the local economic and cultural power of the landed gentry and in deep inequalities in land ownership. In some parts of Britain, indeed, the same families still control much of the land, even if they do not appear, publicly, to be as locally active political, economic and legal agents as were their ancestors (Newby, 1987). This deep inequality in land ownership and the related inequalities in access to housing and other services still provide a context for understanding social conflict. In rural Buckinghamshire the political apparatus has for long been dominated by the values and interests of the articulate middle classes, yet conflicts and frustrations over control of the land and its fruits rumble on and remain in popular consciousness, even if the discontents of the poor are rarely articulated into effective lobbying within local political systems. As a Buckinghamshire country saying has it: ''Tis a crime to steal a goose off the common, but not to steal the common from under the goose.'

Secondly, as in earlier periods of history, rural social conflict and change can become crystallized in fears and anxieties about the perceived risks, posed by those defined as 'other', to the persons, homes and neighbourhoods of 'respectable' folk (Pearson, 1983). However, these conflicts and fears are filtered through new prisms and, while manifold in origin, tend to become coded in concerns about crime, disorder and related social problems (Sparks, 1992; Stenson, 1998). National TV and other media reinforce the effects of fluid demographic shifts between town and country by fostering awareness, through drama as well as news, of the real or imagined impact of crime (Sparks 1995), in addition to pollution, increasing road traffic and other hazards which follow urban escapees. These developments blur the demarcation lines between rural and urban life, even if fantasies of the separate, terror-free, rural idyll persist.

In social theory, ubiquitous fears and the new modes of governance, which have developed within it, have been given recognition by theorists of the risk society (Beck, 1992; Ericson and Haggerty, 1997). These theorists stress that the optimistic political agendas of post-war welfare states focused on the inclusive, socially just distribution of goods, the expanding rights of citizenship. But, by contrast, since the 1970s more pessimistic agendas have emerged. Anti 'Big-Government' neo-liberal political movements and administrations, feeding on declining confidence in the capacity of nation-states to meet rising demands on government for security against life's risks, have urged citizens to assume greater responsibility for managing them (Garland, 1996; Stenson, 1996). Heightened attention to the risks of techno-logical breakdown, environmental damage and criminal threats by perceivedly feral human males, has given rise to new 'mentalities' of government: new rationalities, strategies and technologies of rule which make populations thinkable and measurable for the purposes of government (Foucault, 1991; Rose, 1993; Stenson, 1999). Hence

> risk society operates within a negative logic that focuses on fear and the social distribution of 'bads' . . . Collective fear and foreboding underpin the value system of an unsafe society, perpetuate insecurity, and feed incessant demands for more knowledge of risk. Fear ends up proving itself, as new risk communication and management systems proliferate. The surveillance mechanisms of these systems create profiles of human populations and their risks to ascertain what is probable and possible for those populations. (Ericson and Haggerty, 1997, p. 6)

This process leads to a progressive partitioning of the population, away from the denuded public spheres (Taylor, 1997). People retreat into private lifestyles or very local, demographically restrictive con-ceptions of inclusive community. In this setting the police and other agencies of local governance play a special role in filtering and brokering information about risks. Information is reallocated between a range of agencies and community groups, and attempts are made to reinstitutionalize the trust which lies at the heart of effective government and the fostering of social solidarity (Shapland and Vagg, 1988; Stenson, 1993; Ericson and Haggerty 1997; Misztal, 1996).

Although the effects of globalizing changes and urban tensions have impacted on rural enclaves, like the subject of our case study in this chapter, this does not eradicate the differences between town and country, both in terms of how problems are conceptualized by official agencies and local populations, and also in the informal and formal practices which have developed for coping with them. Ericson and Haggerty's analysis of the government of risks focuses on the role of well-resourced official agencies of governance, particularly in urban settings, with increasingly sophisticated high-tech means to map the geography of trouble (pp. 7–9). However, in our case study setting, as in many other rural locations, the resources of the police and other governing agencies can be stretched almost to breaking-point in the attempt to control a broad geographical area. Also CCTV and other high-tech innovations, though readily available in large urban complexes, are scarcer and less effective in this rural space. This scarcity interacts with and reinforces both a marked reluctance to report troubles to the police, and the practice of informal, sometimes even brutal, methods of dispute resolution (and see also Peay, chapter 11).

Agents of official government employ the rhetoric of community empowerment, helping people to help themselves. But this is with the proviso that they behave in ways of which the statutory authorities approve (Crawford, 1997). Some of the coping mechanisms and informal governing practices employed by poor people may be deemed unsavoury and divisive by these lights, but they nevertheless constitute a flexing of collective muscle which can have a profound impact both on local populations and on the work of official agencies (Johnston, 1996). Through analysis of a rural case study, this chapter explores how pervasive global anxiety reaches into the countryside, where there are deep inequalities in wealth and power. But these areas are likely to provide a significant contrast with urban areas in the range and effectiveness of the measures available to impose official social discipline. (For a general discussion of some of these issues see Dingwall, chapter 6.)

Outville

This chapter analyses how risks related to crime and disorder are perceived and managed in the pseudonymous Outville, a village sharply divided spatially along class lines, in which urban nightmares seem to have followed those who tried to escape them. This large village of over 3,000 people is situated several miles from the old market town and industrial centre of High Wycombe in Bucking-hamshire and is located in the broader Wycombe District Council area. The official reported crime figures were high in the Outville parish even in comparison with those of High Wycombe town, whose rates for most offence categories tend to be significantly higher than in the surrounding district. For example, in 1996:

(1) The burglary/theft from a non-dwelling rate was nearly a third higher than for the town sector.
(2) Criminal damage, at 16.7/1,000 of population, was significantly higher than the whole Police Area average (13.5) and a little higher than the town sector (15.2).
(3) Actual and grievous bodily harm, at 5.2/1,000, was higher than that of the town sector (4.1) and about a third higher than the Police Area average.

On first encounter with the village it appears to have all the hallmarks of a traditional, albeit somewhat gentrifying, south Buckinghamshire village: an old village hall with a lively amateur dramatics group; an active community association and parish council, with articulate middle-class members; a varied collection of traditional shops along with several pubs; smart detached houses and cottages; a stripped-pine shop and a computer graphics company. For the parish as a whole 30 per cent of all economically active heads of households were individuals in the Registrar General's Classes I and II (professionals and managers), according to the 1991 census.

If one side of the village is predominantly affluent, the other side of the village, the 'estate', consists of council housing constructed at various periods since the 1930s. While the earliest inhabitants included the local rural poor, increasingly subsequent cohorts were dispersed from urban locations in High Wycombe (many having been originally relocated from London). This geographically isolated site was consistently unpopular with council tenants in the District. A large number of houses on the estate have been sold under the 1980 Housing Act, the 'right-to-buy' legislation. According to census data, whereas in 1981 nearly half of all the properties in the parish were council-owned, this had declined to just over one-quarter in 1991. The council estate part of the village is invisible from the high street. It is also physically cut off from the rest of the village by the existence of a large spiked fence erected by employers to prevent vandalism from young people living on the estate. The existence of the fence also prevents estate residents from crossing the industrial park to get to the village shops and amenities, and means that instead they have to make a circuitous road journey, or use the warren of alleyways, narrow footpaths and car parks. These were often described as fear-inducing by adults and especially by women, because they were perceived as territory for bored youths. Hence the fence came to represent both a symbolic and a physical/spatial boundary between the two sides of the village.

Outville as a Problem Area

Long-standing concerns about social relations in the council-estate part of the village and complaints from more affluent residents about the behaviour of their poorer neighbours had focused on issues of crime and incivilities, especially by young people. These concerns about crime in Outville had been signalled in a pen-portrait in an unpublished survey of youth crime and victimization, conducted by the Home Office-sponsored agency, Crime Concern, in Wycombe District in 1994:

> Outville. An isolated estate causing considerable concern. Family networks are believed to be involved in crime together. There are lots of

complaints about vandalism, noisy parties, drugs and car crime. There are no youth facilities on the estate.

After decades of Conservative local government in Wycombe District, a Labour/Liberal Democrat administration was elected in 1995. This led to the promise to provide a community/youth centre in Outville, followed by heated local debates about whether to site the centre in the poorer or middle-class areas of the village. Wycombe District Council commissioned a small community report from a commercial research consultant, then a more extensive study of social deprivation in the village. The latter was completed in 1997 by the present authors. The overall aim of the deprivation study was to analyse the extent of deprivation in the Outville parish with reference to a range of established indicators. It drew upon a variety of data sets, including crime and criminal justice statistics, and also involved interviews with local employers, local residents, council officials and elected councillors, as well as front-line personnel from the statutory agencies serving the local population. The community report and our deprivation study can be seen on the one hand as disinterested and objective social scientific analyses. On the other hand, they could also be considered to be part of the process whereby risks are made opera-tionally visible and quantifiable – and thus whereby this perceivedly troublesome local population was rendered thinkable and measurable for the purposes of (official) government (Foucault, 1991; Stenson and Watt, 1999).

The Divided Village

Outville is not among the worst examples of a multiply deprived estate in either urban or rural locations (Power and Tunstall, 1995; Rural Development Commission, 1992). Nevertheless, our study demonstrated that on most indicators of deprivation the estate part of the village scored higher than the average for the District as a whole, and in the case of some indicators compared unfavourably with the national picture. For example, in 1997 over one in four households living in the estate area of the village contained someone in receipt of income support, compared with only 6 per cent of households in the rest of the parish and 22 per cent in the urban area of High Wycombe. Data from the 1991 census indicated that nearly a quarter of children on the estate were living in households with no adult in employment, compared with only 10 per cent in the District as a whole. About 20 per cent of children at the local primary school were in receipt of free school meals – almost certainly a significant underestimation of true levels of need – against a Buckinghamshire average of 11.6 per cent. Data from the 1991 census also indicate that overcrowding, unemployment and the proportion of lone-parent families were noticeably higher on the estate. These deprivation factors are exacerbated by the isolated location of the village and sparse and expensive transport services, restricting access to shopping, public services and leisure facilities located in High Wycombe and Marlow.

Furthermore, apart from the primary school, the only community facilities in the estate were a small, bleak parade of shops, which was in the evening an assembly point for young people and hence avoided by adults. During an interview the head of the primary school, which mainly serves families from the estate, pointed to an aerial photograph of Outville. He indicated that the housing-estate area is invisible from the main roads leading to the old village, the high street and the shops, suggesting that this was a major attraction to the original planners: 'out of sight and out of mind'. He also echoed the claims of most of our interviewees that at every phase of development the priority to build housing forestalled the provision of community facilities to serve the new populations. The senior youth officer responsible for youth work provision in the area, offered only sporadically, identified zoning policies and the refusal of the local landowner to sell his land as the key constraints preventing the development of youth provision.

There was a large evangelical Christian church on the estate built on a site originally owned by Buckinghamshire County Council, which had earlier been earmarked for community facilities. This was still resented by many residents because it was seen to serve only a small, religious section of the population, rather than functioning as a general, civic resource. This was used as a site for a family centre for infants and their carers (open to all), and sporadically for youth work sessions, although theft and vandalism by club members led to bannings of individuals and periodic closure of the club. At the time of our study there was no youth provision on the estate. Moreover, many people on the estate refused to enter the church because they felt that attempts would be made to convert them. For example, one estate resident, Mrs A, said: 'These things are perceived as religious and they're out to get us . . . you know people are very realistic. They know evangelism for what it is.'

Development land was at a premium in Outville. This area is surrounded by rolling, wooded Green Belt land, some council-owned, but mostly the property of the local aristocratic family, who have owned the land for centuries. The naïve observer may have proposed the obvious solution: the acquisition and re-zoning of adjacent, Green Belt land for the construction of community youth centres, sports halls, pubs or other community facilities. But this was not a thinkable item for the political agenda (Lukes, 1974). Conservationist political agendas within the district, hostile to the zoning of land for industry and social housing, had been prioritized in recent years, and so Green Belt land was considered to be sacrosanct. This probably reflected the confluence of interests linking the landed gentry with the new rural middle class (Stenson and Watt, 1999). Predominantly white commuter villages like this in the Home Counties of south-east England have become spaces in which upwardly mobile urban escapees, while still hooked into the high-tech global economy, attempt to live out dreams of a nostalgic, trouble-free, middle-class English rural way of life (Murdoch and Marsden, 1994). The residents with high incomes and access to a car who lived in the older part of the village were unlikely to experience Outville as an isolated or deprived area, but rather could enjoy the middle-class rural lifestyle it offered. Their children were, in the main, sent to highly rated primary schools in neighbouring villages with middle-class intakes, to the grammar schools in High Wycombe and to schools in the independent sector. In all, there were few reasons for the middle-class population to come into positive, social contact for work, education, worship or pleasure with poorer residents in the area.

In summary, the village combined a traditional Buckinghamshire village setting with a relatively large council estate, in effect a peripheral estate (Geddes, 1993) of High Wycombe, whose social composition and internal relations were increasingly a product of mixed housing tenures and housing allocation policies. Within this wider context, let us now examine the ways in which local officials conceptualized the area as a site of social problems.

Crime, Policing and Control Talk

Within the world of the local police, local council and criminal justice officials at management level there was a discernible pattern in the 'control talk': the imagery and narratives used to depict the area, its population and culture. These made up elements of a cognitive framework which not only depicted problems of crime and disorder, but also provided dominant interpretive accounts to explain these phenomena (Cohen, 1985). A picture was painted of an inward-looking, poor population with limited education or intellectual ability, unstable family structures, little parental control over unruly and scholastically underachieving children and adolescents. A local employer in a nearby industrial estate, who did not employ anybody from the housing estate, described it thus: 'a bad housing estate . . . there's a hooligan element, and we had to put the fence up (providing a barrier against the estate's residents) and there's been a few problems'. The research consultant's community report crystallized the prevailing image of the area in the following terms: 'an isolated, immobile and introverted community, in which deviance comes younger than is normal'. The population was described by a local police sergeant as 'a forgotten people' and by a youth worker as 'a disposable community, certainly disposable kids', typical descriptions employed by professional workers in contact with this neighbourhood.

With the exception of senior housing officers, a major theme within the control talk was the claim that the District Council Housing Department was using the estate area as a 'dumping ground' for 'problem tenants'. These were often said to be headed by single parents and people with teenage children who had been in conflict with neighbours in their previous residence and involved with the criminal justice system (Bottoms and Wiles, 1997, p. 335). The rapid diminution of the council housing stock in the 1980s and 1990s throughout the district, as a result of the 'right-to-buy' policy, had reduced the discretionary scope for council allocations, though this was not always understood by those complaining about the movement of families:

the Council are dumping people here, every misfit. (Police constable)

As we understand it Wycombe dumped problem families on the estate and we didn't know that when we came. (Local employer on industrial estate)

Even a housing official, in a department which was very sensitive about the charge of dumping, admitted that it was an area on the cusp of serious decline:

We want to do something now before it turns into a Castlefield [a perceivedly troubled estate in High Wycombe, later the topic of a BBC documentary programme]. Outville is not in the same realms as Blackbird Leys [Oxford] or inner London estates. However, it has the potential to be a dumping ground. (Housing officer)

Noisy and critical Police–Community Consultative Group meetings in the area could be bruising, unpleasant experiences for the council officials and senior police officers charged to attend:

some of the people there are pretty ignorant . . . you hear people outside the area referring to Outville village idiots. Previous youth initiatives and other community ventures have failed because of apathy and lack of support by parents. They gripe a lot, but they always want someone else to do it for them. (Council officer)

The parents don't seem that bothered about controlling the kids. The behaviour of the younger kids is getting worse, what are they going to be like in their teens? . . . People are not prepared to take action, for example to run young people's activities. (Police constable)

The older people see the area as going down . . . the young people who we see just hang around in each other's houses, out of control, drinking and getting into drugs . . . There is a lack of motivation to explore employment. (Female probation officer)

As our study manifested, official concerns also focused on burglary, under-age drinking, incivilities, domestic violence (rarely reported to officialdom), intimidation, bullying and violence perpetrated on those deemed not to 'fit in' to the prevailing culture:

There are a lot of disputes between adults over kids' behaviour, over burglary, one picks on another. There is a lot of score settling and intimidation. But you don't tell the police, it's difficult to get people to come forward. And yet when something really bad happens they want the police to do something. (Police constable)

Despite the perceptions of the area among officialdom as problematic, police resources for Outville remained limited. The small team of officers located in a local small town were responsible for patrolling Outville in addition to a range of villages in a wide geographical area. Hence the village lacked its own dedicated beat officers. This resulted in a rather minimalist approach to law enforcement. One police officer defined the deeper problems of the area as 'a social job', requiring long-term involvement by the council. This seems to confirm Ericson and Haggerty's view that the police are often involved in filtering information about risks and reallocating this to other agencies of government:

It's really social work, for example a woman has trouble with her neighbours, you liaise with the housing department. They can wield a hammer that we don't have . . . There are lots of single-parent households, with no car. Mum can't get to see her friends, she gets depressed, the children are unruly. There is hostility shown by the older families to the new kids coming in. Then there are feuds. (Police sergeant)

The absence of officers with a full-time beat commitment to the area, and the difficulty in obtaining information which could be used in criminal prosecutions were compounded by the fact that, as the constable said, 'it is very difficult to do observation up there, even if we had the manpower'. This point was widely seen as crucial. In the words of a local employer, 'there is no police out here, that's a terrible thing.' Lack of information flow reinforced obstacles to the development of trust between police and public and led to an implicit policy in which deviance was contained and condoned (see Kinsey et al., 1986). Whatever the intention, this may have helped to consolidate a monopoly position for particular dealers who brought the police few hassles and helped to maintain discipline in the local drug market. For example, local police officers played down the problems of hard drugs in the area:

> Cars sometimes come in to sell individuals crack, but mostly the kids smoke spliffs (cannabis) . . . no needles about, no heroin and no crack houses . . . There is one dealer on the estate who has been established for years . . . he doesn't cause major hassles, there are no gangs hanging around outside the house . . . and this keeps the lid on other dealers. (Police constable)

This rather low-key assessment of the drug scene was not shared by a youth worker who had developed close links with young people in the area:

> [there are young people] involved in crime to pay for drug use . . . it's a main priority for their lives as they see it, that has all the attendant features of drug use. I think there's been a lot of money borrowed and people being chased. There are people trafficking drugs and who have had to disappear . . . cannabis, amphetamines, LSD, ecstasy, cocaine. (Female youth worker)

Resisting Government?

These accounts are reminiscent of the theories of social disorganization developed by sociologists to explain the clustering of social problems in areas where traditional familial and community authorities have crumbled or have failed to develop (Bottoms and Wiles, 1997, pp. 307–14). Yet, despite the depiction of the culture as disorganized, in its inability to socialize and control children and adolescents in conformity with middle-class and respectable working-class standards of behaviour, there was also a recognition of a form of social organization which is resistant to official authority and to those identified as outsiders. This provides a form of explanation for the capacity of some to bully, intimidate or impose rough justice on those deemed to be deviant: 'It's a very cliquey place – if you fit in you're all right, but if you don't . . .' (Housing officer).

Extended family networks were often seen as at the root of this alternative, rival mode of organization, an ironic point, given that earlier generations of urban planners had been criticized for breaking up the support systems of working-class extended families (Young and Willmott, 1957): 'Unfortunately, there are long-standing families in the area who wield a lot of power and like to get their own way' (Council officer). This rather disorderly image of the area was, to some extent, echoed in a survey in 1996 of ninety-six young people in Outville, conducted by the Youth Service-sponsored Outville Youth Council. Only 46 per cent of the sample thought that Outville was a safe place, 58 per cent were concerned about drugs in the area, 55 per cent about crime and 63.5 per cent about violence.

However, the legal and official governmental gaze on social life can be myopic. As noted earlier, and as radical criminologists have argued, it is misleading to reduce complex social conflicts to the simple, legal categories of 'crime', measured in discrete incidents (e.g. de Haan, 1991). Even as we recognize the scale of human suffering involved, it is important to unpack the simple characterization of people and neighbourhoods in terms of crime and fear. This way of reducing social reality can conceal the complexities underlying easily digestible notions about the links between youth, crime and social threats (Ferrell, 1996, 1998). In order to explore this complexity, let us examine the social and spatial structures of Outville in greater depth.

Inner World

Among senior officials and police officers views about Outville crystallized around the notion that there was a polarized class difference between estate and old village. However, perceptions of the area *within* the estate were more complex. The narratives of residents provided an implicit challenge to the view of the estate's population as uniformly deprived and disorderly. This has also been found in studies of urban-council housing estates (Foster, 1997). Negative labels were deflected and retargeted towards particular sections of the estate and particular social categories (Damer, 1974). In part this was based on length of residence, as well as differences in age and housing tenure:

> Outville consists of several communities . . . There is a settled community scattered throughout together with quite a few transient council families . . . most of the families in the newer part of the estate are under thirty-five, whereas in the older part they're more in their fifties and sixties. (Mrs A, resident)

> A lot of the houses here [in this section] have been bought, so they care a bit more about them. 'Hilltop Road' is . . . that's the [worst area in the estate] around the trouble and things . . . you know families that need a lot

of help really. They're just all down there . . . On the estate down the bottom here there's a couple of families that need a lot of help really . . . kids are left out all day and night, you don't feel safe going down there. (Mrs B, resident)

This description of social complexity was accompanied by narratives which depicted social change as decline, with perceivedly troublesome families moving between the least desirable areas of social housing in Wycombe, and with gossip about those families circulating among residents between the Wycombe estates:

A lot of the families coming up here now seem to be troubled families, whose kids cause a hell of a lot of trouble . . . new kid on the block, got to make a way for himself . . . families that sort of got a reputation of being moved from one area to another for causing trouble so they've been put in this area. Well they're starting trouble all over again and eventually they'll get moved out of this one for causing trouble and put in another one. But yeh it is getting known as a dumping ground . . . My kids are all right at this age, but as they get to teen age, what is there for them to do but get in with the wrong crowd, break into people's houses and do drugs? . . . because there's absolutely nothing up here. (Mrs B, resident)

Informal Governance

Yet these narratives of decline and disorganization are tempered by a recognition of what could be defined as informal governance. This involved claims about a degree of trust, mutual support and exchange of information about risks, which operated within this population. This could be viewed as partially filling the vacuum created by the perceived lack of proactive official policing and local service provision by the local authorities. For example this resident was involved in organizing what was described as a family group, which pragmatically worked with the grain of the varied household structures of the estate. It was set up, in part, because the mothers-and-toddlers group on the 'toffs'' side of the village was perceived as unwelcoming to people from the estate:

(it is) more for those that haven't got a lot, unemployed . . . we call ourselves a family group because anyone looking after a child can come . . . the dad or the aunty . . . or nan. The mothers-and-toddlers group is basically the mother and child. (Mrs B, resident)

This ethic of mutual support, particularly among women, can also be deployed to negotiate trust relationships with those (often, though not always, male) who may otherwise be seen as threatening. According to the same resident:

> We've been here three years and we've had no trouble, no break-ins, no one's stolen our car . . . We know a lot of the youth around here. Whether that's played a part in the fact that we give 'em the time of day and we're not nasty to them. So they respect us . . . if you're one of these that complains every five minutes then you're gonna have a lot of things happen to you, cause they do it out of spite.

It can also be deployed to provide informal defence against criminal victimization:

> There is some sense of community . . . we are always in and out borrowing things, if somebody's kids have something happen, others will rally round. So . . . if somebody nicks something from me, somebody else will have a pretty good idea who it is . . . there's no neighbourhood watch, only for the posh part. I think it's because they think it's because we're seen as not having much to protect anyway . . . we do it for each other. Turn each other's lights on . . . it's watching out for each other, because no one else is going to do it. (Mrs A, resident)

This may appear to be a positive response to the official policies fostering greater personal and communal responsibility for crime prevention (Garland, 1996; Stenson, 1996). But there was also a darker side to this communitarian ethic (Evans et al., 1996; for further consideration see Peay, chapter 11). Bullying tactics and rough justice were applied to those who were perceived to fall outside the particularistic criteria used to identify those with 'insider' status, for example, in terms of length of residence, ethnic status or whether residents accepted the prevailing patterns of informal authority within the population. There could be disputes over many issues ranging from debts arising out of drugs transactions, to family feuds, to resentment of newcomers from other estates failing to control the perceivedly criminal or disorderly behaviour of their children: 'It's the type of neighbourhood where things would be resolved privately by people getting visited' (female youth worker). A local councillor recounted examples of bullying from his constituency case file. For example, a young mother recently moved from another part of Wycombe said that her kids were bullied at school and 'had things like dead chickens thrown at her front door . . . she'd been out with her kids and a crowd had gathered round jeering at her' (male councillor).

This kind of informal governing practice on the part of some residents can take on a racist dimension and can function to maintain a degree of racial segregation in council housing estates (Smith, 1989). Senior officials were reluctant to view bullying practices in overtly racial terms:

> There is no ethnic problem in Outville . . . they don't choose to go there, because it's so isolated and there's no Mosque. (Senior housing officer)

> Ethnic minorities don't want to go there, there are no religious facilities. It's predominantly a white place. (Housing officer)

> There is no racial tension in Outville. (Senior youth officer)

Notwithstanding these claims by senior officials, this view was not shared by all the residents. In a predominantly white estate, many of the recent families who had been moved contained non-white members, for example mixed-race children of white mothers:

> [they] tend to move away because the children get bullied . . . I've known of at least three families who have had severe taunting. It is basically a white area, therefore children of mixed race, children who are Afro-Caribbean have a tough time . . . they stand out. (Mrs A, resident)

In addition, a study of young people in the urban areas of Wycombe District, conducted by the authors, revealed that among sections of south Asian and Afro-Caribbean young people Outville was perceived to be a white territory and a place to avoid (Watt and Stenson, 1998).

A typical case, reported in the local newspaper, involved a single black mother who had pleaded with the council to rehouse her away from the estate. This was after her three children had, over a five-month period, experienced sustained racist abuse near their home and at school, and with one daughter having been assaulted with a stick. The youth worker emphasized the problems encountered by young people of mixed race. While she ran a club, of the twenty-five regular members one was Asian, two were African and six of mixed race (i.e. with one Afro-Caribbean parent): 'A lot of their anger and personal feelings are around that very issue. They identify as black (and) . . . they feel racism, especially through school . . . they suffer in isolation' (female youth worker).

Conclusion

The dreams of rural peace pursued by the middle-class residents of the village were disturbed by the flow of poor urban people who were the casualties of an increasingly unequal social structure and whose problems were compounded by lack of community facilities in an isolated and confined rural space. While the middle-class residents were active in the parish council, Neighbourhood Watch and other committee-based organs of community organization, the estate residents were less involved, or tended to be seen as disruptive at the public meetings they attended. For both adults and children, the ability to use these settings effectively requires requisite education to foster the necessary knowledge and skills. More deeply, it requires the fostering of the kind of ethically reflective subjectivity which facilitates inclusion in a liberal citizenship. As the youth worker put it, in talking about the young people from the estate, 'It's about frustration, disempowerment . . . it would be a long-term project to bring them on board and empower them and speak for their community.'

Nevertheless, it is important for theorists of risk and government, as well as for the control agencies themselves, to recognize that governance does not operate only through the medium of sophisticated committee knowledge and skills. Nor is it simply the preserve of the complex of paternalist, tutelary agencies: statutory agencies, commercial firms, voluntary/not-for-profit agencies, or community associations given official recognition and sanction (O'Malley, 1996; Stenson, 1999). In rural settings, particularly, where official agencies are poorly resourced there are more informal modes of governance, emanating from diverse sites and sources, including kinship networks. These are filtered through local structures of feeling about place and reinforce both visible and invisible social and geographical boundaries (Taylor et al., 1996; Girling et al., 1997). Risks, including those relating to criminal victimization, are conceptualized, communicated and managed through informal oral cultural channels. Yet, given the rhetoric of partnership with the community (Husain, 1995, and see also Gilling and Pierpoint, chapter 7), a reliance on, or tolerance of, these informal modes of governance raises awkward questions for the police and other official agencies of government, whose remit is to provide a universalist, equitable and socially solidaristic framework of security for the management of risks (Shapland and Vagg, 1988; Stenson, 1993). Where there is tolerance of informal modes of governance, two key questions remain for public agents of government: whose social order is being protected, and who has the local power to assign the status of 'insider' or 'outsider'?

References

BECK, U. (1992) *Risk Society: Towards a New Modernity*, London: Sage
BOTTOMS, A. E. and WILES, P. (1997) 'Environmental criminology', in

Maguire, M., Morgan, R. and Reiner, R. (eds), *The Oxford Handbook of Criminology*, 2nd edn, Oxford: Oxford University Press

COHEN, S. (1985) *Visions of Social Control*, Cambridge: Polity Press

CRAWFORD, A. (1997) *The Local Governance of Crime*, Oxford: Oxford University Press

DAMER, S. (1974) 'Wine Alley: the sociology of a dreadful enclosure', 22 *Sociological Review*, 221

ERICSON, R. and HAGGERTY, K. (1997) *Policing the Risk Society*, Oxford: Oxford University Press

EVANS, K., FRASER, P. and WALKLATE, S. (1996) 'Whom can you trust? The politics of grassing on an inner city housing estate', 44 (3) *The Sociological Review*, 361

FERRELL, J. (1996) *Crimes of Style: Urban Graffitti and the Politics of Criminality*, Boston: Northeastern University Press

FERRELL, J. (1998) 'Youth, crime and cultural space', 24 (4) *Social Justice,* 21

FOSTER, J. (1997) 'Challenging perceptions: community and neighbour-liness on a difficult to let estate', in Jewson, N. and MacGregor S. (eds), *Transforming Cities: Contested Governance and New Spatial Divisions*, London: Routledge

FOUCAULT, M. (1991) 'Governmentality', in Burchell, B. et al. (eds.), *The Foucault Effect: Studies in Governmentality*, Hemel Hempstead: Harvester

GARLAND, D. (1996) 'The limits of the sovereign state: strategies of crime control in contemporary society', 36 *British Journal of Criminology*, 445

GEDDES, M. (1993) *Local Strategies for Peripheral Estates*, Initial Review and Issues Paper, Coventry: Local Government Centre

GIRLING, E., LOADER, I. and SPARKS, R. (1997) 'The trouble with the flats: CCTV and visions of order in an English Middletown', Paper delivered to the British Criminology Conference, Queen's University, Belfast, July

de HAAN, W. (1991) 'Abolitionism and crime control', in Stenson, K. and Cowell, D. (eds), *The Politics of Crime Control*, London: Sage

HAY, D., LINEBAUGH, P., THOMPSON, E. P. et al. (1975) *Albion's Fatal Tree: Crime and Society in Eighteenth Century England*, London: Allen Lane

HUSAIN, S. (1995) *Cutting Crime in Rural Areas: A Practical Guide for Parish Councils*, Swindon: Crime Concern

JOHNSTON, L. (1996) 'What is vigilantism?', 36 *British Journal of Criminology*, 220

KINSEY, R., LEA, J. and YOUNG, J. (1986) *Losing the Fight against Crime*, Oxford: Blackwell

LUKES, S. (1974) *Power: A Radical View*, London: Macmillan

MARSDEN, T., LOWE, P. and WHATMORE, S. (1990) *Rural Restructuring: Global Processes and Local Responses*, London: Wiley

MISZTAL, B. A. (1996) *Trust in Modern Societies*, Cambridge: Polity Press

MURDOCH, J. and MARSDEN, T. (1994) *Reconstituting Rurality: Class, Community and Power in the Development Process*, London: UCL Press

NEWBY, H. (1987) *Country Life: A Social History of Rural England,* London: Weidenfeld and Nicolson

O'MALLEY, P. (1996) 'Indigenous government', 25 (3) *Economy and Society*, 310

PEARSON, G. (1983) *Hooligan: A History of Respectable Fears*, London: Macmillan

POWER, A. and TUNSTALL, R. (1995) *Swimming against the Tide: Polarisation or Progress on Twenty Unpopular Council Estates*, York: Joseph Rowntree Foundation

ROSE, N. (1993) 'Government, authority and expertise in advanced liberalism', 22 (3) *Economy and Society*, 283

RURAL DEVELOPMENT COMMISSION (1992) *1991 Survey of Rural Services*, Salisbury: Rural Development Commission

SHAPLAND, J. and VAGG, J. (1988) *Policing by the Public*, London: Routledge

SMITH, S. (1989) *The Politics of Race and Residence*, Cambridge: Polity Press

SPARKS, R. (1992) *Television and the Drama of Crime*, Buckingham: Open University Press

SPARKS, R. (1995) 'Entertaining the crisis: television and moral enterprise', in Kidd-Hewitt, D. and Osborne, R. (eds), *Crime and the Media: The Postmodern Spectacle*, London: Pluto Press

STENSON, K. (1993) 'Community policing as a governmental technology', 22 (3) *Economy and Society*, 373

STENSON, K. (1996) 'Communal security as government – the British experience', in Hammerschick, W. (ed.), *Jahrbuch für Rechts- und Kriminalsoziologie*, Baden-Baden: Nomos

STENSON, K (1998) 'Displacing social policy through crime control', in Hanninen, S. (ed.), *Displacement of Social Policies*, Jyvaskyla: SoPhi Publications

STENSON, K. (1999) 'Crime control, governmentality and sovereignty', in Smandych, R. (ed.), *Governable Places: Readings in Governmentality and Crime Control*, Aldershot: Dartmouth

STENSON, K. and WATT, P. (1999) 'Governmentality and 'the death of the social'? A discourse analysis of local government texts in the south-east of England', *Urban Studies* (forthcoming)

TAYLOR, I. (1997) 'Crime, anxiety and locality: responding to the "condition of England" at the end of the century', 1 (1) *Theoretical Criminology*, 53

TAYLOR, I., EVANS, K. and FRASER, P. (1996) *A Tale of Two Cities: Global Change, Local Feeling and Everyday Life in the North of England. A Study in Manchester and Sheffield*, London: Routledge

WATT, P. and STENSON, K. (1998) ''It's a bit dodgy around there': safety, danger, ethnicity and young people's use of public space', in Skelton, T. and Valentine G. (eds), *Cool Places: Geographies of Youth Cultures*, London: Routledge

YOUNG, P. and WILLMOTT, M. (1957) *Family and Kinship in East London*, London: Routledge and Kegan Paul

6

Justice by Geography: Realizing Criminal Justice in the Countryside

GAVIN DINGWALL

The solution to increasing complexity, diversity, and plurality, became for many a retreat into common sense or managerialism; into denying the need to theorise totality, whilst taking comfort in easier, more apparent entities or geographies.

(Morrison, 1995, p.456)

The aim of this chapter is to consider the official response to criminal activity in rural areas against a theoretical discussion of changes in criminal justice and sentencing policy, primarily in England and Wales, since the Conservative election victory in 1979. In policy terms this is a convenient starting-point; the populist appeals to stronger law and order measures in combination with a drive towards increasing personal responsibility evident in pre-election propaganda (Downes and Morgan, 1997) gave way to increasingly reactionary penal policies and crime control strategies (see generally Dingwall and Davenport, 1995) as the rate of reported crime escalated alarmingly (Home Office, 1979–91). It was, in general terms, a period when the respective roles, rights and responsibilities of individuals, local communities and the state evolved (see generally Ewing and Gearty, 1990; Loveland, 1996), yet traditional social, political and economic disparities deepened (Andrews and Jacobs, 1990). This combination of an appeal to the supposed morality of the 'good old days' on the one hand coupled with pressure to revolutionize the power of central government on the other was particularly evident in the Conservatives' strategy towards controlling crime. A process of accountability and centralization gained momentum which offered, at least theoretically, less discretion at the local level to respond to particular crime problems. The changes that were introduced, however, were largely a response to the more visible, more political and quantifiably more serious problem of crime in urban areas. In the popular imagination the crime problem was synonymous with inner-city rioting in Brixton or Los Angeles, joyriding in urban council estates and violence on the street. The reasons behind this urbanization of deviance are various, but it is apparent that 'modernity up-rooted populations, took them out of their ritualised and "natural" locality into the city' with the consequence that contemporary society is often perceived as 'urban and individualist' (Morrison, 1995, p. 237).

Yet, despite an unprecedented legislative interest in criminal justice matters and a number of impressive large-scale empirical studies into the operation of the criminal justice system, little systematic attention has been paid, by either policy-makers or academic researchers, into how criminal justice agencies work in the rural environment. The neglect of the rural perspective represents a serious omission in contemporary criminological research, not least because rural residents appear to have genuine and, in some respects at least, justifiable concerns about crime and law enforcement (Koffman, 1996). Ironically the postmodern acceptance of the urban norm (Morrison, 1995) exists despite a greater willingness to accept that the world is becoming a 'plurality of heterogeneous spaces and temporalities' (Heller and Feher, 1988, p. 1). Given our greater understanding of rural crime (Anderson, 1997, chapter 3; Koffman, 1996, chapter 4) and the centralization of criminal justice policy, which will be documented further below, it seems reasonable to ask whether measures designed for the urban experience are practicable and theoretically justifiable in the rural setting. It will be argued that the process of centralization evident in the period under consideration masks considerable disparity in the operation of criminal justice services and that a more pluralistic approach in responding to crime would both reflect more clearly the current reality and allow a more communitarian response to develop. Implicit in this argument is the premise that the terms 'justice' and hence 'criminal justice' are relative and need to be assessed in terms of the values of the community in question (Walzer, 1983). Consequently, any attempt to standardize and rationalize such concepts on a national basis without sufficient sensitivity to the inherent diversity in British society represents a failure to address real needs and real problems.

This chapter will be primarily concerned with what could conventionally be termed 'official' responses to crime. Nevertheless the importance of 'unofficial' diversionary strategies for responding to criminal activities should not be underestimated (Dingwall and Harding, 1998). In country areas where the victim and the offender are more likely to be acquainted it is not unreasonable to surmise that there may be more of an incentive to resolve disputes without involving state agencies (see further Stenson and Watt, chapter 5; Peay, chapter 11), a factor which may help explain the marked differences between the low rates of reported crime in such areas and the amount of crime reported in victim surveys in the same localities (Koffman, 1996). Although crime surveys generally show that the most common reason for non-reporting is that the criminal incident was regarded by the victim as too trivial (Jones et al., 1986; Koffman, 1996), victims are clearly also diverting a considerable proportion of minor offences from the official arena, thereby setting the parameters of the official response to criminal activity (Dingwall and Harding, 1998). In a penal system where the primary determinant of punishment is offence severity (Criminal Justice Act 1991, ss.1(2)(a), 6 and 18) it would appear that decisions regarding reporting are often also based upon notions of proportionality. This is of relevance to the current discussion for two reasons. Firstly, rural victims' perceptions of seriousness may differ from the views of urban victims because of variations in crime patterns between the city and the countryside, and this may result in differences in reporting rates. Secondly, decisions on seriousness may also be affected by the relative practical difficulties of reporting the incident to the police and for the police in responding to it in an area of low population density. Diversion is also important in that it appears to have popular support in country areas: a higher proportion of victims in the Aberystwyth survey favoured the use of diversionary measures on the person(s) responsible for the crime(s) than those who favoured a fine, community sentence or a custodial sentence (Koffman, 1996, Appendix, table 5.17).

The chapter will start by considering the manner in which criminal justice agencies operate in country areas before turning to recent developments in sentencing policy. A particular emphasis in the first section will be given to policing, as the police represent the extent of most citizens' experience of the criminal justice service in both city and country areas.

The Provision of Criminal Justice Services in Rural Areas

It is clear that government strategy makes little provision for geographical distinctions in criminal justice policy, despite the fact that the application of the same policies in different areas is likely to produce different results. Since the Conservative election victory in 1979, two themes have become dominant in the provision of criminal justice services: an increased move towards managerialism and centralization (Hudson, 1996; James and Raine, 1998). There were obvious philosophical reasons why the Conservatives wished to make the provision of services more accountable in the 1980s; applying the principles of the market would, it was claimed, provide key services more efficiently than a bureaucratic civil service whose perceived inefficiencies were seen as symptomatic of the national malaise. From an economic perspective, reducing the size of the bureaucracy appealed to a government committed to reducing national expenditure. Although the most obvious changes occurred in the late 1980s and early 1990s with the introduction of the Citizen's Charter and the Next Steps initiative (Lewis, 1993; Theakston, 1995), the Conservative administration started to reform the provision of services almost as soon as it gained office (Drewry and Butcher, 1991). In 1979 an 'Efficiency Unit' was set up in the Cabinet Office under the chairmanship of Sir Derek Raynor to improve the cost effectiveness of government departments, including those responsible for criminal justice matters. This was followed in 1981 by the abolition of the Civil Service Department and in 1982 by the establishment of the Financial Management Initiative, which aimed at improving links between departmental budgets for government departments. These measures resulted in the civil service being reduced from a staff of 732,000 in 1979 to 554,000 in 1991 (Dorey, 1995, p. 239).

The most radical reforms came with the Next Steps initiative, which arose out of the Ibbs report (1988). The report's primary recommendation was that new semi-autonomous agencies be set up to carry out the executive functions of government within the terms of a policy framework drafted by the relevant government department (ibid., para. 44):

The aim should be to establish a quite different way of conducting the business of government. The central Civil Service should consist of a relatively small core engaged in the function of servicing Ministers and managing departments, who will be the 'sponsors' of particular government policies and services. Responding to these departments will be a range of agencies employing their own staff, who may or may not have the status of Crown servants, and concentrating on the delivery of their particular service, with clearly defined responsibilities between the Secretary of State and the Permanent Secretary on the one hand and the Chairman or Chief Executive of the agencies on the other. Both departments and their agencies should have a more open and simplified structure.

Given the constitutional issues involved, it is noticeable that the programme was subject to remarkably little parliamentary debate (Lewis, 1993) despite a body of perceptive contemporary literature on the changes (Chapman, 1988; Drewry, 1988; Kemp, 1990). By the end of 1996 there were 129 Next Step agencies in operation employing a total of 348,529 people (McEldowney, 1998, p. 325).

The transition to agency status has not been without problems, most notably in the criminal justice sphere where lapses are particularly sensitive politically. On 1 April 1993, both the Prison Service and the Scottish Prison Service were given executive agency status and became accountable to the Home Secretary and the Secretary of State for Scotland for the implementation of prison policy in their respective jurisdictions. A series of embarrassing security lapses led to the dismissal of the first Director General of the Prison Service. The wrongful early release of a number of multiple offenders caused further strain in the relationship between the Prison Service and the Home Office, exposing the practical and theoretical difficulties in separating the formation of policy from the implementation of policy (Dingwall, 1998).

This reform of the provision of services is important to a discussion of rurality and the work of criminal justice agencies for four reasons. Firstly, several key criminal justice agencies have received agency status, most notably the Court Service Agency. Secondly, rural residents have become increasingly dependent upon Next Step agencies, such as the Social Security Benefits Agency, the Employment Service and the UK Passport Agency, for the provision of services generally and hence have become used to such concepts as consumers' charters and success being measured in terms of economic efficiency. Thirdly, the pervading culture of managerialism upon which the rationale for Next Steps rests creates particular problems in rural areas owing to the higher costs associated with the sparsity of the population (Anderson, chapter 3; Davies, chapter 9). Such strategic problems are not new. Jones (1989), for example, reported that the distance from appropriate medical facilities in Gwynedd and Clwyd hampered the successful use of probation orders with requirement for treatment in north Wales. However, an increasing necessity to be publicly accountable and to include financial considerations in the delivery of services could clearly exacerbate the belief amongst agency staff in rural areas that they are under-resourced (Davies, chapter 9) and reduce the possibilities for more resource-intensive initiatives. Finally, and most crucially, Next Steps altered both the role of the state and of citizens (Lewis, 1993). The market became the provider of key services, the individual became the consumer of such services, and, crucially, both parties acquired new rights and duties. This contracting state is a consistent response to the postmodern belief that state intervention can only provide a limited response to social problems because of their inherent complexity (Aronowitz, 1988), and consequently the increasing reliance on managerial objectives in the provision of services offers a more realistic set of aspirations (Morrison, 1995).

Other criminal justice agencies were also radically reformed as part of the 'crime control' policies that the Conservatives adopted (James and Raine, 1998; Windlesham, 1993). However, these reforms were more often prompted by the urban than the rural experience. The first major manifestation of disorder to which the Conservatives had to respond was peculiarly urban in character. In 1981 rioting broke out in Brixton, leading to popular concerns about lawlessness in inner-city areas and the breakdown of notions of community in such areas. The violent clashes between the police and the predominantly black demonstrators had clear political ramifications, not least because urban policing had become highly politicized as a result of the election of radical Labour councils in many English cities, leading to conflict between chief constables and their police authorities (Loveday, 1985; Reiner, 1992). In conjunction with a reappraisal and extension of police powers in the Police and Criminal Evidence Act 1984 (see Zander, 1995), the police became subject to increasing central control. This was not all of the government's making. In the far-reaching decision of *R. v. Secretary of State for the Home Department, ex p. Northumbria Police Authority* [1988] 2 WLR 590 it was held that, under both the Royal Prerogative and the Police Act 1964, the Home Secretary had a duty to do what he felt was necessary for preserving the peace. In effect this meant that the Home Secretary could override the view of the local police authority. Following this case, Reiner (1991) found that chief constables tended to regard Home Office policies as binding, even if technically they were only of an advisory nature.

The Police and Magistrates' Courts Act 1994 continued the trend towards centralization by increasing the Secretary of State's involvement in the organization of police authorities, perhaps most visibly by granting the Home Secretary the power to determine the objectives of each police authority and to set performance targets for authorities to meet (Leishman et al., 1996; Loveday, 1994). Further reforms were contained in the Police Act 1996, the most controversial of which relate to the structure and functions of police authorities. The Act provides that the normal size of a police authority should not exceed seventeen members (s.4) unless the Home Secretary exercises discretion to increase the membership. This restriction quite clearly detracts from the notion that the police authority should be a local body and makes no allowance for the differences between different types of force. Section 6 of the Act states that the police authority is responsible for ensuring that the force is 'efficient and effective', in other words that the police authority delivers value for money (Leishman et al., 1996).

All of these developments in policing appear to have been driven partly by the ideological discourse of the New Right which favours centralization and partly as a pragmatic 'crime control' response to urban disorder, given the Conservatives' manifesto pledges to be tough on crime. However, it would be wrong to state that the rural played no part in the development of policing powers at this time. The concern generated by hunt saboteurs, ravers and New Age Travellers (see further Hester, chapter 8) resulted in the police being given sweeping new powers in the Criminal Justice and Public Order Act 1994. The belief that these groups were threatening the rural equilibrium and therefore needed to be 'effectively' policed is reminiscent of earlier times, where the symbolic battlegrounds for testing the loyalties of the police were rural rather than urban (Radzinowicz, 1968). The 'outsiders' may have changed, but the underlying issue, namely the competing interests in rural areas, remained essentially the same.

These reforms have impacted upon all police forces (Reiner, 1997), but Hirst (1994) has argued convincingly that many of the reforms introduced in this period have proved especially problematic for rural forces to implement. She cites the logistical problems of holding suspects in police custody after the implementation of the Police and Criminal Evidence Act 1984 as an example. The Act differentiates between 'designated' and 'non-designated' stations in an attempt to use resources more effectively. Unless stringent criteria are met, a suspect must be taken to a designated station if custody is required. These designated stations have the requisite facilities for prisoners provided by the Act. In urban centres this differentiation of stations may well have led to a more sensible allocation of resources. However, in rural areas the distance between designated stations may cause practical problems. She takes the example of Lampeter, a non-designated station situated a considerable distance from the nearest designated stations at Aberystwyth and Carmarthen. The distance is compounded by the poor road network in the area: any transfer of prisoners involves two officers in a round trip of approximately two hours. However, staffing levels at Lampeter are such (between 1 a.m. and 6 a.m. there are only two officers on duty, and between 6 a.m. and 9 a.m. there is only one officer on duty) that such trips at best place a severe restriction on resources and, at worst, cannot be undertaken without help from officers stationed elsewhere. There has apparently been talk of upgrading Lampeter station, but this would have serious resource implications owing to the stringent requirements of the Act.

Given the geographical and sociological factors, there would appear to be recognizable differences in the way that country police forces interact with the local community. Young (1993) studied the cultural identity of a rural force and found that it varied markedly from the urban model (compare with Holdaway, 1983; Graef, 1989; Young, 1991). In particular he found that senior police officers corresponded to some extent with the squirearchical hierarchy traditionally found in rural communities. To a large extent this study built upon earlier studies which had suggested that country police officers were strongly integrated into the local community, whereas urban officers often had little direct connection with the areas that they policed and tended instead to identify with other police officers (Cain, 1973; Shapland and Vagg, 1988). This integration with the community may help explain the fact that rural police forces generally enjoy the support of the communities that they police. Out of the Aberystwyth sample 64 per cent stated that the local police did 'a good job' (Koffman, 1996, Appendix, table 5.4). Similarly, Shapland and Vagg (1988) reported a high degree of popular support for the police from rural respondents (see also Anderson, chapter 3).

Jones and Levi (1983) compared policing in Devon and Cornwall with Greater Manchester and found that the public in Devon and Cornwall were more favourable towards the police than the population in Greater Manchester. They also stated that the police in Devon and Cornwall had a more informed view of the public's concerns, which suggested a greater sense of integration. The authors, however, rejected a simple explanation on the basis of a rural/urban divide. Although popular support for the police in Devon and Cornwall was lowest in Plymouth (the largest centre of population), the level of support there was still higher than in smaller settlements in the Greater Manchester area. They concluded that the rural/urban divide was accentuated by the different policing philosophies adopted by the respective chief constables, John Alderson and James Anderton.

The functions of criminal justice agencies are continually evolving as a response to the needs of both government and the community that they are serving. At a time when, at least at a formal level, policing is becoming increasingly centralized it is still readily apparent that, whilst there are many common functions that police officers in central Glasgow share with police officers in Caithness, the manner in which these functions are realized may vary. Urban policing is increasingly remote, reactive and specialized (Uglow, 1988), with the consequence that contemporary society requires a variety of styles of policing:

> In this context, the British conception of the police as a body with an omnibus mandate, symbolizing order and harmony, becomes increasingly anachronistic. The British police are likely to move more towards the international pattern of specialist national units for serious crimes, terrorism, public order, large-scale fraud, and other national or

international problems. Local police providing services to particular communities will remain, but with sharp differences between 'service' style organisations in stable suburban areas, and 'watchman' bodies with the rump duties of the present police, keeping the lid on underclass symbolic locations. (Reiner, 1997, p.1039)

Paradoxically, we may be witnessing an increasing bifurcation in policing practice between rural and non-rural areas notwithstanding the clear centralization present in government policy, a process that again accords with the postmodern experience of increasing diversity despite a move towards centralization (Morrison, 1995).

Issues of Proportionality and 'Desert'

If criminal justice practice was subject to a process of increasing centralization, penal policy and sentencing also underwent significant changes in the period under review. Once again, the primary reason given for such a change by the government was the perceived need to bolster consistency in sentencing decision-making, given the near legendary disparity between different courts in sentencing matters (Home Office, 1990). The policy adopted in the Criminal Justice Act 1991 could potentially be interpreted as a postmodern retreat, insofar as it relied upon commonsensical notions of 'desert' and espoused a more managerialistic attitude towards the need to conform whilst failing to acknowledge key theoretical difficulties brought about by the pluralistic nature of contemporary society. The retreat to retributivism and the adoption of 'just deserts' and 'proportionality' as the primary determinants of both the type and scale of eventual punishment (Ashworth, 1995; Cavadino and Dignan, 1997; Dingwall and Davenport, 1995) originated in part from an increasing awareness of the limits, and associated libertarian dangers, of intensive state-based rehabilitative programmes (von Hirsch, 1976; Bottoms and Preston, 1980). The penal optimism of the post-war years had become increasingly difficult to sustain owing to the lack of empirical proof that such potentially invasive techniques had any demonstrable utilitarian benefit. Such intensive state interference was adjudged to be an ineffective way to manage social problems (Garland, 1996) and the failures generated by such methods in turn created what Habermas (1976) famously termed a legitimation crisis. Moreover, it is clear that retributivist concepts would be philosophically attractive to a Conservative administration which made great play of personal responsibility and blamed 'liberal' policies for the increase in reported crime.

The 1991 Act was deliberately stated in bold terms (Home Office, 1990) and, broadly speaking, provided that the sentence imposed by a court should reflect the gravity of the offending conduct (more detail can be found in Ashworth, 1995; Walker and Padfield, 1996; Wasik, 1998). To take one example, s.1(2)(a) provides that a custodial sentence can be imposed only where no other sentence would adequately reflect the gravity of the offence, and s.2(2)(a) states that the length of such a sentence should be proportionate to the gravity of the offence, but little specific guidance is given on how the gravity of an offence is to be quantified. In an attempt to appease judicial concerns about the erosion of judicial independence, it was envisaged that further guidance on determining matters of seriousness and proportionality would be provided by appellate courts in a series of so-called 'guideline judgements' (Home Office, 1990). Yet, despite a series of such judgements from the Court of Appeal, it has been argued (Dingwall, 1997) that these pronouncements have frequently preferred the general to the particular and have often avoided the most complex theoretical questions. In fairness, the all-too-familiar judicial caveat that all cases are different and that therefore it is difficult to provide detailed sentencing guidance at least recognizes the complexity of salient issues that desert theorists need to consider.

This policy, in itself, may appear to be of little direct relevance to our current discussion on the operation of criminal justice agencies in rural areas but there are a number of theoretical issues that need to be addressed before one can consider rural sentencing practice. For example, to what extent, if at all, can the gravity of the offence, and hence the punishment that the court will impose, be influenced by localized factors under the 'desert' model? In the case of *Bibby* (1995) 16 Cr.App.R.(S.) 127 the offender targeted rural building societies as, having watched an episode of *Crime Watch* on television, he believed that they were particularly vulnerable to robbery. The Court of Appeal appeared to be influenced by the increased vulnerability caused by the rural location when reviewing the sentence that Bibby had originally received in the Crown Court. This, however, is merely a recent example of a traditional sentencing practice, namely that the courts treat the vulnerability of certain categories of individuals as an aggravating factor when determining sentence (Walker and Padfield, 1996).

A more theoretically challenging scenario was considered by the Court of Appeal in *Cunningham* [1993] 1 WLR 183. Could a sentencer take into account the prevalence of an offence in a given area in determining the harm that was caused by the offender? The Court answered this in the affirmative and considered not merely the direct harm to the immediate victim but the aggregate harm to the local community:

The seriousness of the offence is clearly affected by how many people it harms and to what extent. For example, a violent sexual attack on a woman in a public place gravely harms her. But if such attacks are prevalent in a neighbourhood, each offence affects not only the immediate victim but women generally in that area, putting them in fear and limiting their freedom of movement. Accordingly, in such circumstances, the sentence commensurate with the seriousness of the offence may need to be higher here than elsewhere. Again, and for similar reasons, a bomb hoax may at one time not have been so serious as it is when a campaign of actual bombings mixed with hoaxes is in progress. (p.187)

Although this reasoning may appear superficially attractive, it exposes considerable theoretical difficulties. Under 'desert' philosophy the gravity of the punishment should be determined with reference to both the harm caused and the offender's culpability (von Hirsch and Jareborg, 1991). Neither of these factors are susceptible to easy quantification, yet it would appear that the prevalence of an offence in a particular locality should only be taken into account in assessing the harm caused if the offender was aware that additional harm would be caused in the circumstances. Adopting the court's example, the hoax bomber would clearly deserve a longer sentence if he deliberately coincided his threat with an actual bombing campaign. However, notwithstanding the additional fear caused by a spate of sexual attacks in a given locality, it seems somewhat perverse to impose a longer sentence on the third attacker than on the first merely because of the other two attacks in which he had no part.

Further analysis of the court's reasoning is outside the scope of this chapter but the judgement raises an important and intriguing question: if a car is more likely to be stolen in Swansea than in Aberystwyth, under a 'desert' model should the rural thief receive the same sentence as his or her urban counterpart? If this is answered in the affirmative, does the theory take adequate account of the differences in locality and consequently the potential differences in harm suffered by both the immediate victim and the community at large? And, if disparity can be theoretically tolerated, should the rural theft be viewed as more serious, and hence deserving of a greater punishment, because such thefts happen less frequently and could cause greater inconvenience to the victim because of in-adequate public transport, or, conversely, should the urban theft be taken as more serious because it is more common and, according to the reasoning in *Cunningham*, harms more people? These questions are intrinsically debatable – might not the first car theft in an isolated village cause more general concern than the latest of many in an area renowned for car crime? – but they raise important questions of sentencing policy and could potentially justify a disparity in sentencing practice between urban and rural courts despite a policy designed to standardize sentencing decisions on a national basis.

This realization that the harm caused can vary through geographical factors, and that consequently the proportionate punishment for apparently identical offences can legitimately vary, makes it problematic to assess sentencing trends in rural courts and to compare such findings with urban courts. Furthermore, it is widely accepted that despite the new legislative framework sentencers continue to enjoy considerable personal discretion, so that generalization remains difficult (Ashworth, 1995).

Robertshaw (1994) studied Crown Court practice in a number of rural courts in the Wales and Chester and Western Circuits, namely Barnstaple, Bodmin, Truro, Caernarfon, Carmarthen, Dorchester, Haverfordwest, Newport on the Isle of Wight, Salisbury, Taunton and Welshpool. As he recognized, his criteria for selection were highly subjective: they included 'some notion of population intensity, isolation from other centres, and agricultural predominance' (p. 52). Certain Crown Courts were excluded from the sample on the grounds that the author was ignorant of the area, the sample of cases was too small or the locality included sizeable centres of population. A further problem with the study was that the author was dependent upon annual returns to the Lord Chancellor's Department for information. These returns did not differentiate between offence type, so only the crudest forms of analysis could be undertaken. Robertshaw analysed the courts' sentencing practice with reference only to the custodial rate (which includes partly suspended sentences) and found that for guilty pleas there was a slight tendency for rural courts to make less use of custody than urban courts. For those convicted at trial there was a far greater range in the use of custodial sentences: in 1989, for example, 15.2 per cent of sentences in this category were of a custodial nature in Taunton, compared with 64.7 per cent in Caernarfon. This clearly demonstrates the dangers in assuming a generic sentencing pattern in rural Crown Courts. Robertshaw concludes with two tentative findings: those who plead guilty in rural courts tend to be treated more leniently than those who plead guilty in urban courts, and there was a tendency for a higher proportion of rural defendants to plead not guilty. The second point is of particular note and raises a number of issues worthy of further consideration. Recent research has highlighted both the importance of 'case construction' by the Crown Prosecution Service (McConville et al., 1991) and the reliance placed by suspects on their legal representatives (McConville et al., 1994); do rural defence solicitors and rural prosecutors operate differently from their urban colleagues? It is not unreasonable to speculate that the professional culture may be very different in a countryside solicitor's office from that in a specialized, and frequently overstretched, urban criminal defence practice.

There have been no other empirical studies on Crown Court sentencing in rural areas. Other academic studies have been very narrow in focus and have been primarily concerned either with the sentencing of a particular type of offence (e.g. business offenders: Croal, 1991; drug importers: Green, 1994) or with a particular class of offender (most notably those from ethnic minority groups: Brown and Hullin, 1992; Hood, 1992). A major Home Office study into sentencing practice in the Crown Court (1988) took account of six extraneous factors other than those relating directly to the offence: (1) the remand status prior to trial, (2) gender, (3) whether the case had been committed for sentence by a magistrates' court, (4) the status of the judge hearing the case, (5) the ethnic origin of the offender and (6) information contained in the social inquiry report, but no consideration was taken of geographical factors.

Similarly, in his important study on the sentencing behaviour of magistrates, Henham (1990) considered a number of personal factors such as sex, age, occupation, education and political persuasion, in an attempt to ascertain whether these variables affected the magistrate's view of sentencing principles. Again no consideration was taken of the geographical setting in which the magistrate operated. Yet, it would appear that rurality can exacerbate some of the variables employed. One rural magistrate, Margaret Gwynne Lloyd, demonstrates this vividly with respect to her bench, Gogledd Preseli in mid-Wales (1994). All eleven members of the bench were drawn either from the farming community or had a background in teaching. She notes that a bench which is overdependent upon members originating from such a narrow professional background potentially lacks the diversity of experience necessary to administer justice impartially, and that the particular occupations represented may have a traditional relationship with the other members of a rural community:

> The issue is rather that both teachers and farmers face subtle potential problems in the exercise of their duties. Teachers would be the first to acknowledge that their connection with a school . . . brings them into frequent conflict with their role as a magistrate. It is often inappropriate for them to sit on a case involving a recent pupil if his/her general conduct has to be considered by the court . . . The possibility of bias arising through analogous interests is something that also faces farmers. Offences involving agricultural pollution is a case in point. Furthermore the farming community is one of the most stable of all social classes and is well blessed with long, well-established and extensive local connections. (p. 69)

The potential problems of unrepresentative benches may well be more acute in rural areas where the benches are especially small and where the range of occupational experience amongst the magistrates may be narrower than in urban areas (on magistrates' backgrounds generally see Henham, 1990). Again, though, more sophisticated research is necessary to establish whether there are consistent sentencing patterns in rural magistrates' courts. One particular methodological problem that researchers face is that such courts often have a very small throughput, often making the sample size too small for meaningful statistical analysis. Gogledd Preseli, for example, deals with an average of only 350 offences annually.

Yet, even if it could be shown categorically that rural magistrates do sentence offenders differently, is this necessarily of concern? There is a danger in research of this nature of seeing consistency as the only worthwhile goal, especially when sentencers are supposedly working in a 'desert'-based environment, thereby ignoring the fact that notions of harm, proportionality and justice vary between different communities. This in no way reduces the need for more systematic empirical research into rural sentencing practice – the identification of particular trends would add greatly to our understanding of the way in which sentencers operate; rather it cautions against seeing uniformity as the overriding concern in contemporary criminal justice.

A Way Forward?

Within the context of democratic values . . . we should be willing to respect diversity by regarding it as a resource and not a defect. Unanimous votes are good news for the recipient victors but not for the long-term health of a democracy. A diversity in a gene pool is a strength, not a weakness. Symphonic music is the richer for the different sounds of the piccolo and the flute. Sameness or unanimity, depending on the context, is often a threat, a weakness, or a bore. (Hill, 1991, p. 151)

The overall picture that emerges is that, despite a determined process of centralization in matters of criminal justice management and penal policy, there remain qualitative differences in how the criminal justice system operates in rural areas (Cain, 1973; Hirst, 1994; Jones and Levi, 1983; Robertshaw, 1994; Shapland and Hobbs, 1989; Shapland and Vagg, 1988; Young, 1993). The simplicity of such a conclusion masks an incredibly complex picture of differential crime patterns, differential informal control networks, geographical, economic and pragmatic differences in how criminal justice agencies operate, different professional cultures, different popular and community concerns and, in turn, different notions of how best justice is served. Moreover, it is arguably of little benefit to delimit areas purely on a rural/urban dichotomy, as this hides the inherent diversity of rural areas in the United Kingdom (Williams, chapter 10). For those who determine criminal justice policy this diversity exposes the difficulties of standardization both at a practical level, in that measures designed as a response to the urban experience may not be practicable in a rural setting, and at a theoretical level, in that different communities may have a different sense of what is appropriate as a response to criminal behaviour (Walzer, 1983). We are left in a state of flux because the complexity associated with postmodern society helps provide an understanding of where we are and yet, simultaneously, highlights the difficulties associated with centralized planning at the state level: 'The post-modern mind does not expect any more to find the all-embracing, total and ultimate formula of life without ambiguity, risk, danger and error, and is deeply suspicious of any voice that promises otherwise' (Bauman, 1993, p. 245).

Rather than looking to the state to provide a comprehensive answer to social problems such as crime, there has been a growing consensus amongst politicians and commentators that the focus should shift to more active forms of social control allied to greater personal responsibility (Clarke, 1987; Garland, 1996, 1997; Newburn, 1997). The views of right-wing writers such as Murray (1998), namely that modernity has provided too many excuses for criminal activity and that individuals and communities need to reclaim moral responsibility from the state, have gained increasing political acceptance and can be seen in the Crime and Disorder Act 1998, which introduced anti-social behaviour orders and abolished the presumption that children under the age of fourteen have no criminal responsibility in England and Wales. What is most notable is that these measures have been adopted not by a Conservative government but by a Labour one. A new political agenda has been set:

[I]ntimations of a possible new intellectual and policy paradigm are not difficult to detect – on the political right as well as on the left. The fall of communism has taken the zest out of the old battles of state against market, and socialism against capitalism. The simplistic universalities of the Cold War no longer resonate; the focus is now on complexity and difference. Persistent divergencies in the fortunes of market economies have focussed attention on the varieties of capitalism, and on their moral and cultural dimensions. Endemic unemployment in Europe, the rise of the working poor in the United States, the transformation of labour markets everywhere and the associated threat of fragmentation and anomie have fostered a new concern with the dangers of social exclusion and the *a priori* necessity for social cohesion. Classic themes from the eighteenth and nineteenth centuries – the role of trust in a market economy; the prerequisites of civil society; the meaning of citizenship; the relationship between duties and rights; the need for and scope of a public domain; the threats to and demands of community – have been rediscovered. (Marquand and Seldon, 1996, pp.9–10)

By recasting the role of the state, the community and the individual, the challenge is to create 'a voluntaristic integration of citizens into a compact of co-operation, compromise, communication and self-policing' (Bergalli and Sumner, 1997, p. 18). Rural communities provide a useful opportunity for testing the extent that such social control mechanisms already operate (Peay, chapter 11; Stenson and Watt, chapter 5) and could prove particularly suitable for new methods of responding to deviant behaviour, such as reintegrative shaming (Braithwaite, 1989). Such a community response, however, assumes that the community is reasonably uniform, a notion which this book challenges. It is clear that there are disparate groups coexisting in the countryside and that the values of these groups may be in direct conflict (see Hester, chapter 8; Peay, chapter 11; Stenson and Watt, chapter 5). The view that a stable community, with a common value set reflects the rural norm may be a source of reassurance (Moody, chapter 1; McCullagh, chapter 2) but it is largely illusory. Those who participated in the 1998 Countryside March were united only in the belief that there was something unique about the countryside and that rural issues were not being adequately addressed at a national level. In reality the composition of the marchers demonstrated the breadth of interests and values found in country areas.

Many of the factors present in the provision of criminal justice – the trend towards Europeanization (Harding et al., 1995) and globalization on the one hand, versus increased calls to local community on the other (Bergalli and Sumner, 1997), the move towards greater centralization yet the continued practice of diversity – are but part of a greater debate concerning the regulation of postmodern society. Parallels can be drawn with the increasing calls for subsidiarity within the European Union and devolution within the United Kingdom. As crime is a genuine concern of rural residents (Anderson, 1997; Koffman, 1996) the most appropriate way to respond to it should be given consideration both at a practical and a theoretical level. Central to this debate has to be a recognition and a respect for diversity.

References

ANDERSON, S. (1997) *A Study of Crime in Rural Scotland*, Edinburgh: Scottish Office Central Research Unit

ANDREWS, K and JACOBS, J. (1990) *Punishing the Poor: Poverty under Thatcher*, London: Macmillan

ARONOWITZ, S. (1988) 'Postmodern and politics', in Ross, A. (ed.), *Universal Abandon? The Politics of Postmodernism*, Minneapolis: University of Minnesota Press

ASHWORTH, A. (1995) *Sentencing and Criminal Justice*, 2nd edn, London: Butterworths

BAUMAN, Z. (1993) *Postmodern Ethics*, Oxford: Blackwell

BERGALLI, R. and SUMNER, C. (1997) *Social Control and Political Order: European Perspectives at the End of the Century*, London: Sage

BOTTOMS, A. E. and PRESTON, R. H. (eds) (1980) *The Coming Penal Crisis*, Edinburgh: Scottish Academic Press

BRAITHWAITE, J. (1989) *Crime, Shame and Reintegration*, Cambridge: Cambridge University Press

BROWN, I and HULLIN, R. P. (1992) 'A study of sentencing in the Leeds magistrates' courts: the treatment of ethnic minority and white offenders', 32 *British Journal of Criminology*, 41

CAIN, M. (1973) *Society and the Policeman's Role*, London: Routledge

CAVADINO, M. and DIGNAN, J. (1997) *The Penal System: An Introduction*, 2nd edn, London: Sage

CHAPMAN, R. A. (1988) 'The next steps: a review', 3 *Public Policy and Administration*, 3

CLARKE, M. (1987) 'Citizenship, community and the management of crime', 27 *British Journal of Criminology*, 384

CROAL, H. (1991) 'Sentencing the business offender', 30 *Howard Journal*, 280

DINGWALL, G. (1997) 'The Court of Appeal and guideline judgments', 48 *Northern Ireland Legal Quarterly*, 143

DINGWALL, G. (1998) 'The Home Office, the Prison Service and the recalculation of release dates for multiple offenders', 49 *Northern Ireland Legal Quarterly*, 74

DINGWALL, G. and DAVENPORT, A. (1995) 'The evolution of criminal justice policy in the UK', in Harding et al. (eds), *Criminal Justice in Europe*, Oxford: Clarendon Press

DINGWALL, G. and HARDING, C. (1998) *Diversion in the Criminal Process*, London: Sweet and Maxwell

DOREY, P. (1995) *British Politics since 1945*, Oxford: Blackwell

DOWNES, D. and MORGAN, R. (1997) 'Dumping the hostages to fortune? The politics of law and order in post-war Britain', in Maguire, M., Morgan, R. and Reiner, R. (eds) *The Oxford Handbook of Criminology*, 2nd edn, Oxford: Clarendon Press

DREWRY, G. (1988) 'Forward from FMI: the next steps', *Public Law*, 505

DREWRY, G. and BUTCHER, T. (1991) *The Civil Service Today*, Oxford: Blackwell

EWING, K. and GEARTY, C. (1990) *Civil Liberties under Thatcher*, Oxford: Oxford University Press

GARLAND, D. (1996) 'The limits of the sovereign state: strategies of crime control in contemporary society', 36 *British Journal of Criminology*, 445

GARLAND, D. (1997) 'The punitive society: penology, criminology and the history of the present', 1 *Edinburgh Law Review*, 180

GRAEF, R. (1989) *Talking Blues*, London: Collins

GREEN, P. (1994) 'The characteristics and sentencing of illegal drug importers', 34 *British Journal of Criminology*, 479

HABERMAS, J. (1976) *Legitimation Crisis*, London: Heinemann

HARDING, C. et al. (eds) (1995) *Criminal Justice in Europe*, Oxford: Clarendon Press

HELLER, A. and FEHER, F. (1988) *The Postmodern Political Condition*, Cambridge: Polity Press

HENHAM, R. (1990) *Sentencing Principles and Magistrates' Sentencing Behaviour*, Aldershot: Avebury

HILL, P. J. (1991) 'Religion and the quest for community', in Rouner, L. S. (ed.), *On Community*, Notre Dame, Ind.: University of Notre Dame Press

HIRST, P. (1994) 'Problems affecting rural policing', in Harding, C. and Williams, J. (eds) *Legal Provision in the Rural Environment*, Cardiff: University of Wales Press

HOLDAWAY, S. (1983) *Inside the British Police*, Oxford: Blackwell

HOME OFFICE (1979–91) *Criminal Statistics*, London: HMSO

HOME OFFICE (1988) *Sentencing Practice in the Crown Court*, Research Study No. 103, London: HMSO

HOME OFFICE (1990) *Crime, Justice and Protecting the Public*, Cmnd 965, London: HMSO

HOOD, R. (1992) *Race and Sentencing*, Oxford: Oxford University Press

HUDSON, B. A. (1996) *Understanding Justice: An Introduction to Ideas, Perspectives and Controversies in Modern Penal Theory*, Buckingham: Open University Press

IBBS REPORT (1988) *Improving Management in Government: The Next Steps*, Report to the Prime Minister, London: HMSO

JAMES, A. and RAINE, J. (1998) *The New Politics of Criminal Justice*, London: Longman

JONES, G. (1989) 'The use and effectiveness of the probation order with a condition for psychiatric treatment in north Wales', 20 *Cambrian Law Review*, 63

JONES, S. and LEVI, M. (1983) 'The police and the majority: the neglect of the obvious', 56 *Police Journal*, 351

JONES, T., MacLEAN, B. and YOUNG, J. (1986) *The Islington Crime Survey: Crime Victimisation and Policing in Inner City London*, Aldershot: Gower

KEMP, P. (1990) 'Next steps for the British Civil Service', 3 *Governance*, 186

KOFFMAN, L. (1996) *Crime Surveys and the Victims of Crime*, Cardiff: University of Wales Press

LEISHMAN, F., COPE, S. and STARIE, P. (1996) 'Reinventing and restructuring: towards a new policing order', in Leishman, F., Loveday, B. and Savage, S. (eds.), *Core Issues in Policing*, London: Longmans

LEWIS, N. (1993) 'The Citizen's Charter and next steps: a new way of governing?', 64 *The Political Quarterly*, 316

LLOYD, M. G. (1994) 'The magistrate in a rural area with particular reference to courts in west Wales', in Harding, C. and Williams, J. (eds), *Legal Provision in a Rural Environment*, Cardiff: University of Wales Press

LOVEDAY, B. (1985) *The Role and Effectiveness of the Merseyside Police Committee*, Liverpool: Merseyside County Council

LOVEDAY, B. (1994) 'The Police and Magistrates' Court Act', 10 *Policing*, 221

LOVELAND, I. (1996) *Constitutional Law: A Critical Introduction*, London: Butterworths

McCONVILLE, M., HODGSON, J., BRIDGES, L. and PAVLOVIC, A. (1994) *Standing Accused*, Oxford: Oxford University Press

McCONVILLE, M., SANDERS, A. and LENG, R. (1991) *The Case for the Prosecution*, London: Routledge

McELDOWNEY, J. (1988) *Public Law*, 2nd edn, London: Sweet and Maxwell

MARQUAND, D. and SELDON, A. (1996) *The Ideas that Shaped Post-War Britain*, London: Fontana Press

MORRISON, W. (1995) *Theoretical Criminology: From Modernity to Post-Modernism*, London: Cavendish

MURRAY, C. (1988) *In Pursuit of Happiness and Good Government*, New York: Simon and Schuster

NEWBURN, T. (1997) 'Youth, crime, and justice', in Maguire, M., Morgan, R. and Reiner, R. (eds), *The Oxford Handbook of Criminology*, 2nd edn, Oxford: Clarendon Press

RADZINOWICZ, L. (1968) *A History of English Criminal Law, iv:, Grappling for Control*, London: Stevens

REINER, R. (1991) *Chief Constables*, Oxford: Oxford University Press

REINER, R. (1992) *The Politics of the Police*, Brighton: Wheatsheaf

REINER, R. (1997) 'Policing and the police', in Maguire, M., Morgan, R. and Reiner, R. (eds), *The Oxford Handbook of Criminology*, 2nd edn, Oxford: Clarendon Press

ROBERTSHAW, P. (1994) 'Rural Crown Courts: are they different?', in Harding, C. and Williams, J. (eds), *Legal Provision in the Rural Environment*, Cardiff: University of Wales Press

SHAPLAND, J. and HOBBS, R. (1989) 'Policing on the ground', in Morgan, R. and Smith, D. (eds), *Coming to Terms with Policing*, London: Routledge

SHAPLAND, J. and VAGG, J. (1988) *Policing by the Public*, London: Routledge

THEAKSTON, K. (1995) *The Civil Service since 1945*, Oxford: Blackwell

UGLOW, S. (1988) *Policing Liberal Society*, Oxford: Oxford University Press

von HIRSCH, A. (1976) *Doing Justice: The Choice of Punishments*, New York: Hill and Wang

von HIRSCH, A. and JAREBORG, N. (1991) 'Gauging criminal harm: a living-standard analysis', 11 *Oxford Journal of Legal Studies*, 1

WALKER, N. and PADFIELD, N. (1996) *Sentencing: Theory, Law and Practice*, 2nd edn, London: Butterworths

WALZER, M. (1983) *Spheres of Justice: A Defence of Pluralism and Equality*, Oxford: Blackwell

WASIK, M. (1998) *Emmins on Sentencing*, 3rd edn, London: Blackstone Press

WINDLESHAM, D. (1993) *Responses to Crime, Penal Policy in the Making*, Oxford: Clarendon Press

YOUNG, M. (1991) *An Inside Job*, Oxford: Oxford University Press

YOUNG, M. (1993) *In the Sticks: An Anthropologist in a Shire Force*, Oxford: Oxford University Press

ZANDER, M. (1995) *The Police and Criminal Evidence Act 1984*, London: Sweet and Maxwell

7

Crime Prevention in Rural Areas

DANIEL GILLING and HARRIET PIERPOINT

Introduction

The last twenty years have witnessed a growing consensus about the importance of crime prevention as a control strategy in its own right. This consensus has been built upon a dissatisfaction with more traditional, and mostly reactive, approaches to crime control and their capacity to curb the increases in officially recorded rates of crime. It is also based upon an increasing recognition, common to other areas of public and social policy, that statutory services alone and in isolation cannot be expected to serve the common good. Crime prevention, therefore, is the responsibility not just of the statutory services, but also of the private and voluntary sectors, and of the general public.

Our purpose in this chapter is to examine the development of crime prevention policy and its relevance to the problem of rural crime, and the nature of rural infrastructures through which such problems might be tackled. Much has already been written in this volume about rural crime, and our task is not to repeat this. Rather, we seek to identify some of the issues – often as much political as practical – which are germane to the development of crime prevention measures and strategies in rural areas.

The Urban Bias in Crime Prevention Theory, Policy and Practice

Crime prevention policy, in its earliest days, had a national focus which was neither specifically urban nor rural. Its origins, in the mid-1950s, reflected the collective concerns of the Home Office and the insurance industry about the level of officially recorded crime, which began its inexorable rise at around the same time, and did not, as had been hoped and expected, return to its low pre-war levels. Both sectors joined forces to launch a publicity campaign encouraging private citizens and organizations alike to be more vigilant with their possessions.

As an approach to crime control, it was, however, extremely small-scale and marginal. The 1950s and 1960s saw the forceful emergence of the so-called 'treatment paradigm' which focused criminological and criminal justice attention upon the individual and family circumstances of the offender. The dominant belief was that the key to successful crime control lay in the treatment of the offender, not in the prevention of the offence. Indeed, other than Terence Morris's observation that rising property crime was not unconnected to the increased availability of consumer goods, there was very little contemporary interest in crime as opposed to criminality. Moreover, beyond a small number of areal studies in urban districts, that carried forward sociology's Chicagoan inheritance, there was little that demonstrated anything in the way of a 'geographical imagination' (Brantingham and Jeffrey, 1991) in the study of crime. The crime prevention of the 1950s and the 1960s was pragmatically, rather than theoretically, informed and as such it lacked scientific credibility.

This situation began to change in the UK in the 1970s, as more information began to be acquired about crime, as the effectiveness of the treatment paradigm began to be called into question by damning research (Brody, 1976), and as alternative theories about crime and crime causation began to be generated. In the first instance, these theories were generated in an American context. Ironically, in the same era as large-scale social programmes were being launched against urban crime and poverty, ideas started to emerge that linked high levels of crime and disorder to urban design. An interesting study by Jane Jacobs (1961), for example, criticized modern planning orthodoxy for creating urban districts that, in her words, were custom-made for crime, because so much public space became un-owned, unused and anonymous. Her solution was to demand design modifications that brought more 'eyes on the street', recreating urban villages which in many ways mimicked a rural ideal or stereo-type.

Far more influential was the work of Oscar Newman (1973), whose notion of defensible space became a powerful critique of new housing projects, particularly those using high-rise blocks. He conducted scientific research, of dubious quality (Bottoms, 1974), that associ-ated features of these high-rise blocks with high levels of crime and disorder, and he set in motion a research paradigm that was followed in the UK by Alice Coleman (1990), who found very similar relation-ships, premised upon an equally dubious science (Smith, 1986). For our purposes, however, the significance of this work was that it helped to shift criminological attention from the offender to the offence, but in so doing located the offence in a specifically urban context. This was because the critique of Jacobs, Newman, Coleman and others was of modern planning and design which had been applied as a solution to demographic problems in urban areas, and simply was not relevant to the rural context.

In the UK of the 1970s the growing crime problem was an urban crime problem, associated in particular with tower-block estates where high levels of crime and vandalism coexisted with other acute social problems. The notoriety of some of these estates – 'sink' estates or 'hard-to-let' estates – soon made them a priority for action, and in the late 1970s the Department of the Environment established the Priority Estates Project (PEP) to tackle these compounded social problems (Power, 1989). The PEP itself set a paradigm of policy intervention, mixing a range of measures, focusing upon design and policy management, and addressing social concerns, which has been copied in other programmes.

Crime prevention was influenced strongly by these developments. Having originated in very unfocused and pragmatic concerns about high rates of crime, by the end of the 1970s it had acquired for itself a new importance, as a result of the new criminological and policy context in which it found itself, and in particular as a result of the contribution of Home Office researchers to the development of a new 'situational' model of crime prevention (Clarke and Mayhew, 1980). This model stressed the importance of tackling crime, as the name suggests, within its specific situational context, rather than simply relying upon universal, unfocused approaches. In other words, it was problem-orientated.

The difficulty for our purposes, however, was that the crime problem was perceived as existing, more or less exclusively, in an urban context. This perception was informed, as noted above, by images of problem estates that were exclusively urban, but it was also given a more solid foundation by the results of the British Crime Surveys of the 1980s (Hough and Mayhew, 1983; Mayhew et al., 1989) which, using the 'Acorn' classification of residential areas, offered tangible evidence of the much greater risk of criminal victim-ization in urban areas, to back up the picture generated by admittedly imperfect police statistics broken down into predominantly urban and rural areas.

Thus it was unsurprising that, while in theory the situational model might be equally applicable to crime in urban and in rural areas, when the model was developed into policy and practice it was applied to urban areas only. The Home Office in the 1980s was under considerable pressure to tackle a crime problem that was a political liability to 'the party of law and order', and in such a context it made sense to focus effort where the problem appeared to be greatest. Indeed, given that areas with high levels of crime also tended to have high levels of social malaise, and that the one might be causally linked to the other, such an approach had the added advantage of simultaneously addressing certain social policy concerns.

Thus the Home Office sponsored a number of projects, from individual demonstration projects through to the Five Towns Initiative and the Safer Cities Programme, which had a strong urban focus (Gilling, 1997). Moreover, they were not alone in so doing, for at the same time as statutory attention was directed at urban areas, voluntary attention was directed likewise. Thus NACRO developed a methodology which was strikingly similar to that suggested by advocates of the situational approach, albeit with a stronger social policy orientation, and applied it, when commissioned to do so, in high-crime estates across the country (Poyner, 1986). One could argue that there was a certain symbiosis between statutory and voluntary effort that helped, in the long run, to combine opportunity reduction, which had been the major focus of Home Office effort, with social crime prevention, which had been NACRO's primary concern. This union led to the birth of a more holistic approach to crime prevention which was officially christened 'community safety' in the early 1990s (Home Office, 1991), and has since become a term which is regarded as more appropriate than crime prevention. Community safety's conception and birth was, however, an entirely urban affair.

To summarize to this point, crime prevention originated in pragmatic concerns about rising crime, but developed over the course of the 1970s and 1980s, as a result of the criminological, criminal justice and social context in which it found itself, into a vehicle intended to address a crime problem which was seen to be urban in general, and linked in particular to modern public-sector housing estates, whether inner-city or suburban. The reader would be excused for thinking that this has no relevance whatsoever for the rural context. However, crime prevention policy has more than one dimension to it.

From the 1980s one can discern a dual strategy within crime prevention. First, as outlined above, there was a deliberate attempt to develop crime prevention initiatives in urban areas which suffered disproportionately from criminal victimization. The rhetoric accompanying this part of the strategy, evident in particular in two Home Office circulars in 1984 and 1990 (Home Office, 1984, 1990), was that local agencies should begin to recognize their responsibilities in terms of crime prevention, and the potential savings they could make from relatively small resource investments. However, in practice a considerable amount of money was spent by central government supporting the local development of crime prevention, particularly through the Safer Cities Programme.

Secondly, however, the tradition of less focused crime prevention through the dissemination of practical advice was maintained through large-scale publicity campaigns, with the addition of a 1980s 'spin' that emphasized the importance of active citizenship, especially through the vehicle of Neighbourhood Watch. The publicity was not specifically urban or rural, but the model of active citizenship it promoted, which mixed individual vigilance and responsibility with mutuality through community surveillance, was, like Jacobs's urban-village solution, more resonant within the rural context. It is a fact, and a source of some disquiet, that, as in other areas of public policy, rural areas receive a disproportionately small amount of public-service resources. In rural force areas, for example, the police may have fewer crimes per officer to process than their urban counterparts, but there are fewer officers per head of the rural population. Moreover, as a result of cutbacks in policing resources in particular, the police have no institutional base in many rural areas, which increases response times and significantly reduces productivity, if offenders have to be processed, because of the distance between approved custodial facilities. The consequence of this is that the message of crime prevention publicity, that crime prevention is largely a matter of individual and community responsibility, has long been the reality in rural areas anyway (see also Anderson, chapter 3; and Dingwall, chapter 6).

A Case for Rural Crime Prevention?

It is undeniably the case that rates of rural crime are far lower than rates of urban crime. In rural police forces, for example, the rate in 1994 was approximately two-thirds of the average for urban forces (Husain, 1995). The 1996 British Crime Survey supports such a picture, showing considerably smaller risks of victimization in rural areas of burglary, vehicle-related theft, vandalism, and violent crime (Mirrlees-Black et al., 1996). For example, while police statistics show that rural force burglary is 50 per cent the rate of urban force burglary, the British Crime Survey shows that 3.9 per cent of rural homes were victimized in 1995, compared with 6.3 per cent in urban areas, and 10.3 per cent in inner city areas specifically (Hansard, 4.2.98, col. 722).

These data would appear to support the view that crime is not a significant problem in rural areas – a view that is also illustrated by the 1996 British Crime Survey, which shows that rural fear of crime runs at half the rate of fear in inner-city areas, despite the fact that rural populations support proportionately more older people, who tend to be the most fearful demographic group (Hansard, 4.2.98, col.

722). Similarly, Sugden's (1998) small survey of farmers in Rutland supports the view that rural crime is not generally regarded as being a serious problem; something which can, on occasion, encourage complacency in terms of vigilance and preventive effort (a problem of which the National Farmers' Union has become painfully aware as the rising costs of agricultural crime have had to be met from the union's insurance pay-outs) (Rural Development Commission, 1996).

Unfortunately, the view that crime is not a problem in rural areas perpetuates certain myths about rural areas in respect of crime. There is, for example, a notion that rural crime involves very different kinds of crime from those occurring in urban areas. Rural crimes, it might be thought, are offences against wildlife, poaching, livestock rustling and so forth. Such a view encourages an ideology of triviality about rural crime, and is mistaken, as, in truth, rural and urban patterns are broadly similar. According to 1993 police statistics, for example, violence against the person stood at 4 per cent of all crime in each type of area; burglary stood at 25 per cent in urban areas and 27 per cent in rural areas; theft of a vehicle stood at 11 per cent in urban areas and 9 per cent in rural areas; and criminal damage stood at 17 per cent in urban areas against 15 per cent in rural areas.

Another myth is constructed around the idea that crime does not occur in rural areas because they are so stable and homogeneous that everyone knows everyone else's business, moral standards and expectations are higher, and strangers stick out like a sore thumb. As with certain other stereotypes, this Durkheimian view may have a kernel of truth, insofar, for example, as the density of acquaintance-ship (Freudenberg, 1986) is often much greater in rural areas, but it is also very misleading, and perpetuates the myth that outsiders and strangers are responsible for rural crime (see also Moody, chapter 1).

Some rural areas have experienced very rapid rates of population change in recent years, especially those which have witnessed a depopulation of young adults in search of better employment opportunities; an influx of commuters for whom better transport and communications networks have expanded their residential horizons; an influx of older, retired populations seeking a better quality of life amidst rural tranquillity; or an influx of affluent people buying second homes but only rarely occupying them. Consequently, it should not be assumed that all rural areas are homogeneous or stable. In Marcus Felson's (1994) terms, it should not be assumed that rural areas are awash with 'capable guardians'.

On a related point, there is a notion that rural areas lack the social conditions which are closely associated with criminality. Again, while there may be a kernel of truth in this, insofar as the concentration of deprivation is not so great in rural areas, it is nevertheless apparent that some rural areas are amongst the most economically depressed parts of the country (see also Moody, chapter 1; Anderson, chapter 3). Indeed it is hardly surprising that the combination of scarce public service provision and the depressed economic conditions which characterize some rural areas may result in severe social problems. For example, Hirst (1997) notes the results of a NACRO survey which demonstrates the problems experienced by rural youths, for whom poor public service provision, poor transport and limited job prospects encourage the formation of a neglected underclass, at risk of crime and disorder. Indeed, there is evidence to suggest that certain rural areas experience drug problems which are easily on a par with their urban neighbours (Henderson, 1998).

Overall, then, crime might be less of a problem in rural areas, but it should not be assumed automatically that this is an inevitable consequence of the stereotyped social structure of rural areas, which is clearly in as much of a process of change, in particular as a result of the changing nature of work, as urban areas. The methodology of situational crime prevention, as noted above, is one of a problem orientation: crime must be analysed in its actual situational context. Such a methodology serves as an important warning for those surveying the criminogenic profile of rural areas: readings must be based upon what is real, and not upon what is imagined. In this regard, crime patterns in rural areas are changing, and these changes must be studied, rather than assuming that rural crime is not a problem.

The 1990s: The Emergence of a Rural Crime Prevention Agenda

For most of the 1980s crime prevention only touched rural areas insofar as they provided an audience for publicity encouraging active citizenship and sensible precautions. However, the risk of crime was not so great in rural areas, and many crime prevention initiatives, such as Neighbourhood Watch and electronic surveillance, sought to recreate, in urban neighbourhoods, conditions of rural life which were natural inhibitors of criminal activity (Felson, 1994), and were thus substitutes for the real thing. Therefore, the impact of the publicity was unlikely to have been particularly significant in rural areas.

However, the end of the 1980s saw the beginning of a concern that perhaps rural areas did after all have a crime problem of sorts. The first manifestation of this was the media-dubbed 'lager lout', a character who had money to spend in the late 1980s boom, and spent it, it would appear, getting drunk and fighting with other young males in non-metropolitan public houses. As is so often the case, the stories about this disorder in Middle England turned out to be exaggerations. The Home Office was moved by the media attention to research the issue, but Tuck's (1989) subsequent study showed that towns with an apparent disorderly reputation were no worse than towns without: in each, there were occasional manifestations of drink-induced disorder and violence, usually after public houses had closed down, and usually on a Friday or Saturday night. Pearson's work in the early 1980s, with its historical analysis of 'respectable fears', also demonstrated that 'it has ever been thus' (Pearson, 1983). In spite of Tuck's findings that sensible preventative measures, such as 'pubwatch', might alleviate the problem of drink-related disorder, she found no evidence that things had suddenly become a great deal worse in rural areas.

In the 1990s, however, the issue of an increase in rural crime has come once more to the fore. It is not immediately apparent from where such an issue arose, although the media have again played an instrumental role, with one tabloid claiming in 1994 that 'Britain's havens of rural calm could soon vanish under a sea of crime' (cited by Thomas, 1994). Stories began to appear in the media of organized criminals roaming the countryside, preying on the easy pickings of vulnerable rural communities. Clearly efforts were being made to put rural crime on the criminal justice, and the crime prevention, agenda.

Thus, in 1994 the first national rural crime prevention conference was held in Gloucestershire, organized by Crime Concern. Police representatives made the most of an opportunity to air their concerns about rural crime to a conference well attended by the media. For example, Tony Butler, the well-respected Chief Constable of Gloucestershire, reported that in his constabulary area the crime rate per thousand of the population was higher than that of Merseyside, although the number of officers per person was considerably lower (*The Times*, 1994). Others – such as a Home Office minister, no less – suggested that the increase in rural crime was a result of urban displacement: successful crime prevention in cities made criminals turn their attention outside the city, to rural areas within easy reach by virtue of improved road networks.

There is no evidence that this is generally the case, although there have been well-reported instances of travelling criminals targeting, for example, the antique fixtures, fittings and statuary of stately homes, not to mention their prized plants. Rather, it is more apparent that the increase in recorded crime in non-metropolitan police areas can be accounted for in the main by increases which have occurred in their most urbanized and suburbanized districts. The division between urban and rural police forces is a very imperfect one, since both are neither fully urban nor fully rural, and their aggregate statistical returns fail to discriminate the location within their force areas of the crimes which are actually recorded.

There is another statistic which appears to support the notion of a significant increase in rural crime, but which is, in fact, highly misleading. Over the decade to 1997 crime in non-metropolitan police-force areas increased by 5 per cent, while in metropolitan force areas the increase was only 2 per cent. The difference appears to be highly significant, but only on first inspection. First, as above, it is not clear in which parts of the non-metropolitan force areas the increases have taken place. Second, since crime in non-metropolitan areas is significantly lower than crime in metropolitan areas a relatively small numerical increase in crimes can manifest itself as a disproportionately large percentage increase – it must be remembered that rural crime starts from a much lower base. Third, the fall in officially recorded crime across the country in the last few years, while it is to be welcomed, is probably not unconnected to the police service developing a stronger performance culture since the implementation of the Police and Magistrates' Courts Act 1994, which instituted a system of national and local performance objectives and targets, backed up by the reclassification of certain offences which have allowed them to become non-notifiable and therefore absent from the official statistics. This point is necessarily speculative, but it is quite likely that metropolitan police forces have been under most pressure to demonstrate a decrease in crime, and have, perhaps unsurprisingly, done so.

Consequently, while the 1994 conference helped to put rural crime prevention on the political agenda, it is not apparent that the threat to rural areas was as great as was portrayed: indeed, the cynic we met above would probably argue that the police part in this consciousness-raising over rural crime was not unconnected to internal police concerns about resource cutbacks, which made it very difficult for chief constables to justify deploying police officers in rural areas, without additional resource allocation from the centre.

While the case for a substantial increase in crime in rural areas remains questionable, what is certain is that rural crime prevention was indeed placed on the political agenda. This forced a discernible change in crime prevention policy, so that what had been, until this time, a strong urban bias began to give way to an approach which, while not establishing a level playing field, at least proved to be more accommodating of rural concerns.

The immediate upshot was that Crime Concern was requested to produce a good-practice guide on crime prevention for parish councils, which was duly published (Husain, 1995), and in 1997 the Local Government and Rating Act was passed with a clause empowering local parish councils (community councils in Wales) to implement crime prevention measures. Also, attempts were made to encourage the formalization of the self-reliance which in any case has been characteristic of many rural localities, by the Home Office's promotion of parish special constable schemes, and parish warden schemes, providing a voluntary local link with non-metropolitan police areas (Department of Environment, 1995). Plans for the expansion of the parish special constable scheme were overambitious: between 1995 and 1996 numbers increased by 1,500, rather than the hoped-for 3,000 (Department of Environment, 1996).

Beyond the active citizenship strategy, changes in centrally supported crime prevention also appeared more favourable for rural areas. The Safer Cities Programme was absorbed within and eventually replaced by the new Single Regeneration Budget (SRB), providing competitive funding for regeneration schemes which included crime prevention within their objectives, and which, unlike its predecessor, was open to rural areas. Also, competitive funding was made available through CCTV Challenge, which has since gone through four rounds, and which provides part-funding for local crime prevention initiatives which can demonstrate a need for CCTV schemes. Much of the funding for successful bids has gone to the high-crime metropolitan areas, but a proportion has also gone to non-metropolitan towns in predominantly rural areas – indeed, there were even allegations after the first round that funding may have been biased towards some of the more vulnerable Conservative parliamentary constituencies (Gilling, 1997).

Perhaps the most important crime prevention development for rural areas is just about to happen. Conservative crime prevention policy was criticized for its failure to locate a statutory responsibility for crime prevention with local authorities (Home Office, 1991). Without such a framework, crime prevention developments appeared ad hoc and confusing. The Conservatives, while encouraging local authorities to develop a strategic responsibility for crime prevention (as many, mostly metropolitan authorities, did), refused to countenance any statutory responsibility, but the new Labour government seeks to do exactly that through the Crime and Disorder Act, albeit without any commitment to the provision of additional resources. The legislation requires the police and District local authorities to establish a statutory partnership, preparing a three-year crime-reduction strategy, drawn up following a crime audit and consultation with other local agencies, including the public. The importance of this for rural areas is clear: for the first time, crime prevention will have to be systematically addressed in all rural areas.

The model and methodology for these envisaged partnerships is taken in large part from the Safer Cities Programme and from an experience of crime prevention strategies which has been largely urban. A question remains, therefore, about how such a model will translate to the rural context. In the remaining space of this chapter we wish to consider a small number of important issues likely to arise from the implementation of the Crime and Disorder Act in rural areas. Our awareness of these issues is informed by some ongoing research evaluating community safety strategy groups in urban and rural areas of Devon and Cornwall. The purpose of our research is to assess, primarily through qualitative interviews, the degree of, and factors influencing, collaboration within these groups. We are considering the nature of effective partnerships and elements which might underpin a successful partnership between agencies in the crime prevention field. We are also seeking to identify any factors that may hinder effective co-operation. It is envisaged that the research will be completed at the beginning of 1999. The proceeding discussion is, therefore, necessarily brief.

The Crime and Disorder Act and the consultation paper that preceded it have generated a vast amount of activity, especially in terms of practical advice, which is necessary in view of the fact that crime audits and crime-reduction plans are expected to be in place by April 1999. Despite all the activity, however, we are concerned that there has been little consideration of the rural context. Practical experience and advice emanate mostly from urban areas, and may not translate unproblematically to the rural context.

In some rural areas local authorities have demonstrated a reluctance to establish partnerships with the police, despite county-wide agreements in favour of them. This is not because of conflict, but because there remains a strong view that crime and crime prevention are the responsibility of the police: many divisional police commanders, for example, will attest to the number of letters or contacts they receive about crime problems from local councillors, and this way of thinking extends to some local authority officers. The police may see the crime problem as most open to solution by local authority action, for example by providing better leisure facilities for youths, but this perspective may not cut ice with the local authority.

Local authorities, especially rural ones, may be reluctant to participate in formal crime prevention strategies if these have resource implications, because the local authorities feel that they have insufficient resources. The government view is that successful crime reduction generates savings to pay for itself, but this may not convince those who see a significant initial expense in the preparation of audits, consultation, and the development of strategies, who do not forecast great savings because the initial costs of rural crime are not perceived as great, and who are not convinced that savings would necessarily accrue to themselves rather than, say, the criminal justice system. We would not wish to overstate the extent of this difficulty, but nevertheless it is apparent that the appeal of partnership may often be more rhetorical than practical.

We have witnessed a contrasting situation, where the police and rural local authorities work very well together, but they tend to do so on an informal, ad hoc basis, rather than through a formal committee structure and a formal strategy. Our concern here, however, is that this informal crime prevention may be threatened by the more formal accountability demands, which extend eventually back to the Home Secretary. Giving informal resourcing decisions greater visibility risks a level of formal commitment that local authorities may find hard to sustain over the longer term. This issue has been anticipated insofar as guidance suggests that existing initiatives should not necessarily be abandoned (Home Office, 1998), but the guidance assumes that such initiatives are or can be formalized, and urges that they be put under the umbrella of the new strategies.

On the issue of resources it is important to emphasize that urban local authorities are generally better placed: they have a broader resource base from which to draw, and more significant crime problems that make the potential savings more worthwhile. Their greater concentration of social problems generally means they are better placed to lever in money from competitive sources such as the SRB, or special government initiatives such as those in the areas of health or drug prevention. They are also more likely to be sites of criminal justice-related voluntary activity, and beneficiaries of private-sector sponsorship, given the latter's stronger concentration in urban areas.

A further issue relates to the spatial distribution of crime. In urban areas crime problems are more likely to be concentrated and more obvious, and, especially because there is likely to be greater coterminosity between the partners, it is easier to agree priorities. This spatial concentration of crime reflects an orthodoxy in crime prevention which is largely environmental, focused on certain places, not others. In rural areas in contrast, crime is often more dispersed and does not so easily fit the environmental model. Rural crime prevention, therefore, may tend towards an issue-based approach (e.g. tackling drug-related crime), rather than an environmental approach.

Even when crime is concentrated within rural areas, the implementation of crime prevention initiatives may be problematic. For example, vehicle-related crime may be concentrated at rural beauty spots, but their remoteness makes the deployment of security personnel or surveillance devices prohibitively expensive. Alternatively, given that rural local authorities cover a larger geographical expanse, small concentrations of crime and disorder, especially when not proven in police statistics, have an inevitable parochial feel about them. There may be causes championed by certain interest groups or councillors from several different areas, in which case the identification of priorities becomes a very political process, rather than a rational, problem-orientated one.

Finally, the structure of local government has important implications for rural crime prevention. The Crime and Disorder Act is clear that strategies must be based on District Council boundaries. In urban areas these may be unitary, where coterminosity makes information exchange easier and more relevant, and partnerships are, therefore, easier to forge. In addition, urban district authorities are usually large enough to possess some sort of strategic capacity, based around the position of the chief executive. Some rural district councils do not possess chief executives, while their status as lower-tier authorities inevitably affects their strategic capacity in crime prevention, especially as this is likely to involve an input from such county functions as education, social services and youth services. In practice, rural district councils are sandwiched between councils, that have had their own crime preventive capacity since 1997, and county councils, which are recognized in the guidance as equal partners, but which, ironically in the name of equality, may be reluctant to tailor their services differentially to meet the crime prevention strategies for each district council, especially if they do not share the same political hue. Again, the guidance recognizes the issue, but offers no obvious solution to this potential political conflict.

Concluding Comments

It should be apparent from the preceding discussion that crime prevention is something that has developed largely in response to urban crime problems, and without much consideration for the rural context, simply because rural crime has not been viewed as serious enough to justify such a preventive response. It has become apparent in recent years, however, that crime can be a problem in rural areas, and this has brought rural crime prevention on to the criminal justice agenda, although its raised profile is also partly attributable to efforts on the part of the police in bringing to light their resourcing difficulties in rural areas.

However, an urban model of crime prevention, premised very strongly upon an environmental approach that targets high-crime areas, cannot be simply mapped on to rural areas without some consideration being given to the changed context. Nevertheless there is no reason why individual crime prevention measures cannot be applied to rural areas when it is cost-effective to do so. Crime prevention boasts an impressive versatility (see, for example, Clarke, 1992). However, it is clear that rural infrastructures and manifestations of typically urban crimes are quite different, and indeed more challenging. For example, it is probable that repeat victimization in rural areas is low because crime rates are low (Pease, 1998). Therefore, repeat victimization is not as promising a base for preventive intervention as it is in urban areas. It is not apparent that this general point has been appreciated by those who have drafted the legislation and the guidance for the Crime and Disorder Act. It needs to be, because underpinning much of this are urban assumptions and urban experience, which give urban areas an advantage in meeting the requirements of the legislation, but leave rural areas at a disadvantage.

By the same token, policy cannot simply proceed on the basis of dubious, stereotyped assumptions about the nature of rural social life. In the recent past, there was a tendency in the parts of crime prevention policy that stressed active citizenship to presuppose a base of self-reliance and mutuality in rural areas, on to which could be grafted such things as special constable schemes. Given the pace of change in rural areas, these things cannot be presumed, and in this regard the extension of routine crime prevention to rural areas, implicit in the Crime and Disorder Act, is to be welcomed. However, the difficulties of applying crime prevention in rural areas need to be thought through, and time needs to be allowed for rural areas, relative to urban areas that effectively have a head start. The anxiety to move forward should not be at the expense of forcing rural areas into hurried decisions, perhaps following inappropriate urban models rather than developing their own expertise. A more considered, long-term strategy is necessary for rural areas, particularly if the government's hope, that investment in crime prevention will generate savings, is going to be realized. The alternative would be disillusionment, and subsequently very half-hearted compliance with the legislation.

References

ACRE (Action with Communities in Rural England) (1995) *Rural Crime*, Cirencester: ACRE

BOTTOMS, A. (1974) Review of *Defensible Space*, 14 *British Journal of Criminology*, 203

BRANTINGHAM, P. and JEFFREY C. (1991) 'Crime, space and criminological theory', in Brantingham, P. (ed.) *Environmental Criminology*, 2nd edn, Prospect Heights, Ill.: Waveland Press

BRODY, S. (1976) *The Effectiveness of Sentencing*, Home Office Research Study No. 35, London: HMSO

CLARKE, R. (ed.) (1992) *Situational Crime Prevention: Successful Case Studies*, New York: Harrow and Heston

CLARKE, R. and MAYHEW, P. (eds.) (1980) *Designing Out Crime*, London: HMSO

COLEMAN, A. (1990) *Utopia on Trial*, 2nd edn, London: Hilary Shipman

DEPARTMENT OF ENVIRONMENT (1995) *Rural England*, London: HMSO

DEPARTMENT OF ENVIRONMENT (1996) *Rural England*, London: HMSO

FELSON, M. (1994) *Crime and Everyday Life*, Thousand Oaks, Calif.: Pine Forge Press

FREUDENBERG, W. (1986) 'The density of acquaintanceship: an overlooked variable in community research?', 92 *American Journal of Sociology*, 27

GILLING, D. (1997) *Crime Prevention: Theory, Policy and Politics*, London: UCL Press

HANSARD (1998) *House of Commons Daily Debates*

HARDING, C. (1994) 'Research into criminal justice in rural areas', in Harding, C. and Williams, J. (eds) (1994), *Legal Provision in the Rural Environment*, Cardiff: University of Wales Press

HENDERSON, S. (1998) *Drugs Prevention in Rural Areas: Final Report to the Home Office Drugs Prevention Initiative*, London: Home Office

HIRST, J. (1997) 'Rural realities', 3 (9 April) *Community Care*, 8

HIRST, P. (1994) 'Problems affecting rural policing', in Harding, C. and Williams, J. (eds), *Legal Provision in the Rural Environment*, Cardiff: University of Wales Press

HOME OFFICE (1984) Circular 8/84: *Crime Prevention*, London: Home Office

HOME OFFICE (1990) Circular 44/90: *Crime Prevention*, London: Home Office

HOME OFFICE (1991) *Safer Communities: The Local Delivery of Crime Prevention through the Partnership Approach*, London: Home Office

HOME OFFICE (1998) *Crime and Disorder Bill: Guidance on Statutory Crime and Disorder Partnerships*, London: Home Office

HOUGH, M. and MAYHEW, P. (1983) *The British Crime Survey: First Report*, Home Office Research Study No. 76, London: HMSO

HUSAIN, S. (1995) *Cutting Crime in Rural Areas: A Practical Guide for Parish Councils*, Swindon: Crime Concern

JACOBS, J. (1961) *The Death and Life of Great American Cities*, London: Cape

MAYHEW, P. et al. (1989) *The 1988 British Crime Survey*, Home Office Research Study No. 111, London: HMSO

MIRRLEES-BLACK, C. et al. (1996) *The 1996 British Crime Survey*, Home Office Statistical Bulletin Issue 19/96, London: Home Office

NEWMAN, O. (1973) *Defensible Space*, London: Architectural Press

PEARSON, G. (1983) *Hooligan: A History of Respectable Fears*, London: Macmillan

PEASE, K. (1998) Personal communication

POWER, A. (1989) 'Housing, community and crime', in D. Downes (ed.), *Crime and the City*, Basingstoke: Macmillan

POYNER, B. (1986) *Crime Reduction on Housing Estates: An Evaluation of NACRO's Crime Prevention Programme*, London: Tavistock Institute

RURAL DEVELOPMENT COMMISSION (1996) Winter 1995/6 *Rural Focus*, 16

SMITH, S. (1986) Review of *Utopia on Trial*, 23 *Urban Studies*, 244

SUGDEN, G. (1998) 'In defence of farms: an agrarian crime prevention audit in Rutland', in Gill, M. (ed.), *Crime at Work: Increasing the Risk for Offenders*, Leicester: Perpetuity Press

THE TIMES (1994) 'Countryside faces criminal overspill', 14 June 1994, 9

THOMAS, D. (1994) 'Country spivving: townies who hanker after the countryside', 19 June 1994, *Sunday Times*, 9

TUCK, M. (1989) *Drink and Disorder: A Study of Non-Metropolitan Violence*, Home Office Research Study No. 108, London: HMSO

8

Policing New Age Travellers: Conflict and Control in the Countryside?

RICHARD HESTER

In the city of reason, there were to be no winding roads, no cul de sacs and no unattended sites left to chance – and thus no vagabonds, vagrants or nomads.[1]

Introduction

New Age Travellers[2] are essentially a bucolic phenomenon. Travellers, on the whole, live in the countryside and many who are called New Age Travellers have a deep respect for the land. Much of the conflict that arises in respect of Travellers is about land, its ownership and the symbolic threat posed by Travellers to a society that views the private ownership of land as normal. This chapter will not, however, focus on this wider debate but instead narrow the focus down to the very specific topography of the conflict between police and Travellers in a rural context.

Before doing so, however, it is important to explain the historical background to the policing of vagrancy, to sketch out the particular difficulties associated with public order policing and to note the impact of the provisions of the Criminal Justice and Public Order Act 1994.

---

[1] Zygmunt Bauman, *Intimations of Postmodernity* (1992), xv.

[2] The media-created term 'New Age Traveller' is unpopular, particularly for Travellers themselves, as it is, in many ways, meaningless. Its meaning shifted between 1985 to 1995 to embrace various groups within the 'DIY culture' such as the 'Dongas Tribe' (McKay, 1996) and those living a semi-nomadic or even settled life in bender communities (Brass and Poklewski, 1997). However it is the term that best describes the groups of people that have been the subject of a specific type of policing. There is, for example, a National Strategy produced by the Association of Chief Police Officers for dealing specifically with New Age Travellers. I therefore use the term with the same caveat and apologies noted by Clark (1997).

The conflict between wanderers and settled people and its association with policing should not simply be viewed in relation to recent incidents such as the 'Battle of the Beanfield'.[3] It has an interesting historical irony. The development of the police as part of a modernist power/knowledge nexus owes a great deal to what happened in the countryside in the 1600s and the subsequent reaction of the settled community to 'paupers and their families, vagrants, gypsies, rogues, vagabonds and idle' (McMullan, 1998, p. 93). For Colquhoun, at the turn of the nineteenth century, the role of the police was, likewise, to civilize the homeless vagrant. And this need to control the vagrant can be traced back to a number of changes that took place over a hundred years before Colquhoun's 'police machine' was envisaged (McMullan, 1998). These changes included increases in the population and in agricultural technology; rearrangement of landed property and the rapid expansion of cities, which in turn led to the sudden appearance of masterless men and the influx of the 'sturdy vagabond'; and the appearance of the illegal underworld. Colquhoun's 'police machine' was designed to ensure *inter alia* 'the enjoyment of property'. This role has continued today, with these contemporary vagabonds, the New Age Travellers, apparently presenting a potent threat to those who live and own the land in the countryside.

Thus changes in the use of the 'countryside' resulting in 'vagabonds from the country' can be seen as being responsible for stimulating the development of modern policing. New Age Travellers remind us that sedentarism,[4] that ancient prejudice against nomadic people, is alive and kicking (sometimes quite literally). They can also, in the context of a postmodern world, expose some of the dilemmas that face the police who struggle to maximize resources in a world of increasing uncertainty and competing values. This chapter is about these specific problems (imagined or real) that arise in the context of one aspect of rural disorder.

Public order policing, as noted by Peter Waddington (1996), has characteristics that set it apart from routine policing. It is highly

[3] Perhaps the best-known site of conflict between police and Travellers was the 'Battle of the Beanfield' in June 1985 as 'the convoy' attempted to meet at Stonehenge. This is generally acknowledged as the most disgraceful incident in the policing of New Age Travellers (see McKay, 1996, Stone, 1996 and National Council for Civil Liberties, 1986). I was also able to interview one of the police commanders involved in the incident enabling me to acquire a perspective from the police on the events that led to this conflict. There were many other examples of such conflicts described to me by Travellers, including Stoney Cross in 1986.

[4] For an up-to-date analysis of the term coined by Jean Pierre Liegoise see McVeigh (1997).

visible and normally takes the form of 'corporate action' under the command of senior officers. It is also, on the whole, concerned with encounters between police and non-criminals. Lastly, public order incidents are generally more likely to be contested as conflicting views of the genesis and development of events often emerge.

It is only in the last twenty-five years that public order issues in Britain have undergone a 'remarkable transformation' (Waddington, 1996, p. 1). The expansion in the role of the police in relation to public order occurred in the 1970s, as evidenced by the foundation of the National Reporting Centre in 1972. This was followed by a sharp increase in the 1980s in the wake of yet more serious disorder, notably some major urban riots and the miners' strike (see Green, 1990; Brake and Hale, 1992; Brewer et al., 1996). These events, and the policing of the 'hippie' convoy of 1985 (National Council for Civil Liberties, 1986), had a major influence on the Public Order Act 1986. Since then further refinements in the strategic response to public disorder by the police have occurred, with, for instance, the Tactical Operations Manual (Northam, 1988), designed to offer guidance to the police in dealing with incidents of public disorder.

It is in public order policing (set in the rural areas of Britain) that the relationship between Travellers and the police is most visible and problematic. Reiner states that 'police activity has always borne most heavily on the economically marginal elements in society, the unemployed (especially if vagrant). Studies of policing in all industrial societies show this to be constant' (Reiner, 1992, p. 771). New Age Travellers possess little economic or political influence, and it is not surprising, therefore, that they have become a focus of police activity. The relationship between the police and New Age Travellers can also be viewed in the context of a crisis of public confidence in the police. This in turn is exacerbated by the emergence of a number of fairly strong 'alternative' lifestyles and coalitions of protesters which are closely associated with the countryside. The problems that New Age Travellers bring to the police are both major public order issues, most notoriously the events at Castlemorton Common in 1992,[5] but also the day-to-day issues of eviction for illegal camping of small groups of Travellers. These two seemingly unrelated issues overlap in attempts to prevent public disorder.

They were brought together in the Criminal Justice and Public Order Act 1994. The Act provided the police with new powers to deal

[5] In the summer of 1992 a large group of 'ravers' (over 30,000) and New Age Travellers congregated at Castlemorton Common. This received much media attention and was instrumental in precipitating the Criminal Justice and Public Order Act 1994.

with hunt saboteurs, environmental protesters, animal-rights activists and ravers. Developments in public order policing are important to New Age Travellers, firstly when the Travellers are also protesters, but secondly in the context of Travellers as part of large gatherings or raves. It is suggested by Waddington (1994) and King and Brearley (1996) that it was as a result of the changing face of public order issues from the monolithic to the diverse, expressed through contemporary protest, that the nature of public order policing itself changed. This was reflected in a more preventative or pre-emptive approach 'based on tension indicators, intelligence gathering and surveillance, and negotiation and co-operation' (Waddington, 1996, p. 2). The developments noted by Brearley and King (1996) include better community liaison; the introduction of tension indicators; the use of detective work pre- and post- disorder, as well as improved evidence-gathering during disorders; and improvements in contingency awareness and training. Reforms have also been made in the arrangements for control over officers on the ground. The range and quality of equipment has improved, giving rise to a greater flexibility in terms of police responses to disorder (Brearley and King, 1996, p. 113).

In addition there are clearly economic constraints which face all police authorities. These are having a dual effect. On the one hand, resources are being targeted when, and only when, a real need arises, and on the other there is a move to what is described as a more pre-emptive approach. This latter development includes an increasing reliance on surveillance, which could bring into question the legitimacy of police action in the eyes of the public, particularly when such surveillance encompasses 'respectable activists'.

These historical developments in public order policing are of relevance to the specific issue of policing Travellers today since the role of the police as arbiters of countryside conflicts is not new. It is important, though, to note that the police may not be neutral arbiters and may well have stereotypical views of Travellers which may, in turn, inform police practice. The next section of this chapter will therefore consider how the police view Travellers, and whether this view is substantiated in statistical material from police records. After this general analysis, five areas of particular concern, drawn from my original research in this area, are analysed in more depth. Certain central themes which emerge are then discussed by way of conclusion.

A Police Perspective on Policing New Age Travellers

Four constabularies, all of which covered large rural areas, were selected for in-depth, semi-structured interviews with officers of all ranks. The majority of those interviewed, however, held some sort of 'strategic responsibility'. In addition to this primary data source, use is made of the research carried out by Michael Brown (1995) on police attitudes to Travellers. As McMullan has noted with regard to Colquhoun's project: 'The nomad, the vagrant, the idle were transformed from symbols of freedom and popularity into a unitary, afflicted criminal archetype whose every move was the reflex of physical, mental, moral and environmental defectiveness' (McMullan, 1998, p. 108).

It is therefore worth beginning with the question of how these 'idle vagrant nomads' are defined in contemporary policing. Brown (1995) used 159 returned questionnaires to ascertain how police officers defined New Age Travellers. Table 8.1 is taken from Brown's research and shows the seven most frequent responses.

Table 8.1

Definition	Respondents	%
Dropouts	65	40.9
Benefit claimants/spongers	61	38.4
Dirty smelly people	41	25.8
Live in vehicles	31	20.1
Live alternative lifestyles	23	14.5
Hippies	19	11.9
Drug users	19	11.9

Source: Brown, 1995, p. 98.

Having looked at definitions we can examine the 'problems' New Age Travellers present, from the police perspective. This is difficult for a number of reasons. Brown (1995) found that, having contacted each of the forty-five constabularies within England and Wales, including the Transport Police and the Ministry of Defence Police, it was difficult to pin down information on arrests, 'process offences' (offences dealt with by way of reporting for summons rather than by arrest) and complaints from the public. Of those interviewed 75.5 per cent said that their forces had no records which would identify New Age Travellers with regard to arrests. In addition, 91 per cent kept no records for 'process offences' and complaints from the public which could be attributed to New Age Travellers. Brown found it difficult to discover specific quantifiable data on the actual problems caused by Travellers. Researching police annual reports between 1990 and 1993 Brown found that 36 per cent had references to New Age Travellers but again the references were not quantifiable. He was also able to access directly information from the Intelligence Units in Devizes and Penrith. His results here are interesting in that they highlight the extremely low number of actual recorded arrests in 1993 and 1994 (seventy-two in 1993 and ninety-three in 1994). The majority of these arrests were for possession of controlled drugs, many of which resulted in cautions. In contrast, the example of finding a Kalashnikov AK47 and high-value drugs was given as a counterpoint to the otherwise minor nature of criminal activity directly attributable to New Age Travellers. Brown's questionnaire to individual police officers provided the picture of the ten most frequently quoted problems given in Table 8.2.

Table 8.2

Personal experience of a problem	Problem	%
None	50	31
Drugs	23	14
Traffic	20	13
Trespass	18	11
Unco-operative or abusive	17	11
Having no fixed abode	17	10
Theft and kindred offences	15	9
Public order	14	9
Begging	11	7
Dogs	10	6

Source: Brown, 1995, p. 99.

Whilst drugs appear high on the list, the majority of police officers had experienced no problems with New Age Travellers. Brown's research suggests, therefore, that the response by the police is out of proportion to the actual number of offences committed by Travellers.

From my own primary data a number of potential or assumed problems, arising out of the lifestyle of Travellers, that were perceived as possible contributors to the disturbance of the normal life of the country were identified by the police.

1 Large Gatherings

The 'invasion' of Castlemorton Common (Baxter 1992) in the summer of 1992 was probably the most significant single event in shaping Part V of the Criminal Justice and Public Order Act 1994. It also appears to have been a catalyst and a justification for the policing and surveillance of New Age Travellers more generally. The view of informant A was that a major part of police intervention was to prohibit large gatherings in order to avoid the potential problems that would occur were they allowed to go ahead:

> Castlemorton Common, the problems down there, where the residents were completely surrounded by the Travellers and the nuisance value, the Travellers were calling to the houses, asking to use their toilets, breaking down fences, causing these sort of problems, minor, trivial things but if they're repeated, as I said, they tend to build up in people's minds, and once they're affected in that way then they're very ready to complain and hope that something will be done about it. (Informant A)

An altogether more serious account of the threats posed by festivals was given by informant B, who used the example of the last free festival at Stonehenge to convey his view of the attendant problems of large parties of Travellers and associated groups. There is a clearly discernible shift here on the part of the police from viewing such events as relatively minor, with the police becoming involved unwillingly as the result of political and community pressure, to a perception that such gatherings can lead to serious criminal activity:

> there wasn't absolute anarchy but it was close to it and there were some serious offences committed on the site and associated with the Travellers that were there, I mean there were robberies and protection rackets, there was open drug abuse, drug dealing, there was violence, there were people shot, there were sixty stolen vehicles were found burnt out on the site after they left. I mean all of those things were partly a result of the way in which the thing was being policed. (Informant B)

Informant C, however, was clear about the logistic and cost implications of attempting to deal with Travellers in large numbers, which he recognized as being intrinsically problematic:

> so my view has changed. The original view was, 'let it develop, let the law take its course, let the landowners take their action and in two or three months the action will be taken and they'll be moved on.' My view has changed on that because of the practicalities of trying to move them . . . but the general principle now would be to try and prevent large sites developing if that is possible. We can't, and this isn't for publication, or at least for attributing, *we can't in all honesty say we will act because the cost-benefit analysis is just not in favour of doing it*, and a chief officer would be foolish to give his senior officers a *carte blanche* to act without regard to the cost, but in principle it will be to try and prevent large numbers gathering. (emphases added)

2   Policing Small Groups

In the light of the difficulties faced by the police in managing large gatherings it might be thought that policing small groups of Travellers would not pose any major problems. However, this was not the case, according to some of the officers interviewed. Informant A, for example, described the problems presented by illegal campers thus:

> The activities there generally started causing problems with one or two local residents who had a couple of businesses that were in that vicinity. Both of those sites caused us concern because at the beginning of the year the New Age Travellers historically have the festivals and our concern then was that these would be the first pockets of another *Castlemorton* so we were conscious that could happen.

The policing of small groups demonstrates a variety of approaches being employed by different forces. Whilst the police have certain powers under the Criminal Justice and Public Order Act 1994, as does the local authority, considerable discretion is retained in operational matters. Clearly some forces adopt what has been termed a 'fortress policy' towards Travellers, designed to restrict their movements through the strict enforcement of the law, whereas other forces adopt more tolerant practices which are not so reliant on the new statutory powers at their disposal. This diversity of approach would appear to undermine the Association of Chief Police Officers' national guidelines which were designed to encourage a uniform approach to policing Travellers. However, with the ever tightening constraints on resources, it is easy to imagine a hardening of police attitudes in those forces operating a more tolerant approach because of the additional costs that such a policy entails.

3   Increased Theft and Criminal Damage

None of the informants provided evidence of Travellers contributing to an increase in theft or criminal damage. Secondary sources of data, such as Brown's study, suggest that in the two years 1993 and 1994 only about thirty such offences were found in the Intelligence Unit database. Only 8 per cent of police returning Brown's questionnaire reported this specifically as a problem. A typical response to this question came from Informant A who said: 'and they go shopping or whatever, and I know that some of them have been arrested for shoplifting and burglary offences in the village near to where the camp is set up.' It was, however, difficult to obtain precise information regarding the link between alleged offences and criminal convictions. In reply to a question on the increase in successful prosecutions for theft and criminal damage Informant A had some difficulties of recall: 'I don't recall, if you want an emphatic answer on that I would have to check, I don't recall that anybody was actually taken to court for any complaint.' Nevertheless, the mere possible appearance of Travellers across the borders of the county was seen by the police as a potential public order issue requiring the Emergency Planning Team of the County Council to prevent Travellers from settling.

4 Drugs

The problems associated with drug dealing were perhaps most strikingly highlighted by a Drugs Squad officer who was interviewed. The following quotation provides an example of his view on this matter:

> New Age Travellers . . . are a little community on site and they probably feel relatively safe on there with regard to any criminal activity they want to be involved in, particularly drugs, safety in numbers I suppose . . . I mean everyone knew that the Travellers were up at [the site] or sites like that and it was just like a magnet to the local users and small suppliers and it is just a question of pulling up on the site and you would be sort of surrounded by a certain number of people offering to sell drugs. It's that blatant and the deal takes place there and then and they drive off. It's as simple as that.

He also mentioned the difficulties in tracking dealers who were not known through the usual intelligence networks. The sale and use of illegal drugs were mentioned by informants in the context of offences associated with Travellers, but their view of the relationship between drug use and Travellers (with the possible exception of the Drugs Squad officer) contrasted sharply with the media view of 'drug-crazed hippies'. From the interviews with the informants the issue of drug use and supply did not seem to be of greater concern than disquiet about drug use among young people generally. However, connections were made between drug dealing, raves and festivals.

5 The Surveillance of New Age Travellers

Methods of surveillance continue to touch a raw nerve with the British public, as they did when Robert Peel first established the police. Whilst surveillance is seen as acceptable if framed in the image of the traditional 'Bobby' walking the beat, keeping a watchful eye on the potential 'wrongdoer', undercover work and 'high-tech' surveillance seem less acceptable. However, as a result of police concerns about New Age Travellers, two National Intelligence Units were set up in 1985 for 'the collation, evaluation and dissemination of intelligence in relation to the movement of potential illegal trespassers' (Informant B). There is obviously some difficulty in discussing in detail methods of surveillance as they are, by their nature, secret. However, there was much information given on the development of surveillance systems and some indications of the methods used. The opportunities for obtaining intelligence cited by one force simply related to day-to-day policing, and such mundane matters as arrests for shoplifting. Clearly other forces use undercover intelligence and informants. Informant B gave a fairly detailed description of the information system:

> We have had an intelligence unit here for years, we had it in 1985 and we've had it ever since. In the earlier years, that is from '85 and in the next few years it was a sort of a temporary thing that would get revived during the summer and then closed down in the winter, and other forces were aware that we had one and we asked them to feed us information and we would feed them information.

Informant D, whilst acknowledging the existence of covert surveillance, emphasized the need to put this into the context of modern policing, where resources were being reduced and the Home Secretary's Key National Objectives, along with the forces' own Key Performance Indicators, were taking their toll:

> I think everyone is aware that we do carry out surveillance . . . Again useful informants in a general criminal sense are seen as a cost-effective way of dealing with it . . . We simply don't have the resources or the time to do that unless we genuinely think that people's actions are going to lead to a large-scale policing operation. It's not that much of a priority for us. We've got so many other priorities of crime and traffic.

Informant C also played down the surveillance of Travellers as an issue for his constabulary. He denied the use of informants in that particular force: 'It's not that kind of intelligence gathering. It's simply being aware of movement that might lead us into problems . . . but there is certainly no intelligence gathering in terms of having insiders or having informants or that kind of thing . . .'

About three years before the most recent interviews there had been some criticism in the press about the use of surveillance techniques by police (Campbell 1994a, 1994b). It is now clear that intelligence and the use of informers is an integral part of policing Travellers. In addition to the two Intelligence Units, the ACPO National Strategy (1996) suggests that each force operate its own intelligence-gathering system, via a designated intelligence liaison officer who is charged with supplying information to the relevant unit. The guidance recommends that this cover all aspects of trespassory assembly and notes that 'cognisance is made of the primacy of interest in the subversive elements by Special Branch'.

Issues of surveillance underline the importance of public support. Public attitudes to the police have changed dramatically over the last few decades, since the 'golden age' of the 1950s. This may be, as Reiner suggests, due to a fundamental shift in our society as it reaches a state of postmodernity as well as to a more specific concern related to the criminal justice system in the wake of several notorious miscarriages of justice, the Royal Commission on Criminal Justice, and the accelerated production of Criminal Justice Acts since 1982. The public's perception of the police has enjoyed a chequered history. The tactics used by the police in the Wapping dispute and the miners' strike showed not only that confrontation was expensive but that it also risked losing public support for police actions. The Battle of the Beanfield is a good example of this. The police perception of the importance of public support at a local and national level and the consequent media strategies are worth examining. Support from the public at large is clearly an aspect of policing by consent. The continued support of the public is an essential part of the policing of Travellers – hence the inclusion of a media strategy in some police action plans on this subject.

There was a considerable difference between the coverage of New Age Travellers by local media as compared with national media coverage. Guidance notes for the police in media relations stressed the importance of highlighting the intention of preserving the peace, maintaining public tranquillity and preventing illegal festivals, as well as dealing rapidly and effectively with lawbreakers. Police guidance also stressed the need to emphasize support from landowners and local authorities and co-operation between police forces. It was also thought necessary to bring to the public's attention the fact that 'preventative' policing was 'less costly'. There appeared to be some evidence that the cost of confrontational, medium- to large-scale operations was not only high on the police agenda but was an issue that it was thought would provoke public sympathy, as ultimately it is the public who pay for these operations. Lastly, it has been suggested that

> any examples of local disruption caused by potential festival goers causing disorder, crime, damage, vandalism, nuisance are all issues which

will consolidate public opinion behind police action, and public figures should be encouraged to express their support. (Appendix 'B', Constabulary C (1996), *Action Guide to Illegal Trespass and Unlicensed 'Rave Parties'*)

Conclusions

New Age Travellers and those involved in contemporary protest have precipitated a different style of public order policing in Britain. In some respects these changes can be seen as the consequences of policing in a postmodern age where the old certainties of class conflict, what the public want, and other meta-narratives dissolve into a miasma of relativism and diversity. Here diversity of view becomes a serious challenge to the legitimacy of police action, as it represents articulate and influential coalitions of contemporary protest focused on environmental issues and competing lifestyles. Public sympathy for environmental protesters has a different feel to it from the public reaction to the easily stereotyped 'drug-crazed' hippies of the 1985 peace convoy. On the other hand, there is still much resentment of the apparent impunity of such contemporary folk heroes as 'Swampy', who are perceived as causing so much public expense.

Clearly the police have a difficult task in responding to Travellers themselves and to public concerns while simultaneously maintaining public order. This is particularly true in their dealings with larger groups of nomadic people congregating together. In the context of diminishing resources, and with the influence of managerialism on constabularies across the country, the thought of valuable resources being spent in a major confrontation at the expense of missing performance-related key targets must seem abhorrent to operational commanders.

In the minds of the informants to whom I talked, New Age Travellers were seen as a potential threat to public order. It was therefore important for the police to engage in surveillance and covert methods of intelligence to assist in the monitoring of suspect groups and individuals. Ultimately there was a perception that failure to act 'preventatively' would lead to more resources being spent in dispersing groups. However, with this move to covert surveillance comes the risk of losing public support.

There was a strong belief that New Age Travellers were organized. The issue of organization is significant in the sense that the police response to an organized group responsible for an illegal festival will be different from their response to small groups of people who have little in common apart from a recent attraction to a nomadic lifestyle.

Even so there was some evidence that groups as small as twenty attracted police attention, primarily through intelligence followed by attempts to move these groups on or break them up. Frequently the police are faced with a relatively sophisticated degree of organization on the part of contemporary protesters, particularly among environmental protesters, involving the use of the Internet and mobile phones, in response to changes in technology and an inherent need for sound communication systems. This was only tentatively implied by informants in 1994 when the fieldwork for this study was conducted, but since the Criminal Justice and Public Order Act 'DIY culture' networks have flourished. Ironically, this increase in organization was one of the unforeseen consequences of the Act itself.

Attempts by Brown (1995) to develop an official picture of the problem through information from the Intelligence Units, constabulary annual reports and a questionnaire sent to individual officers demonstrated conclusively that there is little empirical evidence to connect Travellers with criminal activity. However, a focus on criminal activity misses the point that it was the large events such as Castlemorton Common that were primarily responsible for fuelling public concern, rather than the presence of small groups of Travellers and suspicion on the part of the sedentary population that thefts might be committed by these nomadic incomers.

However if, as Brown suggests, New Age Travellers are not responsible for large-scale prolific criminal activity, why are New Age Travellers excluded from certain counties and included on intelligence databases? The answer is probably attributable to the fact that many officers view Travellers as a potential threat, partly through deeply felt 'sedentarist' prejudice, the roots of which lie in the symbolic threat that Travellers pose to the ownership of land as well as the obvious practical difficulties of keeping an eye on nomadic people. New Age Travellers are a symbolic threat to the status quo of the countryside, where all can appear to be natural, peaceful and in its place, structurally as well as spatially.

Police opinions on the issue of drug dealing varied from those who felt that the nature of the lifestyle lent itself to this activity, and those who considered that such behaviour simply reflected contemporary youth culture in a more general sense. The detailed piece of research undertaken by Brown into police perceptions of the frequency and nature of offending by Travellers was helpful in illuminating this aspect of police–Traveller interaction.

All informants alluded to the need for co-operation with other individuals, agencies or organizations, and this is supported by the ACPO Strategy for New Age Travellers. There was reference to the need to deal with the issue of unlawful camping, using an inter-agency approach and involving the local authority in drawing up joint action plans.

Ironically, the response of the media to the surveillance techniques employed by the police in respect of Travellers has been to regard them with a significant degree of alarm. In 1993 a case was taken to the Police Complaints Authority based on information leaked to a former Traveller who sued for malicious falsehood. The Intelligence Units based in Cumbria and Wiltshire were the focus of media disquiet following this incident. The result may have been to encourage a swing of support towards the plight of Travellers in tandem with a swing away from support for some of the measures brought in by the Criminal Justice and Public Order Act 1994.

Linking co-operation and intelligence, it seems that before the Criminal Justice and Public Order Act 1994 police forces were more likely to co-operate in a relatively ad hoc way, simply by sharing information about the movement of Travellers, as in Operation Nomad and Operation Snapshot. After 1994, however, they began to adopt a proactive and co-ordinated response to the 'problem' of Travellers. There now seems to be a much greater awareness (in some areas at least) of the need for inter-agency and intra-agency co-operation which is supported by the ACPO National Strategy.

There was also the recognition that a degree of tolerance from the public, as well as the police themselves, was necessary if policing was to be effective. Within the context of a rapidly changing countryside with increasing rather than decreasing levels of suspicion, and tensions between competing interests, this may be a difficult task. The police regarded draconian responses as being counter-productive since they increased 'interest' (that is, public support) in the group and, at the same time, acted as a possible stimulus for resistance. The events that took place subsequent to the implementation of the Act have borne out this concern.

Robert Reiner, in pessimistic mood, suggests a stark choice for our society: barbarism or social justice. In a postmodern world he advocates, *inter alia*, local policing which is 'adjusted to the plural priorities and cultures of a much more diverse social world' (1992, p. 782) but concludes that the odds seem strongly to favour barbarism. King and Brearley's response to this notes that 'given the dynamic relationship between policing and dissent, new forms of both [will] develop' (1996, p. 105).

Attitudes towards Travellers and awareness of their lifestyle and of their differences must be important factors in making sure that policy is reflected in practice. The attitudes of many police constables show a high degree of prejudice against New Age Travellers which in any other context could result in disciplinary action.

The fact that the police operate in a world that they cannot wholly control seriously undermines the validity of allegations about organized or structural oppression perpetrated by them against Travellers. Can meta-narratives of oppression really capture the difficulty of policing an increasingly complex form of alternative lifestyle and protest? There seems some justification for the view that influences far more threatening than the Travellers themselves, under the rubric of managerialism, may call into question not only police effectiveness in controlling Travellers but the ability of the police to control their own destiny.

The policing of this relatively small and vulnerable group can, nevertheless, act as the map of a battleground in British public order policing, its resistance to militarism and separate specialisms, its faith in the 'holy grail' of policing by consent, its continued public support and its ability to respond to cultural pluralism. Sensitivity to cultural pluralism will need to form a central plank in rural policing policy in response to the growing road protest and associated movements, such as Earth First! The policing of New Age Travellers may also demonstrate ways in which the police will attempt to avoid Reiner's potential dystopia, or it may indicate that, in the context of the postmodern world, the intentions of those who seek to develop policing strategies to 'deal' with Travellers will be lost in the fight to maximize resources, appease a sometimes hostile public and be seen to be dealing effectively with crime.

References

BAXTER, J. (1992) 'Castlemorton and beyond: problems caused by gatherings of New Age Travellers cannot be solved by legislation alone', 8 *Policing*

BRAKE, H. and HALE, C. (1992) *Public Order and Private Lives: The Politics of Law and Order*, London: Routledge

BRASS, E. and POKLEWSKI, K. (1997) *Gathering Force: DIY Culture – Radical Action for those Tired of Waiting*, London: The Big Issue Writers

BREWER, M. et al. (1996) *The Police, Public Order and the State: Policing in Great Britain, Northern Ireland, The Irish Republic, the USA, Israel, South Africa and China*, Basingstoke: Macmillan Press

BREARLEY, N. and KING, M. (1996) 'Policing social protest: some indicators of change', in C. Critcher and D. Waddington, *Policing Public Order: Theoretical and Practical Issues*, Aldershot: Avebury

BROWN, M. (1995) 'Do police officers base their assumptions of "New Age" Travellers on stereotypical images rather than empirical evidence?', unpublished thesis for Master of Arts degree, University of Plymouth

CAMPBELL, D. (1994a) 'Police track Travellers by computer', *Guardian*, 25 February

CAMPBELL, D. (1994b) 'Police watch on Travellers to go before European Court', *Guardian*, 1 March

CLARK, C. (1997) ' "New Age" Travellers: identity, sedentarism and social security', in T. Acton (ed.), *Gypsy Politics and Traveller Identity*, Hatfield: University of Hertfordshire Press

COLQUHOUN, P. (1800) *A Treatise on the Police of the Metropolis,* (*c.*1795; 6th edition), London: Mawman

CRITCHER, C. and WADDINGTON, D. (1996) *Policing Public Order: Theoretical and Practical Issues*, Aldershot: Avebury

CRITCHLEY, T. A. (1978) *A History of Police in England and Wales 1900–1960*, London: Constable

GREEN, P. (1990) *The Enemy Without: Policing and Class Consciousness in the Miners' Strike*, Milton Keynes: Open University Press

HOBBS, D. (1988) *Doing the Business*, Oxford: Oxford University Press

KING, M. and BREARLEY, N. (1996) *Public Order Policing: Contemporary Perspectives on Strategy and Tactics*, Leicester: Perpetuity Press

MCKAY, G. (1996) *Senseless Acts of Beauty*, London: Verso

MCMULLAN, J. (1998) 'Social surveillance and the rise of the "police machine" ', 2 (1) *Theoretical Criminology*, 93

MCVEIGH, R. (1997) 'Theorising sedentarism: the roots of anti nomadism', in T. Acton (ed.), *Gypsy Politics and Traveller Identity*, Hatfield: University of Hertfordshire Press

NATIONAL COUNCIL FOR CIVIL LIBERTIES (1986) *Stonehenge*, London: National Council for Civil Liberties

NORTHAM, G. (1988) *Shooting in the Dark: Riot Police in Britain*, London: Faber and Faber

RADZINOWICZ, L. (1948–68) *A History of English Criminal Law*, I–IV, London: Stevens

REINER, R. (1992) 'Policing a postmodern society', 55 *Modern Law Review*, 6

REINER, R. (1996) 'Have the police got a future?', in Critcher and Waddington, *Policing Public Order: Theoretical and Practical Issues*, Aldershot: Avebury

STONE, C. J. (1996) *Fierce Dancing Adventures in the Underground*, London: Faber and Faber

WADDINGTON, A. J. (1994) 'Coercion and accommodation: policing public order after the Public Order Act', 45 (3) *British Journal of Sociology*, 367

WADDINGTON, D. (1996) 'Key issues and controversies', in Critcher and Waddington, *Policing Public Order: Theoretical and Practical Issues*, Aldershot: Avebury

9

The Probation Service in a Rural Area: Problems and Practicalities

PAM DAVIES

Policy

In recent decades the role of the probation service has been a topic of considerable debate in political, professional and academic circles (James, 1995; Lewis, 1991; McWilliams, 1987; Mair, 1997; May, 1991; Spencer, 1995). Prior to the introduction of the Criminal Justice Act 1991 the service had witnessed periods of confidence and uncertainty as the efficacy of the rehabilitation and treatment models, initially embraced with enthusiasm as the way forward in dealing with offenders, was increasingly called into question (most notably by von Hirsch, 1976). Influential publications by writers such as Martinson (1974) in the United States and Brody (1976) in the United Kingdom contributed to an existing mood of no confidence in rehabilitative programmes (see further Cavadino and Dignan, 1997; Dingwall and Davenport, 1995). Further, the 1980s witnessed the Thatcher government adopting increasingly reactionary law-and-order policies, as well as demanding elements of financial accountability and effectiveness from criminal justice agencies (see Dingwall, chapter 6). Such a climate led to serious implications for the Probation Service (Harris, 1992; May, 1991; Raynor et al., 1994). According to Mair (1997, p. 1202), applying the criteria adopted by the Conservatives, the probation service had been ineffective in the past: 'It had failed at rehabilitation; it had failed to reduce the prison population, and it was committed to "soft" social work values which meant that offenders who deserved punishment received help instead.'

However, it could also be argued that the probation service had, by the 1990s, established a pivotal role within all aspects of the criminal justice process, providing information on bail decisions, submitting pre-sentence reports (or social inquiry reports as they were then termed), in the supervising of clients, and in the through- and aftercare of prisoners:

In relation to other criminal justice agencies, the significance of the probation service has been underestimated, yet by virtue of the number of offenders supervised, its costs, and its central position at the very heart of the criminal justice process, the probation service occupies a vital role. (Mair, p. 1197)

Following the implementation of the Criminal Justice Act 1991 that role moved to centre stage. The legislation introduced a 'just deserts' philosophy, i.e. the severity of the sentence had to reflect the seriousness of the offence (Dingwall, chapter 6; Ashworth, 1995; Wasik, 1998). It also redefined 'alternatives to custody' as 'community penalties', as well as introducing a new community penalty, the combination order, which was a combination of community service and probation (Home Office, 1990). This had, at least theoretically, the effect of elevating probation 'up tariff' as many more serious offenders could theoretically be given a community penalty rather than a custodial sentence (Mair, 1997).

However, despite these new opportunities for the service, it was reported in the period following the implementation of this legislation that the ethos of the service experienced a change, leading to a lowering of morale generally among main-grade officers (May, 1991). This change in ethos may initially be traced back to the mid-1980s and the publication of *A Statement of National Objectives and Priorities* (Home Office, 1984), which established a list of priorities and overall objectives for the service. It was seen by many as the introduction of centralized government pressure on the service to be more accountable, more managerially orientated, and more aware of its effectiveness (see Dingwall, chapter 6). Immediately following the introduction of the 1991 Act the Home Office published a Three Year Plan (1993), in which the service was subjected to performance indicators and considerable financial restraints. According to Nellis (1995, pp. 23–4):

The unleashing of market forces in society in general, and in the Criminal Justice System in particular, brought notions of utility and profit to the fore, and it was largely from these that concern with efficiency, economy, and effectiveness derives . . . Every agency and every action must serve some demonstrable purpose, must be measurably effective, and must fulfil its objectives as cheaply as possible.

The climate of opinion within the service at this time was expressed by one practitioner thus:

Chief Probation Officers have abandoned our profession and betrayed their working staff. We are retiring early, dying early, off sick with

mysterious illnesses, demoralised, depressed, and overstretched to cope
with these new regressive Criminal Justice Act provisions. We are keen to
work as probation officers, but we must be allowed our vocation, our
discretion, our independence – we cannot function without those things.
(letter to *The Times*, September 1993)

Given this prevailing climate, the work of the probation service is now
undertaken amid a philosophy and policy that have been amended with
a frequency indicative of panic, as successive governments have striven
to implement and maintain an effective criminal justice system
(Cavadino and Dignan, 1997). While the probation service in England
and Wales is divided into fifty-five separate services (based on the
counties created in the reorganization of local government in 1974),
policy development is directed from the centre by the Home Office.

Areas of Work

In order to understand the problems encountered by a rural
probation service, a brief outline and explanation of the service's
main areas of work needs to be established (see generally Osler, 1995).
Firstly, the service is responsible for preparing pre-sentence reports.
Following a plea or finding of guilt, and in order to assist them with
sentencing, magistrates and Crown Courts request a report on almost
all people who commit serious offences. Pre-sentence reports provide
information on circumstances surrounding an offender's attitude
towards his or her current offence, previous patterns of offending, the
offender's personal circumstances, and an assessment of the risk in
respect of reoffending, together with the degree of possible danger to
the public that the offender appears to present. Bearing these criteria
in mind, the reports usually contain sentence recommendations which
are frequently followed by the court, but need not be.

After sentence the probation service is involved in the practical
implementation of three types of community sentence. The mainstay
of community penalties is the probation order, which lasts between
six months and three years, and requires the offender to report to the
probation officer and receive a number of home visits as instructed,
as well as notifying any change in residential or employment circumstances and complying with any additional supplementary conditions. Community service orders require the offender to complete
between 40 and 240 hours of unpaid work in the community, and
combination orders also entail supervision by the probation service.
Furthermore, all those under the age of twenty-one, and adults
serving custodial sentences of over one year, are supervised on release
by the probation service for a specified time depending primarily on

the length of the custodial sentence. Contact with the offender, his or her family, and custodial establishment staff, including probation officers, is maintained throughout the sentence to facilitate through-care and release plans. Ideally, the prisoner is visited periodically, and sentence-review meetings involving the prisoner and prison staff are regularly held.

Those offenders serving less than four years are automatically released after half of their sentence has expired, although they face possible recall should they breach their licence or reoffend before the full sentence has expired. For those serving four years or longer, excluding life, discretionary release or parole is considered after half the sentence, and thereafter, if not granted, at regular periods up until automatic release after two-thirds of the sentence has expired. A report from the home probation officer is essential to the parole board in its decision in respect of release. Such a report contains full details of the prisoner's home, family and possible employment circumstances. It will also consider community attitudes to the offence(s), and positive and negative influences which are likely to prevail. Importantly, the victim will, if possible, have been contacted in respect of his or her views regarding the possible release of the offender (see Williams, chapter 10). Similar, although usually less detailed, reports are prepared for consideration of home leave prior to the release of any prisoner serving a sentence of over one year, with, again, the victim being contacted in serious cases. The probation service contacts all victims of serious violence and sex offences if the perpetrator receives a custodial sentence of four years or longer, informing them of the proceedings, and asking whether they wish to be continually informed of the prisoner's progress during sentence, most notably if he or she is transferred to a different category of prison.

Life-sentence prisoners are a special category (see generally Padfield, 1996), with a complicated tariff system which, quite apart from their behaviour and progress during sentence, is important in determining any release. If released they are subject to licence, and possible recall, theoretically for life, but this is frequently discharged after a number of years. Finally, certain categories of mentally disordered offenders, detained in secure hospitals for indeterminate periods, are subject to supervision by probation officers on discharge (see generally Peay, 1997). Again, contact with patient and hospital staff is maintained during hospitalization.

The Research Study

This brief overview highlights the variety of functions that have to be undertaken by the probation service in all locations. How does a rural probation service meet these demands and operate in an increasingly centralized system where policy is determined by legislators and administrators who have little affinity with the countryside and, consequently, little understanding of the specific problems likely to be encountered in a rural area? Many probation officers operating in an urban environment are equally unaware of the challenges faced by their 'country colleagues' and see a landscape characterized by leafy lanes and mischievous yokels as opposed to urban deprivation, pollution and a serious crime problem. Depending on personal desire, enthusiasm for new developments, and, probably, length of service, these beliefs tend to be held with a mixture of amusement and envy.

For the purposes of this research, an empirical methodology was adopted which primarily involved a number of interviews with both probation officers and probation ancillaries working within a large rural area in Wales. In providing an illustration of the problems encountered by probation personnel 'in the field', the work aims to provide a reflection of a rural service's ability to accommodate and respond to the demands made upon it by central government. The experiences, thoughts and feelings of the officers concerned were, on occasion, forcefully expressed, and the difficulties encountered provide a useful insight into the day-to-day operation of a rural probation service. The interviews were designed to test a number of initial hypotheses regarding the way in which probation staff operate in the country. For example, is the quality and effectiveness of the probation service's task affected by the financial, logistical and demographic implications of rurality? Do distance and scattered population invariably lead to higher proportional costs of resources to the extent that often these are not provided or realistically available? How does a rural service accommodate staff specialization? Given their geographical isolation, do rural probation services possess greater freedom to use their initiative without the constraints of an interfering bureaucracy? Do the offenders with whom rural services have to deal have particular characteristics and needs? In order to ascertain the perceptions of the staff themselves a semi-structured format was adopted to the interviews which, it is hoped, struck an appropriate balance between allowing the interviewees to focus on their particular concerns whilst setting the overall parameters of the inquiry.

Financial Concerns

The issue of financial resources was of primary concern to those interviewed. A culture had developed which saw efficiency within the service as laudable whilst the frittering of scarce resources was deemed unacceptable (see further May, 1991; Mair, 1997). Had the current 'accountant mentality' within Whitehall (Pratt, 1989; Rutherford, 1993) placed its trust in experienced practitioners who live and work in this kind of environment considerable time and resources could have been saved. However, this does not appear to have happened. Unfortunately, some (although not all) senior managers in these areas, promoted from, and on the stepladder back to, the city, are perceived to possess little incentive to fight their corners. There is a belief that many senior managers may not have had sufficient opportunity to familiarize themselves with the specific problems and difficulties which may prevail in their particular areas. In a large rural patch probation headquarters, with its assistant chief officer, information and technology officer, secretaries and clerks, together with maps of dubiously small and misleading scale, in itself becomes a mini-Whitehall. It could be argued that in urban areas siting offices at regular intervals from each other provides a satis-factory solution for client and court convenience. In contrast, rural centres of population, where the scattered populace gathers for shopping, signing on, leisure activities, or transport to the wider world, are frequently not geographically equidistant or central. Transport and time costs for home visits and fares for clients, when appropriate, are high. Significantly, it does not cost proportionately less, in terms of programme-devising and resources, to run a group of six suitable clients in a rural patch than a group of twelve similar clients within a city. Attempts to save administrative costs by opening offices in geographically central but demographically unimportant towns, even with outlying reporting centres, may create further difficulties, as well as being resource-intensive:

> Clients find it hard, physically and financially, to come in for appointments. There is little reception work for our secretaries to carry out, and we waste much valuable time travelling around between offices – time which could be more effectively spent on client contact. (Officer A)

Prison throughcare can, as we have seen, play an important part in the future community supervision of prisoners, some of whom may be potentially dangerous (Raynor et al., 1994). However, this aspect of probation work frequently receives minimum priority within many rural probation services because of the cost implications and the absence of any immediate, mandatory deadlines, such as those required in report-writing for the courts or community supervision. The distance and poor road infrastructure mean that visits to penal establishments have obvious resource implications in terms of time, money and energy:

Frequently, when you get authorization for a rare visit, you are usually asked by a colleague, 'as you are going to Dartmoor, can you interview Jones and Evans for me?' Restricted, not just by time, but occasionally by the vagaries of the prison's official visiting policy, the quality of the visit declines as we attempt to complete our quota. (Officer B)

Logistical Problems

In both rural and urban areas specialization can create unnecessary logistical difficulties. Probation officers in urban areas, with sufficient supervisors and report-writers in the same office, may nevertheless complain about the lack of flexibility which can arise when one area becomes overloaded and has to ask a neighbouring office (often located no more than five miles away) for support, even when colleagues based in the same office appear to be available. This situation is considerably exacerbated in a rural area. The following scenario was witnessed during the course of this research. In one probation office there were two clients present; one was waiting for a pre-sentence report whilst the other was under supervision. The same situation existed in another office thirty miles away. After seeing the client for their speciality in one office, two officers, both of whom were capable of undertaking the two tasks, travelled in opposite directions to see the similar client in the other office. They then both returned to their homes, situated some miles from their first ports of call. This situation resulted in two officers spending a total of six hours travelling 160 miles at considerable cost to the service. Specialization, whatever its merits in an urban setting, clearly creates a considerable financial drain in rural areas.

In order to facilitate offenders behaving positively on their release, the probation service offers a variety of programmes dealing with such issues as employment, anger management, drink/drug problems and budgeting (Mair, 1997). These sessions may be undertaken on a one-to-one or a group basis, and may be held weekly or on a more intensive block schedule. Organization is either under the direction solely of the probation service, or in partnership with other statutory or voluntary bodies. The Home Office (1993) encourages such inter-agency liaison, emphasizing the importance of the timely sharing of information. It is envisaged that local services should be planned on the basis of clearly assessed local needs, that there should be joint training for staff and that systems for recording information between and within agencies should be established in order to monitor the effectiveness of such programmes (Cross, 1997). However, given the competition for funding and the juggling of limited resources, in some cases it is the rural areas which may miss out on their share of resources and funding as allocation is dependent not upon local need but upon the existence of interested and sufficiently motivated personnel.

On the positive side, in a rural area where client numbers are so small that group exercises and discussion are impractical or unworkable officers may well introduce clients into community-based groups rather than call upon in-service resources. Thus, for example, a large urban probation office may form a football team for offenders whereas a rural office may encourage a client to join a local football team. Although such a procedure may be considered a disadvantage in that clients in rural areas do not have the opportunity to discuss their problems and share their experiences with each other to the same extent, the advantages are that clients experience a wider perspective in dealing with their problems and may be introduced back into the community earlier than those clients who remain in offender-based groups (see further Dingwall, chapter 6). According to Lacey et al.,

> [I]t is basic to the aim of the service to create conditions in which responsibility can be accepted and consequences faced, and that this is done with as much community participation as possible . . . [because] in the end it is the community, not the individual probation officer, who can make or break the offender in terms of his changing, adopting, and shouldering of responsibility. Thus the community needs to be involved in and aware of the learning process, and to develop confidence in the work of the probation service. (1983, p. 123)

Demographic Issues

Rural probation officers often find themselves operating in an extremely large geographical area. This can be a particular problem when the probation service needs to liaise with social services, mental health services, the Department of Social Security or other bodies. Officers highlighted the importance of local knowledge:

> Given the large area that we are expected to cover, little wonder that on occasion clients fail to understand why an officer, particularly if they are covering for a fellow specialist from the neighbouring patch, has no idea where the 'cheese factory' or the 'Black Lion' are located, or that Monday is market day. Therefore a good probation officer needs to know the district, its resources, agencies, places of work and recreation, and its traditions. (Officer C)

There was a perception amongst officers that rural teams need to be generic, based on areas of population and services, with reporting offices located in smaller towns or large villages. Isolated, often with minimal supervision, these teams need a majority of experienced officers who are able to work on their own initiative. Careerwise, the rural probation officer is likely to have to move home in order to achieve promotion or gain further experience, as a neighbouring office may be many miles away. Conversely, an urban colleague may possess not only a choice of offices but possibly of probation areas within a relatively small radius. Furthermore, probation officers wishing to make the transfer from urban to rural may well experience feelings of isolation due to a lack of contact with colleagues and seniors. However, on the positive side, rural officers recognized that the invariable necessity for immediate personal initiative could prove to be a great training experience for the fledgling officer.

While not required to make home visits within some of the vast urban housing estates, the probation officer operating in a country town may experience inadequate multi-occupancy dwellings as equally uninviting and dangerous as any to be found in a city. They may also have to visit remote houses which, according to one officer, requires skills of 'orienteering, rallying and animal taming'. He maintained that 'even if they do exist, country signposts inevitably point directly across fields, the cartographer's marked metalled roads having occasionally disappeared under the plough'. On a more serious note, officers maintained that they were strictly instructed never to interview in an office whilst alone with a client in the building. However, they stated that in their area they were expected to visit clients by themselves at isolated, sometimes officially deserted farmhouses and cottages. Mobile phones were not provided, and would probably prove to be ineffective in the mountainous terrain found in the area under study. This left staff feeling vulnerable:

> The inhabitants of these isolated properties tend to be incomers, rather than locals, many of whom are involved in the drug scene and, frequently, its associated violence. Although we are advised that clients are far less likely to be violent in their own homes, in some instances it is not the clients themselves but their 'business associates' and dealers who may present the greatest possible danger. (Officer E)

There can also be demographic difficulties for offenders. In a situation where an offender may appear vulnerable or unmanageable within the community, he or she may be required to spend the initial part of the probation order resident in a probation hostel where offenders are offered considerable practical and emotional support. However, such establishments are few and far between in a rural patch and offenders may find themselves resident in hostels some distance from family and friends and community. Nevertheless, despite the obvious geographical difficulties, their removal from possible disruptive peer-group influences may give time for reflection and allow staff to provide beneficial help and guidance.

The Rural Caseload

In respect of the caseloads of the probation officers interviewed, nearly all of the clients were reported as possessing low self-esteem, were deemed unmanageable, and were experiencing problems in forming and maintaining relationships. These personality difficulties almost invariably led to drink and/or illicit drug habits. Officers emphasized the fact that continued protection from the consequences of their actions, or the allowance of the excuse of deprivation, however genuine and debilitating, merely reinforced feelings of inadequacy and low self-esteem and that 'quality time' working with clients was what was required, although such intensive work was not encouraged by an increasingly managerialistic approach to probation:

> Much painful heart searching and practical trial and error has to be experienced by these people. Until and unless they are motivated, we can only continue to constructively confront and let go. Change cannot be enforced, the only criteria that we can enforce are the reporting, visiting, and other requirements of the various community penalties and licences supervised. What is required is quality supervision time spent with our clients. Given the existing ethos within the service, sadly, this is the very element that is being marginalized. As long as we tick the boxes, and our files look neat and tidy, then management are happy. We accomplish a great deal of effective casework, but this never gets measured in statistics and tables. (Officer B)

How are these drink/drug and personality problems manifested in a rural setting? As in a city, the criminal population tends to be both indigenous and transient (see Bottoms and Wiles, 1997). While some individuals seek the supposed opportunities, activities and bright lights associated with large cities, others prefer the perceived tranquillity of rural life. Officers appeared to believe that this lifestyle choice affected the type of crime found in rural areas:

> Possibly due to a less materially conscious environment, serious theft and dishonesty involving domestic victims is rare within this patch. This is not to say that we have an easier time. Serious beer-fuelled or drug-related violence, including murder and unlawful killing, both by incomers and locals is not unknown. (Officer D)

Officer D further maintained that drink- or drug-related dishonesty involving commercial and institutional victims was common and that sex offences involving children both inside and outside the family unit appeared, worryingly, to be on the increase.

As well as the more obviously 'alternative' clients, officers also drew attention to the supposedly more 'conventional' incomers, who were seen as almost certainly possessing alcohol problems and probably as involved in the drug scene as 'alternative' incomers. Many individuals admitted to their probation officers that they thought escaping the city might in some way help them to stop using drugs or drinking:

> These clients may be young, having recently left care or an unhappy, unstable although not necessarily financially poor home. Others may be more mature, escaping from broken relationships, failed employment and unsavoury reputations. However, their ideals frequently shatter and previous patterns created on urban estates and city streets are repeated in country towns and seaside resorts. (Officer A)

As one such individual, on probation for a serious assault on a police officer, told the author,

> All I do in the city is drink and fight because that is all there is to do. I came to the country, where I am not known, and the police will leave me alone, to get away from bad influences, and perhaps find a seasonal job. I have given up drinking, but had one or two to celebrate a friend's birthday. I did not mean to cause any trouble. (Offender A)

Interestingly, officers maintained that theft in their area by indigenous locals tended to be comparatively rare. However, fuelled with alcohol they readily capitalize on the carelessly insecure door or window, and may also do so when sober if they are short of money to buy drink. In the caseloads of the officers interviewed drink-related offences of violence and public order occurred frequently. These caseloads contained many hard-working, skilled individuals who were respected in their regular employment but who were inclined to the occasional serious fight or public order incident. Reasonable lifestyles were maintained for substantial periods of time and, paradoxically, a short custodial sentence often resulted in elevating their immediate status amongst their peers. There were, however, longer-term problems: 'The problem is that, in some cases, damage slowly increases and this can result in considerable health and social difficulties through alcohol and drugs, if not through further offending' (Officer D).

Rural towns and villages tend to produce their share of local 'celebrities', people such as councillors or sports people, 'big fish in little ponds', who would melt into the urban crowd. Occasionally copybooks are blotted, either by them or by their families, and strings are sometimes expected to be pulled on their behalf in order to cause a minimum of embarrassment or inconvenience:

> Some years ago, two members of a local football team were convicted of an assault. They succeeded in persuading the supervisor of their resulting community service orders to organize a special midweek working group so that the 'town', not just the football club, would not be let down on Saturdays. Then there was the local councillor and parliamentary candidate who refused to allow a probation officer to visit his son at home in case the neighbours found out and his respectability was jeopardized . . . [a colleague] was surprised at how quickly and co-operatively a politically motivated, potentially rebellious twenty-year-old sailed through her community service order, until she later discovered a near relative was a Crown Court Judge. (Officer C)

Concluding Comments

In conclusion, according to the opinions of those probation officers interviewed in this study the clients of a rural caseload and the reasons why they offend are not markedly different from those found in urban caseloads (see also Koffman, chapter 4). On occasion, it would appear that the quality and effectiveness of the service's task may be affected by the financial, logistical and demographic implications of rurality. However, by far the greatest difficulties faced by probation officers are those imposed by a business-minded, centralized bureaucracy (see Dingwall, chapter 6). Officers repeatedly complained that they received little backing from senior management and commented upon the distance of management from the day-to-day operation of probation within their area. It would appear that the main aim of management is to formulate policy and set objectives, rather than provide a supportive role in which the professional skills of probation officers and the quality of their work are monitored by a specific type of casework supervision (Nellis, 1995).

However, although the interviews highlighted officers' frustration in their attempt to plan and carry out their work within a framework of accountability and cost-effectiveness, it was also possible to detect an emphasis on the part of main-grade officers towards a more 'traditional' approach which emphasized the need for sufficient quality time spent with clients, dealing with their problems and difficulties rather than cosmetically maintaining files and paperwork to National Standard requirements. This accords with a study undertaken by Ford et al. (1997) which indicated that, in their area of research, probation practice had changed less than originally thought and that 'the 80 year old injunction on officers to advise, assist and befriend their clients is continuing to find expression' (p. 59). The researchers found that 'although probation officers' ability to assist with practical problems might be limited by scarce resources, they are clearly seen as competent [in dealing] with family problems, and the listening aspect of counselling' (p. 57). Undeniably, this is not a particularly rural phenomenon, and the same could be said of many urban services. However, it could possibly be argued that, given a greater freedom to use their initiative without the constraints of an interfering bureaucracy, rural officers are able to pursue a more personally rewarding and potentially more successful approach in dealing with offenders. The officers interviewed recognized practical difficulties associated with rurality but also acknowledged that the quantitative and qualitative differences in the practical operation of probation in rural areas afforded scope for increased opportunities.

References

ASHWORTH, A. (1995) *Sentencing and Criminal Justice*, 2nd edn, London: Butterworths

BOTTOMS, A. E. and WILES, P. (1997) 'Environmental criminology', in Maguire, M., Morgan, R. and Reiner, R. (eds), *The Oxford Handbook of Criminology*, 2nd edn, Oxford: Clarendon Press

BRODY, S. (1976) *The Effectiveness of Sentencing: A Review of the Literature*, Home Office Research Study No. 35, London: HMSO

CAVADINO, M. and DIGNAN, J. (1997) *The Penal System: An Introduction*, 2nd edn, London: Sage

CROSS, B. (1997) 'Partnership in practice: the experiences of two probation services', 36 *Howard Journal*, 62

DINGWALL, G. and DAVENPORT, A. (1995) 'The evolution of criminal justice policy in the UK', in Harding, C. et al. (eds), *Criminal Justice in Europe*, Oxford: Clarendon Press

FORD, P. , PRITCHARD, C. and COX, M. (1997) 'Consumer opinions of the probation service: advice, assistance and befriending and the reduction of crime', 36 *Howard Journal*, 42

HARRIS, H. (1992) *Crime, Criminal Justice and the Probation Service*, London: Routledge

HOME OFFICE (1984) *Statement of National Objectives and Priorities for the Probation Service*, London: HMSO

HOME OFFICE (1990) *Crime, Justice and Protecting the Public*, Cmnd 965, London: HMSO

HOME OFFICE (1993) *The Probation Service: A Three Year Plan*, London: HMSO

HUMPHREY, C. (1991) 'Calling on the experts: the financial management initiative, private sector management consultants and the probation service', 31 *Howard Journal*, 31

JAMES, A. (1995) 'Probation values for the 1990s – and beyond?', 34 *Howard Journal*, 326

LACEY, M. , PENDLETON, J. and READ, G. (1983) 'Supervision in the community: the righting of wrongs', 147 *Justice of the Peace*, 120

LEWIS, P. (1991) 'Learning from industry: macho management or collaborative culture?', 38 *Probation Journal*, 21

LUCAS, J. , RAYNOR, P. and VANSTONE, M. (1992) *Straight Thinking on Probation One Year On*, Bridgend: Mid Glamorgan Probation Service

McWILLIAMS, W. (1987) 'Probation, pragmatism and policy', 26 *Howard Journal*, 97

MAIR, G. (1997) 'Community penalties and probation', in Maguire, M., Morgan, R. and Reiner, R. (eds.), *The Oxford Handbook of Criminology*, Oxford: Clarendon Press

MARTINSON, R. (1974) 'What works? Questions and answers about prison reform', 35 *Public Interest*, 22

MAY, T. (1991) *Probation: Politics, Policy and Practice*, Milton Keynes: Open University Press

NELLIS, M. (1995) 'Probation values for the 1990s', 34 *Howard Journal*, 19

OSLER, A. (1995) *Introduction to the Probation Service*, Winchester: Waterside Press

PADFIELD, N. (1996) 'Bailing and sentencing the dangerous', in Walker, N. (ed.), *Dangerous People*, London: Blackstone Press

PEAY, J. (1997) 'Mentally disordered offenders', in Maguire, M., Morgan, R. and Reiner, R. (eds), *The Oxford Handbook of Criminology*, 2nd edn, Oxford: Clarendon Press

PETERS, A. (1986) 'Main currents in criminal law theory', in Van Dijk, J. (ed.), *Criminal Law in Action*, Arnhem: Gouda Quint

PRATT, J. (1989) 'Corporatism: the third model of juvenile justice', 29 *British Journal of Criminology*, 236

RAYNOR, P., SMITH, D. and VANSTON, M. (1994) *Effective Probation Practice*, London: Macmillan

RUTHERFORD, A. (1993) *Criminal Justice and the Pursuit of Decency*, Oxford: Oxford University Press

SPENCER, J. (1995) 'A response to Mike Nellis: probation values for the 1990s', 34 *Howard Journal*, 344

von HIRSCH, A. (1976) *Doing Justice: The Choice of Punishments*, New York: Hill and Wang

WASIK, M. (1998) *Emmins on Sentencing*, 3rd edn, London: Blackstone Press

10

Rural Victims of Crime

BRIAN WILLIAMS

The Academic Neglect of Rural Victims[1]

Victims of crime have attracted increasing political and academic interest in recent years, and a range of services has grown up to meet and draw attention to their needs. Increasingly, there has been a trend towards emphasizing victims' rights as well as their needs, and considerable attention has been paid to specific groups of crime victims (including women, ethnic minorities and people with disabilities). Victimology has existed as an academic discipline since the 1940s, and has begun to take a growing interest both in the practical issues involved in providing effective support to victims and in questions of implementing research findings in practice. To date, however, little attention has been paid to the specific issues affecting victims of crime in rural areas. An unhelpful assumption that the urban experience is the norm against which the non-urban should be measured underlies much of the academic literature on rural crime.

Although academic interest in things rural has revived in recent years, most of the activity is taking place in disciplines other than criminology (see Moody, chapter 1) and in countries other than the United Kingdom. The research that has been undertaken on crime in

[1] I would like to thank Gavin Dingwall and Sue Moody for giving me the idea for this chapter, for pointing out relevant literature and putting me into contact with other researchers, and for their helpful comments upon earlier drafts; I am also very grateful to colleagues in probation, social services and victim support agencies for agreeing to be interviewed. They are usually not named, for reasons of confidentiality, but they are the source of much of the unattributed information in the chapter – for whose accuracy the author nevertheless accepts responsibility. I am also pleased to acknowledge the help of Tina Atkins, the Community Safety Co-ordinator of the Forest of Dean District Council, and of Ian Hankinson of Shropshire Probation Service. My colleague Ray Fabes made very helpful comments on an earlier draft of this chapter.

rural areas has tended to focus upon crime patterns and policing, with very little attention paid to the rural victim. There is a need for critical research on the differences between crime and victimization in urban and rural areas. The present chapter consists of a review of the relevant literature, and was also informed by semi-structured interviews with probation staff involved in work with victims of crime in rural areas. As such, it represents only a pilot study – and a very tentative contribution to the literature. Much more research is needed – a subject discussed further towards the end of the chapter.

It is not clear exactly why the interests of rural victims have been neglected in the academic literature, but a number of possibilities suggest themselves. First, there is the matter of funding. Research funding priorities are driven to some extent by political concerns (Koffman, 1996), and urban rather than rural disorder, crime and incivility have driven political rhetoric about crime in recent decades in the United Kingdom (see Dingwall, chapter 6). Without external funding, large-scale research studies are very difficult to do – and researchers tend to economize by undertaking their work locally, which usually means carrying it out in urban centres (Harding, 1994).

Secondly, and linked to the funding issue, is the question of topicality. While there is considerable popular and media interest in the problem of crime in the inner city, such concern has only inter-mittently – and not always accurately – focused upon rural areas (Tuck, 1989). One might expect some academic interest in the relatively low level of rural crime, given the possibility that this might improve our understanding of overall offending rates, but it remains a minority concern.

Thirdly, the most powerful advocacy groups which express views on the needs of victims of crime are city-based. Although Victim Support, for example, has achieved national coverage, its largest local schemes are in cities, and its national office and secretariat are in London. Smaller, provincial Victim Support schemes are run differently from their city counterparts, and national office policies are not always seen as relevant to the rural setting (Kosh and Williams, 1995), but the organization naturally responds to the concerns expressed by the areas where the need is seen as greatest. Indeed, there can be difficulties in convincing people of the need for services such as support for victims in rural areas, where there is a tendency to believe that people look out for each other because they belong to a real community (Newby, 1988).

Although sexual and domestic violence occur in all walks of life and all parts of the country, organizations such as Women's Aid and Rape Crisis tend to find it easier to obtain funding in densely populated areas, and sometimes struggle to provide a service to the surrounding rural area (Henderson, 1997). They, too, have national offices in cities (but not in London), and they have insufficient resources to provide a fully national service, although they have undertaken some outreach work with a view to improving their coverage of rural areas.

Also, victims of crime in rural areas are in a minority, and as such are less likely to attract research interest, particularly if there is a general belief that crime in rural areas is relatively rare. Hardly anybody believes that crime is falling, despite the statistical evidence, but there is a widespread common-sense belief that crime is not a major problem in the country. There is relatively little hard data about victimization rates in rural parts of the UK – but there are notable exceptions, which are drawn upon in what follows (Koffman, 1996; Anderson, 1997; Shapland and Vagg, 1988).

Finally, there may also be cultural reasons for the re-emergence of interest in rural crime and victims in some countries rather than others. A number of brutal attacks on older people in isolated parts of Ireland led to a rapid change in policing priorities and to increased academic interest in rural crime there, perhaps because the countryside has such a central place in the national self-image in Ireland (McCullagh, chapter 2). Rural crime may come to symbolize the spread of urban malaise to hitherto sacrosanct areas, and reflect wider anxieties about the urbanization process. Much of the research on urban crime since the 1930s has been undertaken in the United States, another country where the cities are perceived as unsettled and dangerous compared with the rural areas, where order and peace are thought to prevail (Moody, chapter 1), but where things are changing rapidly in some places (Krannich et al., 1989). Rural issues have recently taken on greater political importance in the United Kingdom, but the rural does not seem to have the same resonance there as in Ireland or the United States, and it may be that there are cultural reasons for the failure of rural crime to emerge as an issue.

The academic neglect of the area in the UK does not mean that research on rural victims is unnecessary or irrelevant. Indeed, as already suggested, it might throw valuable light on some of the questions which currently arouse concern. For example, what is it about the urban setting which leads to high crime rates, and what aspects of policing and victim support in rural communities might helpfully be emulated in the cities? In what ways are the experiences of victims in rural areas different from those of their urban counterparts, and how might such distinctions inform future service provision? At present 'theories of crime that purport to be general theories are too often theories only of urban crime' (Weisheit and Wells, 1996, p. 394).

Unfortunately the dearth of information about victims in rural areas has led, in practice, to their specific needs being neglected. Before considering the impact upon policy in relation to rural victims, we now turn to the research evidence on rural victims and how their experience differs from those in urban areas.

Differences Between Rural and Urban Victimization

In contrasting the experiences of rural victims with those in urban areas, it is important to make it clear that there are definitional problems with the urban–rural distinction (see also Anderson, chapter 3; Koffman, chapter 4). Not the least of these is the fact that there is a continuum between rural and urban areas, with suburban districts as an obvious mid-point. For the purposes of the present discussion, it is probably sufficient simply to note that there is no clear, binary divide between rural and urban areas or victimization. Some of the confusion in the literature (for example, in relation to relative crime rates) seems to arise from a failure to define the terms clearly (Shapland and Vagg, 1988; O'Connor and Gray, 1989; Tuck, 1989). As some of these authors have pointed out, aggregate crime or victimization figures covering predominantly rural areas need to be further broken down before they can be used to make definitive statements about the rural experience. Some of the more recent research uses more sophisticated statistical techniques to make this possible (Anderson, 1997). Rural areas also differ widely amongst themselves: it might be argued that the experience of living on a remote Scottish island is as different from living in a large suburban village in Oxfordshire as living in a city such as Durham is from living in another such as Birmingham.

In a sense, the dissimilarities between the experience of criminal victimization in rural and urban areas are not particularly surprising. They are affected by factors such as geographical remoteness, cultural differences between cities and countryside, the sparse population of many country areas and consequent isolation, and the extent to which individuals are aware of and interested in the activities and welfare of their neighbours. While this may seem a matter of simple common sense, all preconceptions about the rural–urban distinction need careful examination before they are translated into decisions affecting victims of crime. This section therefore attempts to analyse the existing evidence about victims' experiences critically.

It is worth noting that there is no consensus about the trends affecting rural crime: while recorded crime in rural areas has not fallen as dramatically as in urban areas, this pattern is not entirely consistent, and differences in reporting practices and recording procedures may partially explain the apparent distinction. Factors affecting the level of reported crime may also impact differently in rural areas. There are likely to be differences in levels of fear of crime, and in the ways in which victimization is experienced, between urban and rural areas.

(a) Isolation

Although rural life has been changing rapidly in the UK in recent years, social change in rural areas nevertheless takes longer than in the cities. It has been suggested that fear of crime may be related to the shock of the new: people's feelings about crime perhaps reflect their attitudes to social change more generally, regardless of their actual experience of crime or knowledge about its prevalence. Thus, distaste for alternative youth cultures and 'the other' may translate into anxiety about young people as potential offenders (Moody, chapter 1). Young people who are simply hanging around and making a noise may be perceived as disorderly in rural areas when they would be accepted as part of the scene in an urban setting (Husain, 1995). People who are not known, or whose demeanour and dress are unfamiliar, are likely to arouse greater concern in more isolated areas, and at times people feel free to take the law into their own hands when they object to the behaviour of young people from marginalized groups. Local people attending consultative meetings organized by police in rural Worcestershire reported concern about increased levels of vandalism and 'all the muggings' when no such offences had been reported in the previous five months (Young, 1993, p. 52), and this is far from atypical.

Geographical isolation also affects the reporting of crime. The police may not have the resources to respond quickly to reported incidents, which go off the boil before any official response is mobilized. Some types of incident may be more likely to be dealt with informally in rural areas (Weisheit and Wells, 1996), not least because a police officer whose nearest back-up is some sixty miles away will be acutely aware of the need to handle things alone (Anderson, chapter 3). On the other hand, the social cohesiveness of some rural communities may make it easier to organize crime prevention initiatives such as Neighbourhood Watch, which in turn allay some people's anxiety about crime (Yarwood and Edwards, 1995). (There is also some evidence that county police forces are relatively generously resourced in some rural areas due to political pressure by powerful landowners (Young, 1993). If so, this might actually lead to higher rates of reported crime in such areas.)

Greater geographical distances obviously lead to delay, not only in police responses to reported incidents but also in the criminal justice process once the decision is made to prosecute. Rural residents express considerable concern about the reduction in police patrols arising from greater centralization (discussed further below). The lack of local access to specialist legal advice may mean that both offenders and victims receive relatively poor advice in rural areas. Courts in rural areas sit infrequently, and the travelling distances mean that police and probation interviews with defendants can take longer to organize, delaying matters further – although this depends on the extent to which services are centralized, and small, local offices can sometimes be very responsive (Harding, 1994; NACRO, 1997). It may be that when delays do occur this contributes to the levels of anxiety about rural crime.

Individuals' actual experiences of victimization also differ in rural areas. Some types of offence have a greater impact simply because they affect people living in isolated places particularly severely. Even offences with no obvious personal victim can have a greater impact in the country: a commercial burglary may, in some circumstances, threaten the existence of a small business whose profitability is marginal (Husain, 1995), and theft from an isolated phone box can cause disproportionate inconvenience and concern if this results in it being out of action. Sentencers are likely to reflect local feeling, and respond accordingly (see also Dingwall, Chapter 6).

Overall, however, people in rural areas are aware that their relative isolation is an advantage in terms of the risk of criminal victimization. The fear of crime is much lower in rural than in urban areas, with some justification (Koffman, 1996).

(b) Changing patterns of settlement

Migrants from the city seem often to bring their fear of crime with them when they move to rural areas. This may partly result from media coverage of urban crime: people worry about things such as 'all the muggings' without necessarily being aware of where such crime is taking place. But some people whose experience of crime derives from city living continue to take similar precautions when they move to the country. Anderson (1997, p. 42) notes that some such incomers contribute to the sense of social malaise in isolated areas where they settle, not only because of their fear of crime but also through their failure to participate fully in rural life. Women, in particular, are cautious about going out at night if they have lived in urban areas, and this does not change when they move to the country. They bring what Anderson (1997, p. 46) calls their urban baggage with them.

Yarwood and Edwards (1995) note the paradox whereby crime prevention initiatives are easiest to organize in the very areas where they are least needed: in rural parts of the country the establishment of Neighbourhood Watch schemes arises, at least partly, from concern about the withdrawal of a police presence in local communities. It is in sparsely populated areas with relatively low crime rates that such community activism is least needed; the number of schemes is relatively higher in areas where the risk of crime is lower (Husain, 1988, p. 43). But crime prevention initiatives have a number of functions apart from primary prevention: if they increase public faith in the police, provide a focus for community organization, and bring people together to raise awareness of specific crime prevention measures, they have clearly served a useful function. Their relatively high concentration in low-crime areas may also serve an ideological function, giving middle-class volunteers a stake in active citizenship (Yarwood and Edwards, 1995, p. 450) and encouraging partnership between statutory and voluntary agencies in crime prevention initiatives (Yarwood and Edwards, 1995; Crawford, 1997).

The literature also suggests that there is greater fear of crime in rural areas which are subject to rapid change. This was first observed in America in the 1980s, where settled communities experiencing rapid population growth and concomitant social change were also characterized by an increase in fear of crime. This did not coincide with an increase in informants' experiences of criminal victimization (Krannich et al., 1989). Similarly, Scottish research suggests that in settled communities, crime and incivility tend to be blamed upon strangers and incomers, including day visitors who are believed to target the rural communities for their depredations (Anderson, 1997). Again, this perception may not be borne out by experience, but it demonstrates that anxiety about crime can sometimes represent a displacement of other social stresses (the social disruption hypothesis).

(c) Discretion, self-reliance and rural cultures

1. Police culture   Rural police practices and traditions are distinctive in a number of ways. First, as suggested above, there are powerful incentives encouraging informal approaches to law enforcement, which can lead in turn to lower rates of recorded crime, at least of the more minor kind. Officers may find themselves mediating between a complainant and an alleged offender, and trying to enforce an agreed compromise between their interests, using the carrot of avoiding formal proceedings. This is probably becoming less prevalent as a result of changes in policing patterns, but persists in the most isolated areas (Anderson, 1997). In many country areas the difficulty involved in escorting and supervising prisoners is likely to act as an additional disincentive to holding people in custody except where absolutely necessary (Hirst, 1994).

The police in rural areas tend to be more fully integrated in the local community than their urban colleagues, who often have little direct connection with the areas they police (Dingwall, chapter 6; Young, 1993). This is likely to accentuate the tendency to favour informal approaches in rural policing.

Police officers are likely to share the common rural belief that country areas pose little or no threat to law and order, and that the cities and their overspill areas are dens of iniquity in comparison (Young, 1993). Given the conservative and punitive culture of many rural courts (Lloyd, 1994), detected crime is thus likely to be treated more seriously than in urban areas where it is more commonplace. Crime is also quite likely to be confused and conflated with other disapproved activities: Neighbourhood Watch schemes in some areas, for example, have taken it upon themselves to monitor the movements of New Age Travellers (Yarwood and Edwards, 1995), and residents of one small Shropshire market town applied for Home Office funding for closed-circuit television because of concern about vandalism, shoplifting and gangs of young people hanging around. Research in Scotland found that there was considerable interest in the possibilities presented by CCTV in small towns in rural areas there, and the main impetus for such initiatives was to 'address public anxiety about crime and to reduce the fear of victimization in town centres' (Anderson, 1997, p. viii).

Valid as these aims may be, their implementation would broaden the net of surveillance considerably: CCTV is normally only cost-effective, and justifiable in terms of the possible infringement of civil liberties, in high-crime areas.

Police culture changes only slowly. The effectiveness of police attempts to keep victims of crime informed of developments in relation to their case has remained poor, both in urban and in rural areas (Koffman, 1996), despite the provisions of the Victim's Charter (Home Office, 1996). Better service to victims became a priority in some metropolitan police areas in the early 1990s, mainly with a view to improving witness care in order to secure a greater proportion of convictions. More recently, the witness care arrangements in semi-rural Staffordshire have met with favourable publicity, and its specialist witness care department serves rural and urban parts of the county equally well. It is now being imitated elsewhere, after being praised by the chief inspector of constabulary (Williams, 1999).

2. Rural culture A number of aspects of rural culture have an impact upon crime and crime victims. It has been argued that rural residents are more conformist (Moody, chapter 1) and conservative (Cloke and Davies, 1992), and that criminal justice is operated differently in rural areas – but that there are few generalizable patterns because rural areas are so heterogeneous (Dingwall, chapter 6). It would seem safe to say that in sparsely populated areas people whose behaviour is out of the ordinary are more conspicuous, and that the level of density of acquaintanceships tends to be higher outside urban areas: people in the country are more likely to know one another personally (Weisheit and Wells, 1996). Although the recent trend towards migration out of the cities has weakened such characteristics to some extent, this has not noticeably increased the degree of social equality in country areas (Francis and Henderson, 1992), and rural conservatism, rooted in a deferential culture, is reflected in local politics: 'Most rural local authorities are conservative in outlook, and tend to spend less per capita on services than their urban counterparts' (Francis and Henderson, 1992, p. 10).

Confidentiality is a difficult issue in respect of both rural offenders and victims. People sentenced to undertake community service are much more visible when carrying out their community work in their own neighbourhood, rural victims (particularly of serious crime) find it hard to avoid questions about the reasons for the visits they receive from representatives of criminal justice agencies, and victims and offenders (and their families) are more likely to be known to one another in country areas, which can cause difficulties (Kosh and Williams, 1995; NACRO, 1997; Harding, 1994). These may include reprisals by offenders against witnesses (Parry, n.d.). In rural environments, people have more face-to-face interactions with one another than urban dwellers do, and maintain close scrutiny of each other's activities and properties (Weisheit and Wells, 1996). There may be a different understanding of the concepts of private and public in rural areas: it may be more than a stereotype to suggest that people living in cities are relatively anonymous, and more tolerant of nonconformity than country-dwellers (Moody, chapter 1).

At times, victims are deterred from using services because of concerns about the lack of confidentiality, an example being the difficulties of gaining confidential access to the services of Women's Aid groups (Henderson, 1997). In Northumberland survivors' groups are held on market days in premises to which members might be going for other reasons, such as GPs' surgeries, in recognition of the need for privacy. It can be very difficult for women in rural areas even to visit the doctor's surgery: if they work at home, as many farmers and agricultural workers' wives do, and if they are poor, as many rural inhabitants are, this isolation and poverty can aggravate the effects of domestic violence. In close-knit communities women may also fear ostracism if they speak out about male violence. In many isolated areas, however, there is also a problem with access to information about the services available: research in Scotland found that many women did not know where to go for help, and this was exacerbated by services' lack of resources and consequent inability to undertake outreach and follow-up work (Henderson, 1997).

Rural dwellers also have, and take pride in, a tradition of self-reliance. Informal justice, and a reluctance to inform on neighbours, may be part of this self-help ethos in many areas (Wood and Schwarz, 1996; Anderson, 1997). It may be that the self-help ethos has been built upon 'the sense of neglect by public authorities that more remote communities have experienced, the feeling that very little will happen unless you do it yourselves' (Francis and Henderson, 1992, pp. 23–4). In practice, its operation seems likely to reinforce existing social divisions, particularly where the same, small group of people runs all the local community groups (Francis and Henderson, 1992).

While the tendency to keep one's own counsel about known offenders has its parallels in urbanized areas, the combination of informality and self-help in rural areas may lead to higher tolerance of some forms of antisocial behaviour. Examples, it has been suggested, include domestic violence (Anderson, 1997) and heavy drinking (NCVO, 1995). Rural communities also seem to tolerate harassment of oppressed groups such as Travellers and black people. While racism may be 'associated in the popular imagination with inner cities', racial harassment appears to be quite a common (though under-researched) rural phenomenon (Koffman, 1996, p. 90). For its victims it is a very isolating experience, and it is likely to be experienced as more personal and more individually targeted in a rural area (Parry, n.d.).

(d) Centralization

The police, the courts, probation and other agencies have increasingly centralized their operations in rural areas, and this has had important consequences for the delivery of criminal justice (see Davies, chapter 9). As small rural courts, police stations and social services and probation offices have closed, victims, witnesses, offenders and personnel all have further to travel. Centralization may mean that specialist services become more difficult to access, although part of the rationale of closing local offices may well have been to improve the newly centralized resources available. Staff who have to travel long distances to see clients may be too busy, or too tired, to practise in innovative ways. In lowland rural areas of Scotland there is concern about reductions in the level of police patrols and low levels of perceived police interest in rural crime problems (Anderson, 1997, citing Shucksmith et al., 1996).

While urban policing was the first to become more remote, reactive and specialized, these trends are being followed in rural areas. Reiner (1994, p. 757) has pointed out that specialization in policing makes the service more impersonal and inaccessible, and that this is likely to increase: 'Local police providing services to particular communities will remain, but with sharp differences between service-style organisations in stable suburban areas, and watchman bodies with the rump duties of the present police, keeping the lid on underclass symbolic locations.' Dingwall (chapter 6) has argued that this process may lead to a polarization between urban and rural policing styles, which are already very different. Indeed, if the trend towards greater centralization continues to mean the withdrawal of police resources from rural areas, the current informality of rural policing will soon become a thing of the past.

Similarly, the centralization of the courts service presents problems in rural areas. After a reorganization in Wiltshire residents of Malmesbury found that they had to travel twenty-six miles (two hours by bus) to their local magistrates' court in Wootton Bassett (Crallan, forthcoming). Court closures in North Yorkshire and in other sparsely populated areas have had similar effects, and bus services there are poorer still. One consequence is that victims of crime are likely to be reluctant to report crimes and to attend court as witnesses (unless the police escort them, as they do in more serious cases), and they may be less likely to receive compensation when this might be appropriate. Where they are required to attend it can be at considerable inconvenience.

In the case of the probation service rural offices are being left alone in some parts of the country and rationalized in others. The increasing tendency to concentrate on the core business of crime prevention and the supervision of more serious offenders has made it very difficult to introduce new services for victims, and the type of training and supervision required by specialists working with victims of crime is harder to come by in rural areas. As a result, some rural and semi-rural probation areas are only now beginning to implement the provisions of the 1990 and 1996 Victim's Charters (Williams, 1996).

Voluntary organizations are not exempt from the pressure towards centralizing service provision. While Victim Support, for example, covers the whole of the UK, it can be very difficult to provide services in remote rural areas to the same level as those provided in urban settings. A Victim Support scheme based in a market town may find it easier to recruit volunteers from that area than in the remoter parts of its catchment area. National policy has favoured collaboration between rural Victim Support schemes in England and Wales; a structural review has emphasized the need for greater co-ordination at a county level, causing some tensions within the organization. There is, for example, a concern among some rural volunteers that resources and policies may become more urban-focused at the expense of the interests of rural victims. In Scotland schemes have been rationalized to make them coterminous with local authority boundaries, necessitating a large number of mergers.

(e) Rural deprivation

Crime creates greater difficulty for victims who are already vulnerable for other reasons (Williams, 1999). The popular image of country life fails to recognize the widespread nature of rural poverty, which 'may compound anxiety about crime, especially for older people, who make up a higher proportion of the population than in urban areas' (Anderson, 1997, p. 2). The context of much rural crime is in fact one of social decay, poverty and deprivation. A fifth, or perhaps even a quarter of all rural residents live in, or on the margins of, poverty (ACRE, n.d; Cloke and Davies, 1992; Crallan, forthcoming). This high level of poverty, combined with other factors such as unemployment, transport difficulties and problems in gaining access to rationalized services, points to widespread rural deprivation and disadvantage. Declining services may have a disproportionate effect upon already disadvantaged rural residents (Francis and Henderson, 1992). In addition 'the in-migration of affluent newcomers . . . can increase the subjective and objective relative deprivation of local, non-propertied households' (Cloke and Davies, 1992, p. 350).

The impact of crime is likely to be greater in the context of rural disadvantage. For example, the theft of a car is more serious when the owner lives in an area where there is little or no public transport: 75 per cent of rural parishes in England have no daily bus service (Ramesh, 1998), and the loss of a vehicle may lead to losing a job. Offences against small businesses operating in rural areas may also have more severe consequences, leading in some cases to the closure of shops or firms which were already operating on tight margins. Burglary may also be more traumatic for victims who live in isolated areas and for whom it is a rare experience, including non-domestic burglaries (Husain, 1995).

Victims of crime may be vulnerable by reason of their age, or because they belong to more than one vulnerable group. The impact of victimization can be heightened for a combination of reasons, of which the victim's age may be one.

Young people, trapped in rural areas by their lack of access to transport, can come to be perceived as problematic by older people by virtue of their mere presence. This is aggravated when there is also a lack of specific provision for their entertainment, and few rural areas have attractive alternatives to the pubs, in which many under-eighteen year-olds spend their leisure time (Tuck, 1989). Indeed, there is some evidence that facilities for young people in rural areas have diminished rather than increased in recent years. Such young people are increasingly likely to be found hanging around and drinking, misusing drugs, making unwelcome noise and committing petty acts of vandalism (Anderson, 1997). While they would conventionally be regarded as a nuisance, and often treated as offenders, these young people are also vulnerable to criminal victimization: 'Young people have long been positioned outside the boundaries of the "ideal victim". Official and popular discourse about crime tends to view young people as "trouble", rather than as regular users of public space vulnerable to its attendant risks' (Loader 1996, p. 93).

The process of criminalization of young people has accelerated in recent years (Davis and Bourhill, 1997), and it has arguably made them more vulnerable, as they receive little sympathy when they report offences to the police (and are correspondingly disinclined to do so). While they are all too visible when their presence or behaviour is seen as problematic, young people seem somehow to become invisible when they are the victims of abuse or crime. Young people in general, and children in particular, are neglected as victims of crime (Loader, 1996; Anderson and Leitch, 1996; Morgan, 1988; Morgan and Zedner, 1992), and this is likely to be as true in rural as in urban areas.

Older people, although generally less likely to suffer criminal victimization than members of other age groups, are often also vulnerable in other ways, and they tend to report that crime has a high and long-lasting impact upon them compared to younger victims. As Wood and Schwarz (1991, p. 73; see also Williams, 1999) found 'victimization patterns are not necessarily age specific but are related to factors which are more common in the elderly such as poverty, dependency and social isolation'.

Constraints upon Service Delivery in Rural Areas

A number of the characteristics of rural areas mentioned in previous sections indicate likely problems in service delivery to victims of crime in such areas. Sparse population levels and Conservative local authorities combine to depress the levels of resources committed to rural criminal justice agencies, and this leads to difficulties in maintaining service provision. Where resources are concentrated with a view to ameliorating such difficulties, this can create new problems of delay and difficulties in gaining access to services (Harding, 1994).

When agencies are prevailed upon to pool their resources this can create new pressures. Hurley (1994, p. 108) gives the example of a shift in policy by the police in Powys. At one time, all domestic-violence incidents were referred to the local Women's Aid group. When the decision was taken to move 'towards a multi-agency approach' and involve Victim Support in responding to domestic violence referrals, this new work was not especially welcome: a sudden influx of referrals requiring unusually intensive contact made considerable demands upon the resources of a small Victim Support scheme, even if it suited the purposes of the police.

On the other hand, national guidelines such as the National Standards which apply to statutory criminal justice agencies seem to have been drawn up 'for some mythical urban client, easily accessible and regular in their habits' (Crallan, forthcoming). The assumptions underlying such standards may be quite wrong in respect of the rural setting: it is likely to take longer for agencies to reach people, and for cases to reach court, owing, for example, to longer geographical distances and longer gaps between court sittings. Nationally imposed standards of service, intended to guarantee a minimum standard across the country, may create unanticipated pressures if applied inflexibly. Indeed, equal opportunities for service users may best be achieved in rural areas through flexibility rather than a uniform approach to service provision. As Crallan (forthcoming) notes in respect of the probation service: 'We could start by including location as part of our Equal Opportunities statement, so that the premise that a repertoire of approaches is needed in a mixed urban and rural county is endorsed at a fundamental level.' One of the probation staff interviewed for this chapter made a similar point, noting that 'Rurality has yet to be recognized as an issue which has implications for all policies – as equal opportunities once was' (senior probation officer, small market town in northern England).

Funding is an obvious constraint upon the provision of services to rural victims. Rural services of many kinds are in decline (ACRE, n.d.), but rural areas attract low levels of government funding, and the formulae by which it is calculated include no weightings in respect of higher transport and other costs. Specialist services may be capable of travelling to visit victims (as in the case of some semi-rural police forces' witness care units, or probation officers in their victim-liaison role) but most are located in urban centres. Until the additional costs of supporting victims in rural areas are recognized, they are likely to continue to have difficulty in gaining access to services, making do with those which have the resources to undertake outreach work or to staff rural offices.

The Deficiencies of Policy on Rural Victims

In summary, two questions arise in considering the deficiencies of existing policies in respect of victims of crime in rural areas. First, have such policies been formulated with reference to the research findings reviewed above? Secondly, is there a recognition that, as suggested above, rural service provision raises specific questions of equal opportunities and equality of access to justice?

Dissatisfaction with police responses to victims of crime arises partly from the failure to respond to the findings of previous research. Koffman (1996) finds the low level of confidence in the police expressed by respondents to the Aberystwyth Crime Survey surprising. Part of the explanation is that 'those who have been recent victims of crime are less satisfied with the police than those respondents who have not been victims' (p. 100).

Previous research has consistently shown that victims expect the police to keep them informed about the progress of the case against their offender, and to explain the workings of the criminal justice system to them. These findings are reflected in the Victim's Charter (Home Office, 1996) and in circular instructions to the police (Home Office, 1988). The Aberystwyth survey revealed that 'victims were more likely than not to be dissatisfied with the amount of information they were given by the police about the progress of their investigation' (Koffman, 1996, p. 107).

Where compensation was an issue, only 12 per cent of victims were given information about how to claim it. Only in 40 per cent of the cases where offenders were identified were victims told what became of them. (Research by a police officer in another rural area found that victims of repeated domestic burglaries were as likely as not to receive no advice about crime prevention, despite Home Office urgings to implement the findings of research which showed that such repeat victimization could be substantially reduced by giving appropriate advice; see Murray, 1997). These findings are surprising only to the extent that one might have expected a rural police force, with a closer relationship with its public than its urban counterparts, to do something about such research findings – which replicate those of previous studies carried out in urban and mixed areas.

Lloyd (1994) notes that rural benches of magistrates are often made up of people who are all very similar to each other, and she suggests possible ways of improving their training and increasing their experience. Yarwood and Edwards's research (1995, p. 457) demonstrates that volunteers involved in rural voluntary agencies are predominantly male, middle-class, retired people, and that Neighbourhood Watch schemes in particular favour 'those people with the time and assets to help themselves and who may be quite often in least need of help'.

It would not be unduly difficult or expensive to initiate projects aimed at broadening the range of people involved in voluntary work in rural areas, and this might do something to increase awareness of issues of equality, but there seems at present to be no national policy steer in this direction.

The probation service's commendable attempts to review the quality of its work in rural areas raised a number of what one internal inspection report called 'questions of equity' (NYPS, 1997). Like a similar report commissioned by Norfolk Probation Service (Graham and Hollyer, 1996), this document reviews only probation work with offenders. This is perhaps not surprising, given the Home Office's failure to translate the provisions of the Victim's Charter into circular instructions, or to incorporate them in National Standards, until the mid-1990s (Williams, 1996). While it is regrettable that the opportunity to review the services received by victims of crime in rural areas has so far been missed, some of the findings of the inspections of work with offenders raise relevant issues, mostly to do with the need for flexibility in working in rural settings, and the extra visibility of offenders and probation staff working in rural areas. Such flexibility should also apply to work with victims, who are also likely to feel very exposed when accessing services.

Criminal justice agencies are sometimes constrained by national policies which appear to have been devised without reference to the specific difficulties of providing a service in rural areas. Hirst's research on the Police and Criminal Evidence Act 1984 gives a good example. The provisions of the Act create real problems in remote areas, requiring prisoners to be escorted long distances by uniformed officers with few obvious benefits in terms of defendants' rights (which the legislation was designed to protect). She concludes that rural police forces 'now operate in a legal regime designed to govern the quite different problems of the inner cities, and it is not one that suits them' (Hirst, 1994, p. 97).

Such legislation should be preceded by research and implemented experimentally before it is introduced. Where this does not happen it is easy to fail to anticipate difficulties in specific areas such as rural west Wales. It can be more difficult to find ways of reacting flexibly once the law is in force.

Services to Victims in Rural Areas – Statutory and Voluntary

We have seen that services can be more difficult for victims to find out about, and gain access to, in rural areas, and that many specialist facilities are concentrated in the cities. However, it is also clear that flexible service provision can overcome some of these difficulties, in a range of criminal justice agencies.

Service provision is affected by the same factors as the rural experience of victimization: isolation, shortage of resources, cultural factors and centralization. Taking Victim Support schemes as an example, this can be briefly illustrated with reference to rural groups. Volunteers may be isolated, receiving few referrals and being expected to cover a large area. They may find it hard to get to the scheme's office or to talk to its co-ordinator face to face, and it is difficult and expensive to bring them together for regular training. In some areas, however, the co-ordinator travels around a large rural area holding several volunteer support meetings with small groups of people each month (Hurley, 1994; Brown and Young, 1995). Small schemes can find it difficult to cover isolated areas where no volunteers live (Parry, n.d.). Some schemes are run from their co-ordinators' homes, and in small, close-knit communities confidentiality can be hard to maintain (Kosh and Williams, 1995; Brown and Young, 1995). Traditions of self-reliance may make some victims reluctant to accept help. Centralization of the court system can pose problems of access (Parry, n.d.).

There may, however, be positive aspects to the rural experience. Agency staff who find it difficult to implement national or regional policies in rural areas develop ingenious solutions and use individual contacts to find creative alternatives (Hankinson, 1998; Mullender, 1996). Small Victim Support schemes operating in areas with low crime levels may not need to filter the referrals they receive from the police in the way busy urban schemes do, and rural victims may thus receive a more personal service (Gill and Mawby, 1990).

On the one hand, people may be particularly isolated in rural settings, and where a victim lives some distance from the nearest neighbour this may increase feelings of vulnerability. On the other hand, 'the potentially invasive nature of rural social relationships may pose problems. For example, a victim of domestic violence may feel inhibited about seeking help because she (or he) does not want the whole community to know' (Anderson, 1997, p. 85). Then again, neighbours who take an interest in one's property and activities maintain informal surveillance and may offer spontaneous support at times of crisis. While much of the literature looks at the problems of rural life, 'the necessity of finding solutions to them can lead to better practice' (Hankinson, 1998, p. 83).

Workers in rural areas tend to form personal relationships with people working in other community agencies, and to seek flexible ways of responding to needs, such as outreach work and mobile office facilities. At times, this kind of collaboration can be frustrated by bureaucratic requirements. One example is the creation of formal partnerships between probation services and voluntary agencies. The need for financial accountability means that such partnerships have to be governed by service-level agreements, which are sometimes too much for small, voluntary agencies to handle. Where such agreements are made, local probation staff may find that formal processes and structures demand considerable time and attention which might have been spent in planning and providing services at a local level (Kosh and Williams, 1995). One county probation service, for instance, made a formal agreement with the Citizens' Advice Bureau in an urban area which gave its staff a wider remit than the geographical area it had previously covered, causing potential confusion in rural areas where informal referral systems already existed to local bureaux. Similarly, local liaison over services for women subjected to domestic violence may be superseded by a county-level Domestic Violence Forum involving more senior staff. This is all well and good if the county forum is initiating services of benefit to the women concerned, but in some cases such groups have been criticized as talking shops. At worst, they can become a smokescreen to disguise inaction (Hague 1997, p. 93), a mere public relations exercise without practical substance, and this is very frustrating for those who have often worked away for years in rural areas building up the relationships necessary for the provision of effective support.

Future Trends

The future of services for victims of crime in rural areas depends to a large extent upon central government policy towards rural areas: the trends identified above, such as centralization and the marginalization of the rural fringes, could be reversed if there were the political will to do so. Local actors also have the potential to influence service provision, however, and this section will concentrate upon these possibilities.

Rural magistrates have been vocal, in some places, in defending rural courts threatened with closure. While it is unusual to see criminal justice services at the centre of such campaigning, it is clearly important that rural areas are served by courts, police, probation and other services which are not only accessible but also identifiably located within the community they serve. Some rationalizations have left service users having to cross into unfamiliar areas to gain access to basic services. Such reorganization can and should be resisted, particularly where there is evidence that decentralized services are effective. As Hankinson (1998, p. 86) puts it, 'I see an opportunity for this insistence on demonstrating effective practice to be a catalyst to shift the Probation Service away from its centralised bureaucratic focus on process and procedure towards a Service focused more on accountable, flexible, locally based practitioners.'

The same argument can surely be made in respect of magistrates' courts, police stations and voluntary agencies (which also have their centralizing tendencies; see Kosh and Williams, 1995). It should be possible to provide specialist services in remoter areas, either by encouraging experienced practitioners to work there, or by devising innovative, often individually tailored, service-delivery methods. This is much more easily done by services which have staff working on the ground in rural areas and by interacting with a variety of other professionals and volunteers to devise solutions to the problems of rural working. Such liaison work may in urban areas be viewed as a specialist community approach, but in rural work it is part of the routine necessary to achieve effective service delivery (Hankinson, 1998).

Thus Crime Concern has helped the Forest of Dean District Council to identify a strategy for preventing the criminal victimization of young people and providing support for victims (Crime Concern, 1996). In a separate initiative, the council has collaborated with the local police, women's refuge, Victim Support scheme and other voluntary agencies to protect and advise women in fear of domestic violence. In such cases, and with other offences involving repeat victimization, electronic alarms are installed, linked to a central control unit. These projects are part of a community safety strategy begun in 1996, and they demonstrate what can be achieved through inter-agency work in a small, rural authority (albeit one which gives a high priority to victim support and protection).

While specialist services cannot always be made easily accessible to crime victims in rural areas, there is demonstrable 'scope . . . particularly in rural areas, for the development of models of service delivery which will take account of the small numbers and variable levels of demand' (Paterson and Tombs, 1998, p. 3). It takes time for new services to put down roots in rural areas, and rural community development involves a greater element of trust-building and outreach work than might be necessary in densely populated urban settings (Brown, 1995). This is likely to be all the more true in respect of services for a sensitive group such as victims of crime, but careful preparation can produce innovative services, as in the Forest of Dean.

It will clearly be necessary for criminal justice services in areas with a significant rural component to review their current practices and policies to ensure that they do not disadvantage rural victims of crime. At present, as we have seen, many policies do so inadvertently and unreflectingly. While it is encouraging to see that some in the probation service, and the police in particular, are researching the needs of rural residents, little of this work has so far focused upon victims of crime, and much more needs to be done. It would be particularly helpful if there were a wider recognition that rural service users have different needs, and that rural living has particular implications in terms of their needs. As noted above, Crallan (forthcoming) has suggested that 'we could start by including location as part of our equal opportunities statement'. This would indeed begin a discussion, which has largely yet to take place, about the distinctive needs of rural victims.

Conclusion

Part of the problem is a lack of relevant research and theory (which the present book will at least begin to remedy). As Phillips and Skinner (1994, p. 43) noted in their report on rural youth work,

> Without a historically legitimate body of knowledge about the needs of rural young people and appropriate responses, rural workers can find themselves cast adrift . . . Colleagues might find it hard to believe the assertion that that there are difficulties about delivering a service in a rural area.

This absence of theory makes it difficult for rural criminal justice workers to establish a need for dedicated resources and distinctive approaches to work in rural areas. National policies are made without consideration of distinctively rural implications. Only when there is more and stronger evidence of the particular needs of rural victims is this likely to change.

Most criminologists have shown little awareness of rural crime and victimization, although the fact that their research is urban-based and may not apply to rural areas is often not made explicit. Meanwhile, 'research that emphasises a distinctly rural perspective is limited' (O'Connor and Gray, 1989, p. 176).

American criminologists have renewed their interest in the question of rural and urban differences in crime (Weisheit and Wells, 1996), and practitioners in this country have begun organizing conferences on rural youth and probation work in recent years (Phillips and Skinner, 1994; Hankinson, 1998). There has been almost no research about the specific experiences and needs of rural victims, and work is also needed on issues such as how to 'build upon the existing capacity of rural communities to deal with [crime] issues without recourse to formal criminal justice' (Anderson, 1997, p. 90).

This chapter demonstrates the need not only for further research, but also for better and more consistent service provision. Funding is unlikely to be made available for large-scale research studies until there is wider understanding of the need for different services for rural victims. Interested groups and individuals may need to join forces and publicize the issues before this can be achieved. At present, the lack of relevant information is in danger of reducing the debate to a polemical one, generating more heat than light, and in view of the particular needs identified by what we do know, this is unfortunate.

References

ACRE (Action with Communities in Rural England) (n.d.). Information leaflet

ANDERSON, S. (1997) *A Study of Crime in Rural Scotland*, Edinburgh: Scottish Office Central Research Unit

ANDERSON, S. and LEITCH, S. (1996) *Main Findings from the 1993 Scottish Crime Survey*, Edinburgh: Scottish Office

BROWN, J. (1995) *The Trinity Project's Outreach Work*, London: National Council of Voluntary Organisations

BROWN, J. and YOUNG, C. (1995) *Substance Misuse in Rural Areas*, London: National Council of Voluntary Organisations

CLOKE, P. and DAVIES, L. (1992) 'Deprivation and lifestyles in rural Wales: towards a cultural dimension', 8 (4) *Journal of Rural Studies*, 349

CRALLAN, K. (forthcoming). 'Rural practice: vive la difference!', in Beaumont, B. (ed.), *Work with Offenders: A Progressive Approach*, Basingstoke: Macmillan

CRAWFORD, A. (1997) *The Local Governance of Crime: Appeals to Community and Partnerships*, Oxford: Clarendon Press

CRIME CONCERN (1996) *Crime Prevention and Young People in the Forest of Dean*, Report prepared for Forest of Dean District Council, Swindon: Crime Concern

DAVIS, H. and BOURHILL, M. (1997) 'Crisis: the demonisation of children and young people', in Scraton, P. (ed.), *Childhood in Crisis*, London: UCL Press

DONNERMEYER, J. F. and MULLEN, R. E. (1987) 'Use of neighbours for crime prevention: evidence from a state-wide rural victim study', 18 (1) *Journal of the Community Development Society*, 15

FRANCIS, D. and HENDERSON, P. (1992) *Working with Rural Communities*, Basingstoke: Macmillan

GILL, M. L. and MAWBY, R. I. (1990) *Volunteers in the Criminal Justice System*, Milton Keynes: Open University Press

GRAHAM, M. and HOLLYER, B. (1996) *Inspection of the Delivery of Equitable Service to Offenders in Rural Areas*, Norwich: Norfolk Probation Committee

HAGUE, G. (1997) 'Smoke screen or leap forward: interagency initiatives as a response to domestic violence', 17 (4) *Critical Social Policy*, 93

HANKINSON, I. (1998) 'Rural probation work and effective practice', 45 (2) *Probation Journal*, 82

HARDING, C. (1994) 'Research into criminal justice in rural areas', in Harding, C. and Williams, J. (eds), *Legal Provision in the Rural Environment: Legal Services, Criminal Justice and Welfare Provision in Rural Areas*, Cardiff: University of Wales Press

HENDERSON, S. (1997) *Service Provision to Women Experiencing Domestic Violence in Scotland*, Edinburgh: Scottish Office Central Research Unit

HIRST, P. (1994) 'Problems affecting rural policing', in Harding, C. and Williams, J. (eds.), *Legal Provision in the Rural Environment: Legal Services, Criminal Justice and Welfare Provision in Rural Areas*, Cardiff: University of Wales Press

HOME OFFICE (1988) Circular 20/1988, London: Home Office

HOME OFFICE (1996) *The Victim's Charter: A Statement of Service Standards for Victims of Crime*, London: Home Office Communications Directorate

HURLEY, L. (1994) 'Non-statutory support for victims and offenders', in Harding, C. and Williams, J. (eds.), *Legal Provision in the Rural Environment: Legal Services, Criminal Justice and Welfare Provision in Rural Areas*, Cardiff: University of Wales Press

HUSAIN, S. (1995) *Cutting Crime in Rural Areas: A Practical Guide for Parish Councils*, Swindon: Crime Concern

HUSAIN, S. (1988) *Neighbourhood Watch in England and Wales: A Locational Analysis*, London: HMSO

KOFFMAN, L. (1996) *Crime Surveys and Victims of Crime*, Cardiff: University of Wales Press

KOSH, M. and WILLIAMS, B. (1995) *The Probation Service and Victims of Crime: A Pilot Study*, Keele: Keele University Press

KRANNICH, R. S., BERRY, E. H. and GREIDER, T. (1989) 'Fear of crime in rapidly changing rural communities: a longitudinal analysis', 54 (2) *Rural Sociology*, 195

LLOYD, M. G. (1994) 'The magistrate in a rural area with particular reference to courts in west Wales', in Harding, C. and Williams, J. (eds), *Legal Provision in the Rural Environment: Legal Services, Criminal Justice and Welfare Provision in Rural Areas*, Cardiff: University of Wales Press

LOADER, I. (1996) *Youth, Policing and Democracy*, London: Macmillan

McCONVILLE, M. and SHEPHERD, D. (1992) *Watching Police, Watching Communities*, London: Routledge

MARTIN, C. (ed.) (1997) *The ISTD Handbook of Community Programmes for Young and Juvenile Offenders*, Winchester: Waterside Press

MORGAN, J. (1988) 'Children as victims', in Maguire, M. and Pointing, J. (eds), *Victims of Crime: A New Deal?*, Milton Keynes: Open University Press

MORGAN, J. and ZEDNER, L. (1992) *Child Victims: Crime, Impact and Criminal Justice*, Oxford: Clarendon

MULLENDER, A. (1996) *Rethinking Domestic Violence: The Social Work and Probation Response*, London: Routledge

MURRAY, A. (1997) *The Forgotten Few: A Study on Repeat Victims in Rural Areas – Domestic Burglary*, London: Home Office Police Policy Directorate

NACRO (National Association for the Care and Resettlement of Offenders) (1997) *Hanging around the Bus Stop: Youth Crime and Young Offenders in Rural Areas*, London: NACRO

NCVO (National Council for Voluntary Organisations) (1995) *Substance Misuse in Rural Areas*, London: Rural Team of NCVO

NETTLETON, H., WALKLATE, S. and WILLIAMS, B. (1997) *Probation Training with the Victim in Mind: Partnership, Values and Organisation*, Keele: Keele University Press

NEWBY, H. (1988) *The Countryside in Question*, London: Hutchinson

NYPS (North Yorkshire Probation Service) (1997) Report of internal inspection into supervision in rural areas, unpublished, Northallerton: NYPS

O'CONNOR, M. and GRAY, D. (1989) *Crime in a Rural Community*, Sydney, New South Wales: Federation Press

PARRY, G. (n.d.), 'Rural crime – victim support', unpublished paper by Victim Support field officer, London: Victim Support

PATERSON, F. and TOMBS, J. (1998) *Social Work and Criminal Justice: The Impact of Policy*, Social Work Research Findings No. 13, Edinburgh: Scottish Office Central Research Unit

PHILLIPS, D. and SKINNER, A. (1994) *Nothing Ever Happens around Here: Developing Work with Young People in Rural Areas*, Leicester: Youth Work Press

RAMESH, R. (1998) 'Going nowhere', 46 *Red Pepper* (March), 20

REINER, R. (1994) 'Policing and the police', in Maguire, M., Morgan, R. and Reiner, R. (eds), *Oxford Handbook of Criminology*, Oxford: Clarendon

SHAPLAND, J. and VAGG, J. (1988) *Policing by the Public*, London: Routledge

SHOEMAKER, R. B. (1991) *Prosecution and Punishment: Petty Crime and the Law in London and Rural Middlesex, c.1660–1725*, Cambridge: Cambridge University Press

SMITH, B. (1933) *Rural Crime Control*, New York: Columbia University Institute of Public Administration

TUCK, M. (1989) *Drinking and Disorder: A Study of Non-metropolitan Violence*, Home Office Research Study 108, London: HMSO

WEISHEIT, R. A. and WELLS, L. E. (1996) 'Rural crime and justice: implications for theory and research', 42 (3) *Crime and Delinquency*, 379

WILLIAMS, B. (1996) 'The probation service and victims of crime: paradigm shift or cop-out?', 18 (4) *Journal of Social Welfare and Family Law*, 461

WILLIAMS, B. (1999) *Working with Victims of Crime*, London: Jessica Kingsley

WOOD, H. and SCHWARZ, S. (1996) 'Structure of rural corrections', in McDonald, T. D., Wood, R. A. and Pflug, M. A. (eds), *Rural Criminal Justice: Conditions, Constraints and Challenges*, Salem, Wis.: Sheffield Publishing

YARWOOD, R. and EDWARDS, B. (1995) 'Voluntary action in rural areas: the case of Neighbourhood Watch', 11 (4) *Journal of Rural Studies*, 447

YOUNG, M. (1993) *In the Sticks: Cultural Identity in a Rural Police Force*, Oxford: Clarendon Press

ZEDNER, L. (1997) 'Victims', in Maguire, M., Morgan, R. and Reiner, R. (eds), *Oxford Handbook of Criminology*, 2nd edn, Oxford: Clarendon Press

11

De Profundis: Criminology at the Water's Edge

JILL PEAY

> Fifty years on from now, Britain will still be the country of long shadows on county grounds, warm beer, invincible green suburbs, dog lovers, and – as George Orwell said – old maids bicycling to Holy Communion through the morning mist.
>
> (John Major, 22 April 1993, to the Conservative Group for Europe)[1]

Once upon a time, a long time ago, one hitherto unknown and otherwise torpid rural community embarked upon the construction of a village pond. Unfortunately, everybody did not live happily thereafter. This chapter makes some tentative observations about the genesis, management and (partial) resolution of conflict in one small community. For in the process of building the pond the village encountered issues of justice and democracy, localism and mobility, feuds and feudalism, planning and risk management, vandalism, homespun conciliation, anonymous letters, threats of violence and funeral networking. Ultimately, the prospect of imminent death was confined below the waterline and amongst the 'lower' species, and other dramas came along to preoccupy the village. This chapter charts that transition and goes on to speculate widely and wildly about the nature and ramifications of control as exercised by 'communities'.

What follows is also written in the context of an awareness of (if not intimate familiarity with) the growing literature on notions of community and communitarianism (Crawford, 1996; Etzioni, 1995;

---

[1] The title of and impetus for this chapter are wholly attributable to Philip Stenning, of the Centre for Criminology, University of Toronto. He bears no responsibility for its more expansive tone, which has evolved from a conversation into a monolith. During its lengthy gestation a number of people were either exposed to it or commented on it, thereby adding momentum and depth to the process. However, I am particularly grateful, as ever, to Andrew Ashworth.

Lacey and Zedner, 1995; Nelken, 1985). That literature has questioned the very notion of 'community'. None the less, the concept has a powerful symbolic value, as illustrated by John Major's invocation above of George Orwell's (1941) *England Your England* with its characteristic fragments of English life. It draws seemingly upon some golden and glorious past and acts as a focus for a future of stability to which we can all look forward and somehow share. Since the events detailed here took place in a quintessential southern English village, and yet bear little real relationship to these notions of a mythical, just-out-of-reach, idyllic community, this chapter seeks to challenge empirically some of the hidden assumptions about how communities function normatively. Finally, and perhaps most controversially, it makes the leap from 'the ecological to the pathological',[2] taking John Major's warm and comforting image and placing it against village life as epitomized by Miss Marple and Agatha Christie, where the darker side of human nature lurks just beyond the opening pages.

On Not So Golden Pond

As devotees of the Ambridge Archers will be aware, village life has the capacity to encompass dramas more readily associated with a bigger stage. Whilst the theatricality and self-sustaining momentum of village life provides a source of and meaning to life therein, the compactness of small communities creates a forum where direct action can have a direct effect, the embodiment of empowerment. In contrast to this broad canvas, villages also have their intimate side. For, as Yolande Bergin pointed out, village life and family life have much in common;[3] both are subject to mythical enhancement whilst their close confines can be, in reality, suffocatingly unendurable. Like 'the family', village life concentrates the impact of informal social control, so we have the opportunity not only to watch over our neighbours, but also to become involved in ever more entangled ways in their lives. 'Anonymity and village life' is a *non sequitur*. Notwithstanding, the names and places have been changed in an attempt to protect the guilty.

The saga commenced at some point after the Enclosure Act 1840 but before the arrival of any criminological antennae. Those events are not of primary concern, other than to note that local memories remained vivid of a child who had drowned in the village some years

---

[2] A phrase memorably coined by Andrew Ashworth.
[3] In response to a presentation of this piece at the British Criminology Conference in Belfast, July 1997.

earlier. Every year such tragedies occur up and down the country; their incidence, however, given the frequency of child–water inter-actions, is rare and their number, in contrast with child deaths on the road, modest.[4] In this context, the construction of a pond away from the centre and on a main route out of the village was unlikely to pose the greatest threat to the safety of straying toddlers. But, every child's death rightly has a powerful emotive impact, and the proposal to dig the pond and thereby introduce an additional hazard into the community proved divisive. It posed a perceived threat difficult to rebut with statistically based arguments.

However, the division, as it emerged, was drawn along more undulating lines and was clearly influenced by a clash of personalities and class. In the pro-pond camp were those who wished to bring water to a desert-like conservation area and encourage biological diversity; those who wanted to enhance the amenity value of the area; those fixed with the knowledge that funds had been obtained some years earlier by the Conservation Committee on the basis that a pond was to have been constructed; and those who merely lined up behind the chief pond agitator, a man whose family could be traced back for generations in the village and whose associations might most crudely be stereotyped along with the Grundy clan (for non-devotees – the wheelers and dealers of traditional rural life). Opposed to the pond were those who overtly worried about risk, management, cost and despoliation, but were primarily those who supported the leading light in the 'anti' camp (more akin to the likes of Linda Snell, enjoying the privilege of having been able to choose to live in the country). The motivations of this leading light were mixed but included a long-term dislike of the leader of the 'pro' camp, the

---

[4] Drowning is the third most common form of 'accidental' death amongst children under sixteen. In 1995 there was a total of 473 accidental drownings (all ages) of which 24 were 0–4 years; 8 were 5–9 and 11 were 10–14; most at risk were males and elderly adults. Boy toddlers are particularly prone, being too young to heed warnings, yet enjoying increased mobility in the context of decreased stability. Of the total drownings 2 per cent took place in garden ponds; but in this category, the risk to toddlers (aged 2–4) came from garden ponds in neighbours' or friends' houses; between 1990 and June 1994 thirty children under five had drowned in garden ponds. Even if these figures are an under-reporting (the methodology used by RoSPA entailed a survey of newspaper reports excluding suicides), they contrast markedly with the risk posed by traffic. In 1994 alone, 160 child pedestrians were killed in road accidents, and a further 42 child cyclists aged fifteen or under died on the roads (*Transport Statistics Great Britain 1995*, p.89, Table 4.14, Road accident casualties by road user type and severity); child pedestrians killed or seriously injured under fifteen: 4,610 for 1994 (DoT, *Road Accidents Great Britain 1994: The Casualty Report*, p.100, table 6c, All casualties: killed or seriously injured by road user type and age). All figures kindly supplied by RoSPA.

origins of which were unknown, but its manifestations had included official complaints about him for various alleged infringements of planning laws and failures to pay assorted taxes. For the record, the pro-pond agitator was not a man of diplomatic inclination, and over the years had alienated many in the village; the anti-pond conglomeration had all the requisite social skills and, moreover, dominated the small Conservation Committee. On the pond issue, the vast majority of villagers supported the development; however, the power to say no seemingly lay in the hands of the few.

Some years went by. The chief agitator resigned from the Conservation Committee in frustration at not being able to operate effectively in that forum (read 'get his own way'). The pond issue was shelved. The chief agitator grew ever more frustrated and angry. He organized a village petition, presented it to the parish council, who effected a swift exit saying responsibility had been devolved to the Conservation Committee and the villagers' wishes should be 'made known' to them (this, in a village of barely 600 people). The aforementioned committee met thereafter without notification and again rejected any movement towards the development of a village pond. When challenged they claimed that villagers were only entitled to attend their Annual General Meeting. Another would not now be held until the following year. This part of the saga becomes a little legalistic, but the motto is, 'She who fights by the rules can be slain by them.' The villagers called for an Extra-Ordinary Meeting which, following a marshalling of the forces, was packed by the pro-pond mob. A working party was established to consider the viability of a pond, draw up plans, raise the necessary funds and then refer back to the Conservation Committee.

All of this was done. One hundred hours later (the working party documented its labour in order to gain the benefit of a Rural Action scheme which matched labour with funds) the pond proposal was approved by the Conservation Committee (whose membership had changed over the intervening months) and digging commenced. Of course, it was not as simple as that, and a series of illustrations of art mirroring life might be mentioned. But that would be to digress.

However, the real problems only started once the water was in the pond, an event which unhappily coincided with the start of the summer holidays (in legal jargon, an inducement; in common parlance, the devil making work for idle hands). Jokes had abounded about the pond being incomplete until it had received its first shopping trolley, but it was only a matter of days after the erection of a sign at the pond site asking children to stay out of the water (not warning of the dangers of drowning but of the mess that contact with the blue clay lining would cause to their clothes) that the wooden placard was taken down and thrown into the pond. Three youths were witnessed leaving the site with the tell-tale signs on their shoes. Word got back to the chief pond agitator, who stormed about the village veering between advocating the need for the reintroduction of corporal punishment (which had never gone out of fashion in his family) and the possibility of contacting the local community policewoman for her to speak to the children/parent(s) directly (of course, the 'culprits' had been identified and convicted with all process due in a small community). The possibility of alerting the parent(s) to a civil claim for compensation was canvassed. The full might of the law was to be invoked. Zero tolerance *par excellence*.

As it happened, on the evening of the incident in question the village was benefiting from the visit of the eminent international criminologist, Philip Stenning.[5] He introduced the work of John Braithwaite (1989) into the discussions as they took place outside the village pub, and proposed that the culprits might be re-employed by the committee for the duration of the summer holidays as 'pond wardens' explicitly charged with protecting the pond from vandalism. Although this solution was put to the chief pond agitator, he none the less preferred 'neck wringing'. However, he was prepared to settle for 'speaking' to the culprits in front of their parents. For this he duly took responsibility.

The immediate consequences of this action, and the possibility that some form of parental discipline was inflicted, are unknown. But as the months passed by the recriminations transformed and escalated. Elder brothers and friends of the culprits and their friends from another village became involved and, like throwing a pebble into a pond, the repercussions rippled outwards. At first, it just entailed name-calling; the lads would pick on the chief pond agitator when they saw him out and about in the village. Later, they took to banging at night on the walls of his property and finally, during the winter, threw snowballs and other items at it. At one level, this might be regarded as harmless boisterous behaviour, but for one individual isolated on the receiving end it was an intimidating experience. Finally the 'victim' chose to confront one of the parents of the then troublesome group; regrettably this was one of his close neighbours. An articulate woman, she could not and would not believe that her privately educated son could have had anything to do with either the pond 'vandalism' (which he did not) or the alleged subsequent intimidation. In the absence of what he felt to be the necessary parental response, the adult 'victim' started to make noises about vigilantes

---

[5] Philip has asked to be described as a visiting meddler, but this seems to me far too modest.

and took to wandering about the village furnished with a home-made catapult with which he said he would defend himself. It remains unclear how real these threats were, but, as a means of alerting the concerned community, they had an immediate impact on villagers who had stood by hoping that matters would calm down. To those who witnessed his behaviour, there was no doubt about the reality of the violence he *threatened*[6] and the real sense of threat he had thus experienced. A genuine and urgent sense of apprehension led to an attempt by a counsellor in school bullying to negotiate between mother and son. In turn, this backfired, as family loyalties took precedence and tentative admissions became flat denials. Matters reached an unhappy impasse with both parties spreading rumours and making allegations about the behaviour of the other. Like most more mundane neighbour disputes, this issue invaded the very privacy of the two parties' homes; neither could escape from the perceived attentions of the other and both festered.

It took a funeral to bring about the climax of the affair. Regrettably, and shortly before Christmas, the boy's mother received the most threatening of anonymous letters. She automatically assumed it was from her neighbour; tearful recriminations followed, together with accusations that this all stemmed from the pond. On learning of the anonymous letter, her neighbour admitted to another that he had told of his troubles to his extended family, who lived in the nearby market town. The clan had recently gathered in the village for a family funeral. It was entirely possible, the alleged perpetrator remarked, that one or more of his family had taken independent action on his behalf. But he had no knowledge of this and no control over them. Frantic shuttle diplomacy between the two warring parties narrowly avoided the involvement of the police. A tacit agreement was reached that both parties would avoid contact with each other, although neither had, of course, been initiating such contact. It would be untrue to say that harmony ensued, for aggravation and its sequelae may well have continued in private, but others in the village were no longer publicly drawn in.

Real Life Reflecting Real Life

The sequence of events reflects much of what we know; the risks which crystallized from the pond were not the high-profile and

---

[6] One feature of the behaviour of the imminently violent remarked upon by forensic psychiatrists (familiar with the literature on the over-prediction of dangerousness) is the aura of danger some individuals manifest at points of crisis; whatever it is that experts under these time-limited conditions perceive, for them it feels real.

dramatic incidents most feared, but petty acts of vandalism by young people.[7] This is not to minimize either their impact on the community or their potential for escalation. But it does illustrate yet again that those matters which seemingly make people most fearful and which also attract media attention – whether they are killings by psychiatric patients or children drowning in icy ponds – are not those objectively about which people ought to feel most at risk. Experts on risk ask us to define more closely designedly nebulous matters. Risk to whom, under what circumstances, with what probability, how far in the future and with what degree of severity of damage? They are right to pose these questions, for in an era when risk has become, and will remain, central to our lives[8] we must be cautious of being seduced and infected by the predictive/preventive-reasoning notions of risk. Indeed, Feeley and Simon have argued that it is 'the management of danger and not the identification and sanctioning of guilty individuals' which is becoming the overwhelming task at hand; moreover, this shift in priorities is contributing to an emergent new criminal law, preoccupied not with 'such concepts as guilt, responsibility and obligation' (1994, p.194) or the treatment of individual offenders, but with techniques for 'identifying classifying and managing groups assorted by levels of dangerousness' (p.173). And, of course, such a paradigm shift is exemplified by the popularity of preventive and incapacitative reasoning embodied in the Crime (Sentences) Act 1997, with its mandatory sentences and 'hybrid orders' for psychopaths (Eastman and Peay, 1998), and in the Sex Offenders Act 1997, which requires convicted sex offenders to report their residential addresses.[9]

Another familiar lesson emerged from the saga; namely, that whilst the young people engaged in the visible offences, the adults were more sophisticated and less easily reprimanded. Identifying the author(s) of a threatening letter would have required forensic services beyond the village's resources; the matter was left satisfactorily unresolved beyond

[7] Illustrating Adrian Ground's observation that there is an important distinction to be drawn between worry and fear; see J. Crichton (ed.), *Psychiatric Patient Violence: Risk and Response* (London: Duckworth, 1995).

[8] For all the reasons Anthony Giddens documents wherein reflexivity – our impact on the world – causes us to create problems, for example BSE, for which we may never have any solutions; see *The Consequences of Modernity* (Cambridge: Polity Press, 1990).

[9] This provision may entail the police keeping track of upwards of 3,000 offenders convicted each year. The sex offenders' register is already encountering problems familiar to those who have worked with the 'Supervision Register': issues relating to confidentiality and the register's counter-productive consequences (namely, encouraging offenders to move with greater frequency and change their names in an attempt to 'go to ground').

a reasonable doubt, and no sanctions followed. Moreover, although community control could be effective, it was time-consuming and had the potential to magnify feelings as well as diffuse them. By and large, a tolerant looking away, even in a small community, was the most popular response. Few could have anticipated how close the community came (if it did) to actual bodily violence, or were able to identify what caused the persisters to desist. Finally, it is worth noting that in the two harsh winters that followed, necessitating 'Danger – Keep Off the Ice' signs to be erected at the pond, both were taken down as the ice melted and thrown into the water by unknown perpetrators. The signs were quietly fished out and no far-reaching inquiry instituted as to how they had got there. The lesson had been learnt that tolerance (without the tariff) had much to recommend it (see Hood, 1974).

Selective Reporting, Selective Enforcement and Victimization

The saga also touches on some broader issues. Although tentative, these observations arguably apply not just to a rural community for which the boundaries can be readily delineated, for even those who live in London are fond of saying that it is just a series of small villages. As Lacey and Zedner (1995; see also Bottoms, 1994; Nelken, 1985) have observed, in order for the notion of community to have any force, there has to be an outside threat which makes membership of the group attractive. Thus, the perception of being part of a community may have little to do with geographical boundaries.

First, self-report studies indicate that offending (and victimization) starts at an early age for both men and women and is widespread, even if primarily of a trivial nature. Yet 95 per cent of offenders go unconvicted and unpunished.[10] Even though one in three of the male

---

[10] The proportion may be even higher; Ashworth, for example, drawing on 'official' statistics argues that only 2 per cent of offences result in the punishment of individuals by the criminal justice system (*Sentencing and Criminal Justice*, London: Butterworths, 1995).This figure, of course, excludes those who agree to a caution, and does not take account of the number of offences which may be committed by individual offenders. For 1994, the *Criminal Statistics*, compiled by the Home Office, reveal that there were some 308,431 offenders cautioned for indictable and summary (non-motoring) offences (see table 116, vol.3 of the *Criminal Statistics*, Supplementary Tables for England and Wales). For the same period those found guilty of comparable offences amounted to 768,000 (rounded to the nearest thousand and taken from *Criminal Statistics*, table 5.10). Thus, approximately two and a half times as many offenders were convicted as cautioned. However, for 1994 the *Criminal Statistics* estimate that only some 27 per cent of crime committed was recorded (see table 2A, p.27, comparing the official statistics with the findings of the British Crime Survey). Thus, of the crimes committed (estimate 11,444,444) only some 6.7 per cent resulted in either cautions or convictions in 1994. The reality of the

population may be at risk of having an indictable conviction,[11] the figures generally indicate that there are huge selective enforcement strategies at work. And selective enforcement is magnified by the criminal justice system keeping its gaze focused on identifiable individuals who commit crime and on their subsequent processing.

There are, however, two sides to this coin. Selective enforcement does not mean just the alienation and potential further criminalization of sections of society; it means also that for some citizens, resort to criminal justice agencies and redress from them are not their solution of choice – even were it to be accessible to them in a society where justice is not democratically regulated. Hence, the community is involved in – whether as perpetrators, witnesses, victims or silent parties – and manages the vast bulk of offending against it and its members.[12]

Secondly, there has also been a dramatic growth in employment in the 'protective service occupations' (Taylor, 1995, p.2) and in what Ian Taylor describes as a 'vast new industry around crime prevention (of agency partnerships, volunteers, Neighbourhood Watch organisations, City Centre Partnerships, Pub Watches and Business Watches etc.)' (pp.19–20). However, such enterprise is arguably using community crime prevention initiatives to deter, displace or apprehend potential offenders who offend primarily against private property. As David Nelken has wryly commented, 'once the goal of reducing crime is being achieved – the criminals moved on and the internal enemy no more – presumably the neighbourhood will return to the quiet pursuit of contented suburban competitive individualism' (1985). So, community crime prevention is a different beast from those activities which attempt to involve and engage members in an investment in the community (for example, the pond, the annual round of village fêtes and other fund-raising activities, the erection of the village Christmas tree, entry into the 'Best Kept Village' competition etc.). Herein lies the divide between private and public. When public amenities and resources become vulnerable to attack, the community may not always respond by resort to the criminal justice agencies. Indeed, it is

criminal justice system is that the overwhelming majority of offences do not lead to official sanction.

[11] *The Criminal Statistics for England and Wales for 1994* note at p. 200, fig. 9.6: '34% of males born in 1953 had been convicted of a standard list offence by age 40.' For the 1973 cohort this figure drops because of the increased use of cautioning.

[12] As Paul Rock has commented, the failure of the police to tackle rising crime, and their ultimate recognition that they depended on the community to report and take an active part in the prosecution of crime, led to a new appraisal of the 'value' of communities. For Kenneth Newman, this meant inventing and co-opting community groups and generally invoking the community as being part of the solution to the problem of crime rather than part of its cause.

paradoxical that whilst Neighbourhood Watch clearly encourages direct contact with the police as a means of redress, it is one which, in turn, may lead to acute disappointment as communities come to recognize that the response of the police is not and cannot be all that it is cracked up to be in the initial enthusiastic stages of setting up a Neighbourhood Watch scheme. Increasingly, the police are coming to see Neighbourhood Watch as a means of community integration – namely, that other beast – regarded as valuable in itself and not as a hot line to police action and the apprehension of 'offenders'.

A further tentative distinction may be drawn. When the community watches over schemes in which it has a mutual rather than personal investment in the 'property', perhaps damage to that facility diffuses the sense of victimization. Does the community feel more able to take responsibility for intervening when it 'fails' rather than involving the police? Despite this caveat, the language of first resort remains the familiar; alternative responses to involving the police are explored only once the obvious have been rejected, and it remains possible that it is the inherent triviality of offences of vandalism against the community (as further diffused by the notion that it is not your property being damaged) which leads people away from the negative effects of becoming involved with the police.

None of this should come as any surprise to those intrigued by the relationship between criminology and the environment. As Brantingham and Brantingham have noted 'crime occurs when four things are in concurrence: a law, an offender, a target and a place' (cited in Bottoms, 1994), and by place they mean the interaction between time and space. To digress: if criminal activity is as widespread as self-report studies suggest, there are few innocents; most of us fall into the categories of the very young, the active or the reformed. How does this affect citizens' preparedness (a) to call the police, (b) to deal with situations themselves? It might be surmised that it is significantly easier to call the police and report stranger crime where the knowledge that any further interaction between perpetrator and victim is likely to be regulated and formalized and occur in circumstances where the victim can maintain the moral high ground. In cases of intra-family victimization or even rape the decision to involve formal agencies of control may be much more problematic; for example, for rape victims there can be no guarantee that their position as victim will be enshrined properly by the adversarial system, whilst for intra-family offences there is a high perceived risk of repeat or secondary victimization and/or other negative consequences which may follow a decision to go public. There is, and will be, a continuing relationship between the parties, and the criminal justice system cannot effectively distance them. Time and space tie the parties together. Bottoms adverts to this in his footnote observation of Brantingham and Brantingham's failure to embrace the study of the location of offender residence in their definition of the ecology of crime (p. 593).

Similarly, informal social control in your own backyard entails a likely enhancement of the 'relationship' between victim and perpetrator. If no formal agency is to create and maintain the distance, and yet homes, facilities and patterns of everyday movement make chance encounters inevitable, are neighbours less likely to intervene – more likely to turn a blind eye? Is crime tolerated as preferable to living with the consequences of perceived 'snitching' – a form of self-preservative tolerance? Thus, although much crime goes unreported through a natural reluctance to 'get involved', the fact that such involvement is likely to be sustained on a daily basis thereafter – not merely encapsulated by a few appearances at court – may further inflate non-reporting. Boundary disputes and noisy neighbours are two of the most acrimonious of legal conflicts, not necessarily arising out of their inherent harm, but because of the impossibility of escaping from them: existence and persistence coincide. Neighbours from hell are hellish because of their *proximity*. There is a perpetual reminder of the source of annoyance; like a sore tooth, one cannot keep from worrying at it.

In this context it is worth noting that current criminal justice policy and the thinking which might arguably inform it, strain in two different directions. New Labour's Crime and Disorder Act has been subject to trenchant criticism, particularly in respect of its introduction (to deal, for example, with noisy neighbours) of Anti-social Behaviour Orders (Ashworth et al., 1998). For this legislative response to community disorder will spread the criminalizing and stigmatizing net wider than ever; moreover, this response is essentially *exclusionary* and in extreme circumstances would result in the eviction of problematic members from a community. Yet, much interest has also concurrently been generated in concepts of restorative justice, designed to bring about more harmonious relationships within the community. Restorative conferences bring together

> offenders, victims and members of their respective communities, in order to discuss how the harm caused by the offending behaviour can be repaired . . . to promote repentence and reparation by the offender, reconciliation between victim and offender, and reintegration of communities damaged by crime.[13]

The intentions, therefore, are primarily *inclusionary.*

[13] R. Young and C. Hoyle (1997). This quotation is taken from their research proposal (published on the c-j-s forum) for an evaluation currently being conducted by the Oxford Centre for Criminological Research into the development of a restorative justice programme by Thames Valley Police. Restorative conferences have been the subject of much recent debate (see below Braithwaite and Mugford, 1994; Blagg, 1997; Braithwaite, 1997).

Fear of reprisals is, of course, one reason why crime is under-reported. It may also be one reason why so many prosecutions result in ordered acquittals, where witnesses or victims fail to show up at court to give evidence. As Block et al. note (1993, p. 12), 'ordered acquittals account for almost 70 per cent of all non-jury acquittals' and non-jury acquittals outweigh jury acquittals. Moreover, there was a steady increase in ordered acquittals during the period 1980–90. Lengthy delays in cases coming on for trial are unlikely to facilitate the ultimate appearance of a victim/witness at court, particularly where there is a pre-existing relationship between the accused and accuser. Indeed, as the researchers note, 'the most common explanation for non-jury acquittals were missing witnesses (14 per cent) and victims (10 per cent) which together accounted for a quarter of all acquittals, usually ordered' (ibid., p.41). A further 11 per cent of the non-jury acquittals notably came about because the victim refused to testify. Whether these victim/witnesses acted from fear, or because they had chosen a path of lesser resistance or because, in the intervening months, the community had in some form taken responsibility for the crime, is not clear.[14] It would be impossible to discern how victims weigh whether or not offenders have had their 'just deserts' before they receive their court-anointed deserved sentences. However, in a context where accused and accuser are known to one another, or become known through the crime, it is difficult to ascertain how the witness/victim's perception of the offender changes over time. There is some evidence that victims are less punitive towards their offender than they are towards the general mass of offenders;[15] and there is evidence that some victims may be satisfied with an explanation (why me?) and an apology, or with reparation without explicit punishment. Not unlike judges responding to counsel, it is easier to accommodate mitigation by an offender in whose presence one is. Again, it would be impossible to tease out responsive strategies based upon notions that an offender has been

[14] Recent Home Office research on high-crime estates found that more than 10 per cent of crimes reported to the police led to victims or witnesses being intimidated by the accused. The use of professional witnesses (council officials) and the extension of the categories of witness who can give evidence anonymously may help, but they cannot readily address witnesses' initial reluctance to involve the police because of the fear of reprisals. See *Speaking up for Justice: Report of the Interdepartmental Working Group on the Treatment of Vulnerable or Intimidated Witnesses in the Criminal Justice System* (London: HMSO, 1998).

[15] See, for example, Mike Maguire's observations on burglary victims in *Burglary in a Dwelling* (London: Heinemann, 1982) and Paul Rock's work with secondary victims of homicide, 'The Inquiry and Victims' Families', in J. Peay (ed.), *Inquiries after Homicide* (London: Duckworth, 1996).

punished enough from those informed by the knowledge that an official response may mean the offender will be punished too much (and may, in turn, turn against the community to the community's obvious disadvantage).

Clearly, victimization needs to be seen in its social context; Tim Hope's (1995) analysis of its distribution is pertinent since it draws together both the reality of the incidence of victimization and the idea that the presence or absence of social bonds within a community can have an impact upon the regulation of offenders. He asserts that victimization is associated with (amongst other matters):[16]

> certain distinctive internal social relations, including little formal or informal community organisation, a lack of control, supervision or guidance of adolescent activity in public space, high levels of anxiety about crime, little sense of community, and high rates of repeat victimisation and offending against local residents.

But, his analysis also incorporates notions of communitarianism: 'Operationalised in criminological research, communitarianism translates into a search for independent community contextual effects on crime . . . those influences that derive from the social situation in which individuals are located' (ibid., pp.17ff.).

Central to this, Hope asserts, is Coleman's notion of social capital, the idea that interdependence within the network generates shared resources of obligations and expectations. These are maintained by drawing on such resources to support community norms or making members subject to them; for example, making members feel shame where they transgress (Braithwaite, 1989; Kornhauser, 1978). Communities with high social capital should theoretically experience little formal reporting of crime and/or actual crime.[17]

Control by the Community: Punishment of the Community

David Nelken (1985) has distinguished between three different manifestations of community involvement in crime control, namely

[16] For example, matters related to particular social and demographic characteristics, notably an ecological combination of youth, poverty, mobility, single-adult households and lone-parent households. Moreover, victimization resembles the spatial trend in the distribution of income and wealth.

[17] One excellent example of this would be island communities. For example, the Isles of Scilly, familiar to a number of criminologists, benefit not only from high social capital, but also from the presence of the sea. This enhances the community's sense of oneness at risk from an adverse environment, whilst underlining the problem of crossing real geographical boundaries. Property crime is almost unknown in Scilly.

'communities as the agents, locus or beneficiaries of crime control'. He illustrates this theme by detailing how control *by* the community, control *in* the community and control *for* the community may all be distinguished. However, there is a further manifestation which is of principal concern here, namely control (for which read punishment) *of* the community. Stan Cohen (1985) has explored the infinitely flexible nature of the term 'community' and has shown how an emphasis on community corrections can become a medium through which ever more intrusive control is exercised over the lives of citizens. He has also suggested (1979) that emptying the prisons can result in more punitive communities. Professionalizing social control has three obvious advantages: first, it may be an attractive (if futile) option where community control has been perceived not to be working – a sort of 'out of sight out of mind' thesis;[18] secondly, handing over offenders may mean that punishment is constrained and fair; and finally, the community does not have to take responsibility for an offender's (possibly adverse) response to punishment. All of these propositions are open to empirical challenge. However, perhaps the most telling contrary argument is based not in a utilitarian context, but a moral one. This is adverted to by Anthony Duff who argues that offenders make moral demands on us; it is easy enough to withdraw or condemn, but we should strive to respond to offenders in 'a way which tries to preserve and repair our relations with them' (1989, p.150). The danger that punishment in the community faces (whether formal, informal or wholly unregulated, as may come about where we turn a blind eye) is that

> it will subject offenders, not to the kind of penance which still treats and respects them as members of the community, but to kinds of hostility and vilification which are destructive of the very social and moral bonds that punishment should, ideally, aim to repair. One does not know how great this danger is: but surely it is real. (ibid.)

From the Ecological to the Pathological

Duff's observations have proved sadly prophetic. The bulk of this chapter has been concerned with the humdrum and trivia of everyday offending. The response to this by a community is most likely to take a form that makes life more difficult for offenders through subtle

[18] See Tony Bottoms's analysis of how individual offenders are 'managed' within a technologically advanced criminal justice system in 'The philosophy and politics of punishment and sentencing', in C. Clarkson and R. Morgan (eds), *The Politics of Sentencing Reform* (Oxford: Oxford University Press, 1995), p. 47.

discriminatory practices. Yet, it is also possible for communities to become more overtly exclusionary in their response to particular individuals or types of offender most open to demonization. Communities have shamefully shown themselves capable of the gravest of crimes against those by whom they feel threatened. Leaking or sharing of information about the location of paedophiles – even in the era before the Sex Offenders Act 1997 came into force – resulted in such individuals being hounded out of communities, occasionally at risk to their own lives and the lives of others.[19]

Offenders and potential offenders can react to this freezing out; when Horrett Campbell used a machete to attack children in an infants' school playground, he did so because, he asserted, the children represented the devil and they had been shouting abusive remarks and jeering at him. Psychiatrists attributed these beliefs to auditory hallucinations. Whether Campbell genuinely had been taunted may be irrelevant; for it is the fact that he 'chose' local children as the source of his auditory hallucinations rather than aliens, God or the television, that made his response make sense to him. So he too was invoking his local 'community'. Communities can exercise informal social control overtly (e.g. through newsletters or exhortations) and through the self-induced perceptions of those who perceive themselves as part of the community. The latter may be particularly telling in small communities.[20]

The increasing politicization of issues of crime and punishment can thus affect not only how voters perceive issues, but also how offenders do.[21] This may prove critical. For when Garland observes the contrast between the criminologies of the self, which depict offenders as rational opportunists, little different from their victims – a criminology which normalizes deviant behaviour – and the

---

[19] Samantha Pennell died in a fire set by those reputedly looking for a paedophile; for details of this and other cases of communities responding to the presence of paedophiles or alleged paedophiles see the *Guardian*, 10 June 1997. See also the murder of Megan Kanka in 1994 by a convicted sex offender in the US. This led to the creation of 'Megan's Law', requiring local communitites to be informed when a potentially dangerous sex offender is released into the neighbourhood. A further twist to this saga emerged with the decision of the Supreme Court (25 June 1997) permitting sexual predators (with a diagnosis of mental disorder or personality disorder) to be confined for life, even after the expiry of criminal sanctions, on a preventive basis.

[20] For example, the remarkable lack of discussion in the Irish press of the personal affairs of politicians/journalists and other public figures; yet, discussion may be unnecessary where 'everyone' already knows about these matters.

[21] Bottoms's concerns about the growing era of 'popular punitiveness' (see above) will extend to offenders as well as politicians.

criminologies of the other, which demonize offenders, portraying them as alien, as 'dangerous members of distinct racial and social groups which bear little resemblance to us', he draws the contrast from our side of the fence (1996, p.461). Punitive policies promoted by politicians and endorsed by a fearful community whose views are expressed for them (not necessarily accurately) by a self-interested press are premised, as Garland observes 'upon characterizations of offenders as "yobs", "predators", "career criminals" [or] "sex beasts"' (ibid.). Such portrayals of offenders as essentially evil or wicked constitute an attempt to seek to justify policies of exclusion, such as long-term protective incarceration. But, not all such offenders can be incarcerated, and even if they could be, at some point they are returned to the community. So, do communities pursue policies of exclusion within the community and not always outwith it?

To term as pathological both the response of the threatened community and that of the recipient (whether intended or merely perceived as such) of informal coercive control, may be peculiarly apt. Certainly both share an absence of health; they may also be represented as diseased in the sense that they no longer function as they ideally (mythically?) should. To take this explanatory analogy one stage further may be to give spurious credence to what are very rare events. However, it is alleged that Campbell chose to liken himself to Thomas Hamilton, the Dunblane killer, and Martin Bryant, who had killed thirty-five people in Tasmania. These isolated incidents, now including Stephen Anderson who killed six and injured five in Raurimu in New Zealand, and, of course, Michael Ryan, the Hungerford killer, involved offenders who all executed their crimes against a community made up of victims sometimes known to or possibly thought by the offender to be connected with him in some warped way. Some of these communities were small and/or rural, arguably with 'high social capital'. Is it that some people even within these communities do not feel part of the network – is their alienation all the greater for its presence – like being the only one not invited to some extra-curricular outing from work? There is some statistical support for the notion that those on the margins of society and the margins of normality drift into an anonymous life in cities. For those in smaller communities who do not move but are tolerated – within limits – does the lack of anonymity contribute to their problems? Such questions almost defy answer, for the perpetrators of these horrendous killings are rarely available for subsequent examination; even if they were, it is hard to conceive of any explanation that we would find satisfactory (Eastman, 1996). But it is perhaps worth noting that these are people who, with hindsight, appear not to have been so much 'loners' (in that they did not live physically isolated lives) but people who lived psychologically isolated and alienated lives – either inaccessible to us or pushed away by us.[22]

Finally, it is worth returning briefly to the mundane, for it is everyday events which, by definition, have the most impact.[23] The cosy notion of community is hopelessly crude; it belies the complex social world of communities within communities, of cross-cutting networks, shifting allegiances and the temporary nature of associations forged within the communities in which most of us live. It also portrays the world as having a shared sense of right and wrong, of clear boundaries between crime and deviance, and of the existence of an appropriate response to such incidents. Yet, this is manifestly untrue. We make calculations about what responses are most suited in any given situation; and those responses may involve complicated cost-benefit calculations with, in some circumstances, clear instrumental goals. In other contexts, the method of resolution may vary, based upon revenge or personal obligation where alliances are very tight; or we may draw in others as mediators or arbitrators; or in cases of stranger crime we may be more ready to resort to law. Ultimately, we may find it easier to live with conflict than adopt the role of mediator. Whatever else is at issue, whatever lies at the root of our anxieties, dealing with minor crime may just be a distraction about which we choose not to become distracted.

The critical coexisting factors appear to be the interaction between the myth and reality of communities, between informal social control and perceived exclusion, between the dominance and presence of both the ecological and the pathological, escape from neither of which can readily be effected, and ultimately the structuring of events not around what happens but around who is involved. It is about people and not problems. And people do not share a common view of

---

[22] MacCulloch et al.'s study of sadistic fantasists found evidence of an upward spiralling of deviant fantasies leading to *in vivo* 'try-outs' and culminating in sexual killings in a small sample of special hospital patients suffering from psychopathic disorder. The authors note the occurrence of deviant sexual fantasies amongst 'normal' men, but are unable to explain why some act out these fantasies whilst the majority do not. The further progression to actual killing to gain pleasure (serial killers) or possibly relief (mass murderers) remains speculative. How much is pathological and how much the killer's ecology preys on his pre-existing vulnerabilities is not known, but the study does illustrate the inaccessibility and complexity of these offenders' inner lives; M. J. MacCulloch, P. R. Snowden, P. J. W. Wood and H. E. Mills (1983), 'Sadistic fantasy, sadistic behaviour and offending', 143 *British Journal of Psychiatry*, 20–9.

[23] Some of these closing remarks draw extensively upon off-the-cuff observations made by Paul Rock and Peter Manning at the end of the first presentation of this work.

the world. They do not find the same activities equally deviant or shaming; and when family loyalties are at stake, their definitional boundaries of what becomes the important 'community' may be very narrow. In this context, is Braithwaite's analysis not just part of the solution, but part of the problem as well? For shaming can only work where people can be shamed (see Blagg, 1997; Braithwaite, 1997). Moreover, as Braithwaite recognizes, shaming can take place without reintegration (Braithwaite and Mugford, 1994). Whilst in the formal setting of a restorative conference the balance of shaming (induced by victim confrontation) and reintegration (provided by the offenders having their families, peer group and significant others present to provide a network of social support which may decertify deviance) can be consciously managed, shaming and social exclusion may not be so readily constrained where communities engage in informal responses to deviance. Thus, Braithwaite's 'community of care' – those members directly implicated in any affair – may need to respond collectively effectively to obviate individual and reactive responses. But collective action may not equally balance a wider collective inaction. It is this, in turn, which may be perceived by its target as punishing and hence not just punishment in the community but punishment by the community. And, like the consequences of more formal intervention, such punishment can have unintended and unwelcome consequences.

References

ASHWORTH, A. (1995) *Sentencing and Criminal Justice*, London: Butterworths

ASHWORTH, A. et al. (1998) 'Neighbouring on the oppressive: the government's 'Anti-social behaviour order' proposals', 16 *Criminal Justice Matters*, 7

BLAGG, H. (1997) 'A just measure of shame? Aboriginal youth and conferencing in Australia', 37 *British Journal of Criminology*, 481

BLOCK, B., CORBETT, C. and PEAY, J. (1993) 'Ordered and directed acquittals in the Crown Court', Royal Commission on Criminal Justice Research Study No.15, London: HMSO

BOTTOMS, A. (1994) 'Environmental criminology', in Maguire, M., Morgan, R. and Reiner, R. (eds), *Oxford Handbook of Criminology*, Oxford: Clarendon Press

BOTTOMS, A. (1995) 'The philosophy and politics of punishment and sentencing', in Clarkson, C. and Morgan, R. (eds), *The Politics of Sentencing Reform*, Oxford: Oxford University Press

BRAITHWAITE, J. (1989) *Crime, Shame and Re-integration*, Cambridge: Cambridge University Press

BRAITHWAITE, J. (1997) 'Conferencing and plurality', 37 *British Journal of Criminology*, 502

BRAITHWAITE, J. and MUGFORD, S. (1994) 'Conditions of successful reintegration ceremonies: dealing with juvenile offenders', 34 *British Journal of Criminology*, 139

COHEN, S. (1979) 'The punitive city: notes on the dispersal of social control', 3 *Contemporary Crises*, 339

COHEN, S. (1985) *Visions of Social Control*, Cambridge: Cambridge University Press

CRAWFORD, A. (1996) Review of *The Spirit of Community*, 21 *Journal of Law and Society*, 247

CRICHTON, J. (ed.) (1995) *Psychiatric Patient Violence: Risk and Response*, London: Duckworth

DUFF, A. (1989) 'Punishment in the community: a philosophical perspective', in Rees, H. and Hall Williams, E. (eds), *Punishment Custody and the Community: Reflections and Comments on the Green Paper*, London: STICERT, LSE

EASTMAN, N. (1996) 'Mad, bad and impossible to know', *Guardian*, 14 March

EASTMAN, N. and PEAY, J. (1998) 'Sentencing psychopaths: is the "Hospital and limitation direction" an ill considered hybrid?', *Criminal Law Review*, 93

ETZIONI, A. (1995) *The Spirit of Community: Rights, Responsibilities and the Communitarian Agenda*, London: Fontana

FEELEY, M. and SIMON, J. (1994) 'Actuarial justice: the emerging new criminal law', in Nelken, D. (ed.), *The Futures of Criminology*, London: Sage

GARLAND, D. (1996) 'The limits of the sovereign state: strategies for crime control in contemporary society', 36 *British Journal of Criminology*, 445

GIDDENS, A. (1990) *The Consequences of Modernity*, Cambridge: Polity Press

HOOD, R. (1974) *Tolerance and the Tariff*, London: NACRO

HOPE, T. (1995) 'Community safety and inequality', unpublished paper presented to the Conference on Justice and Democracy, Centre for Criminal Justice Research, Brunel University, 13–14 June 1995

KORNHAUSER, R. (1978) *Social Sources of Delinquency*, Chicago: University of Chicago Press

LACEY, N. and ZEDNER, L. (1995) 'Discourses of community in criminal justice', 22 *Journal of Law and Society*, 301

MacCULLOCH, M. J. et al. (1983) 'Sadistic fantasy, sadistic behaviour and offending', 143 *British Journal of Psychiatry*, 20

MAGUIRE, M. (1982) *Burglary in a Dwelling*, London: Heinemann

NELKEN, D. (1985) 'Community involvement in crime control', *Current Legal Problems*, 239

ORWELL, G. [1941] (1962) *The Lion and the Unicorn*, Part I: 'England Your England', London: Secker and Warburg

ROCK, P. (1996) 'The inquiry and victims' families', in Peay, J. (ed.), *Inquiries after Homicide*, London: Duckworth

TAYLOR, I. (1995) 'Justice, social anxiety and place: the condition of England', unpublished paper presented to the Conference on Justice and Democracy, Centre for Criminal Justice Research, Brunel University, 13–14 June 1995

Index